Péter Losonczi, Aakash Singh (Eds.)

Discoursing the Post-Secular

Schnittpunkte – Intersections

herausgegeben von/edited by

Jutta Hausmann, Tamás Lichtmann, Péter Losonczi

Band/Volume 2

LIT

Discoursing the Post-Secular

Essays on the Habermasian Post-Secular Turn

edited by

Péter Losonczi and Aakash Singh

LIT

Bibliographic information published by the Deutsche Nationalbibliothek
The Deutsche Nationalbibliothek lists this publication in the Deutsche Nationalbibliografie; detailed bibliographic data are available in the Internet at http://dnb.d-nb.de.

ISBN 978-3-643-50152-3

A catalogue record for this book is available from the British Library

Krotenthallergasse 10/8
A-1080 Wien
Tel. +43 (0) 1-409 56 61
Fax +43 (0) 1-409 56 97
e-Mail: wien@lit-verlag.at
http://www.lit-verlag.at

LIT VERLAG Dr. W. Hopf
Berlin 2010
Fresnostr. 2
D-48159 Münster
Tel. +49 (0) 2 51-620 320
Fax +49 (0) 2 51-922 60 99
e-Mail: lit@lit-verlag.de
http://www.lit-verlag.de

Distribution:
In Germany: LIT Verlag Fresnostr. 2, D-48159 Münster
Tel. +49 (0) 2 51-620 32 22, Fax +49 (0) 2 51-922 60 99, e-Mail: vertrieb@lit-verlag.de

In Austria: Medienlogistik Pichler-ÖBZ, e-mail: mlo@medien-logistik.at

In Switzerland: B + M Buch- und Medienvertrieb, e-mail: order@buch-medien.ch

In the UK: Global Book Marketing, e-mail: mo@centralbooks.com

In North America by:

Transaction Publishers
New Brunswick (U.S.A.) and London (U.K.)

Transaction Publishers
Rutgers University
35 Berrue Circle
Piscataway, NJ 08854

Phone: +1 (732) 445 - 2280
Fax: + 1 (732) 445 - 3138
for orders (U. S. only):
toll free (888) 999 - 6778
e-mail: orders@transactionpub.com

CONTENTS

ACKNOWLEDGEMENTS

The editors would like to acknowledge the financial and technical support of the Hungarian Ministry of Education and Culture and Gál Ferenc Theological Academy, Szeged, Hungary.

This project was undertaken within the framework of the International Research Network on Religion & Democracy (IRNRD).

NOTE ON CONTRIBUTORS

NICHOLAS ADAMS is Senior Lecturer in Systematic Theology and Theological Ethics at the University of Edinburgh. Before joining Edinburgh in 1998, he had pursued post-doctoral work on Jürgen Habermas' account of religion at the University of Cambridge. His research is currently focused on the relation between nineteenth century German theology and twentieth century theology. He is author of *Habermas and Theology* (CUP, 2006).

EDMUND ARENS is Professor of Fundamental Theology at the University of Lucerns, Switzerland. Among his numerous books in the disciplines of theology, Christology, communicative theory, and philosophy, are: *Gottesverständigung. Eine kommunikative Religionstheologie* (2007), *Geistesgegenwärtig. Zur Zukunft universitärer Bildung* (2003), and in English: *Christopraxis. A Theology of Action* (1995) and *The Logic of Pragmatic Thinking. From Peirce to Habermas* (1994).

MICHAEL HOELZL is Lecturer in Philosophy of Religion and Director of the Centre of Religion and Political Culture at the University of Manchester. His books include: Carl Schmitt. *Dictatorship: From the Beginning of the Modern Concept of Sovereignty to the Proletarian Class-Struggle.* Translated and introduced by Michael Hoelzl; Carl Schmitt. *Political Theology II. The Myth of the Closure of any Political Theology.* Translated and introduced by Michael Hoelzl & Graham Ward; *The New Visibility of Religion. Studies in Religion and Cultural Hermeneutics* and *Religion and Political Thought*, both edited and annotated by Michael Hoelzl & Graham Ward.

DEVRIM KABASAKAL is Lecturer in political theory and political science at the Department of International Relations in Toros University, Turkey. She is interested in political liberalism, pluralism, toleration, the role of religion in politics and secularism. She has published on John Rawls's idea of toleration and is currently working on issues concerning toleration and its international aspect with a particular focus on Rawls and Habermas.

PATRICK LOOBUYCK is Professor at the University of Antwerp and guest professor at Ghent University (Belgium). His research interests include multiculturalism, church-state relations, and secularization. He is author of several books (in Dutch) and has published in journals such as *Ethnicities* and *Metaphilosophy.*

Péter Losonczi was educated at the ELTE-BTK (Budapest) and the Catholic University of Leuven. He teaches philosophy and religious studies at the University of West Hungary (Szombathely) and is scientific collaborator at Centrum Pieter Gillis, University of Antwerp. His publications include: *Reflecting Diversity: Historical and Thematical perspectives in the Jewish and Christian Tradition* (Lit Verlag, 2007); *Philosophy Begins in Wonder: An Introduction to Early Modern Philosophy, Theology, and Science* (Pickwick, 2009) and *From Political Theory to Political Theology: Religious Challenges and the Prospects of Democracy* (Continuum, 2010).

Gábor Viktor Orosz is Assistant Professor at the Evangelical-Lutheran Theological University, Budapest, and former research fellow of the Hungarian Academy of Sciences, Research Group for Social Ethics and Ecumenism. His book *Alien Dignity. Preimplantations, Genetic Diagnosis and Human Dignity in the Context of Theology* was published in 2009 by L'Harmattan (in Hungarian).

Matthias Riedl taught at the University Erlangen-Nuremberg (Germany), Duke University (North Carolina), and currently holds the Chair of Comparative Religious Studies at Central European University (Budapest). His research focuses on the relation of religion and politics in intercivilizational perspective. Since 2003, he has been Co-editor of the proceedings of the Eranos-Conferences, publishing *Joachim von Fiore – Denker der vollendeten Menschheit* (2004), *Propheten und Prophezeiungen* (2005), and *Die Menschen im Krieg, im Frieden mit der Natur* (2006).

Stefan Rummens is Assistant Professor in Political Theory at the Radboud University Nijmegen (The Netherlands). He obtained his PhD in Philosophy at the University of Leuven (Belgium) with a dissertation on the normative presuppositions of Jürgen Habermas's deliberative model of democracy. His current research interests include deliberative democracy, populism, religion in the public sphere, agonistic politics, representation and global democracy. He is co-author of a monograph on Habermas (in Dutch) and has published articles in journals such as *The Journal of Political Philosophy*, *Philosophy & Social Criticism*, *Ratio Juris*, *Constellations* and *Political Studies*.

John Rundell is Associate Professor, Reader and Director of The Ashworth Program for Social Theory at The University of Melbourne, Australia. He is an Editor of the journal *Critical Horizons* and *The Social and Critical Theory Book Series* and his publications include *Origins of Modernity*, *Blurred Boundaries Migration Ethnicity Citizenship* (edited with Rainer Baubock), *Critical Theory After Habermas* (edited with Dieter Freundlieb and Wayne Hudson), and *Work, Recognition, Politics. New Directions in French Critical Theory* (edited with Jean-Philippe Deranty, Danielle Petherbridge and Robert Zinnerbrink).

Aakash Singh is Research Professor at the Center for Ethics & Global Politics, LUISS University, Rome. He is author of *Eros Turannos*, on the debate between

Leo Strauss and Alexandre Kojeve, and editor of *Indian Political Thought* (Routledge, 2010), and a Critical Edition of B. R. Ambedkar's *The Buddha and His Dhamma* (Oxford University Press, 2010). He is currently completing a manuscript collecting and analyzing G. W. F. Hegel's writings on Indian philosophy, religion and culture, entitled *Hegel's India.* Singh is also General Editor of the Routledge book series, *Ethics, Human Rights & Global Political Thought.*

EDITOR'S INTRODUCTION: DISCOURSING THE POST-SECULAR/ POST-SECULAR DISCOURSES: ANALYSIS AND CONTEXT

Certain thoughts are prayers.
– Victor Hugo, *Les Misérables*

Which term to use, 'Postsecular', 'Post-Secular', 'postsecular', or 'post-secular'? The orthography remains as aporetic as the referent, albeit within manageable, even discursive limits. In this volume, we have neither *imposed* a consistent spelling of the term throughout, nor attempted to *expose* a hegemonic conception of its meaning across the disciplines; rather, we have *proposed* more chromatically to allow the phenomenon of the post-secular to reveal itself through and across disciplines and discourses, from the social studies (Chapter 1) whence it primarily arises, to political theory and political philosophy (Chapters 2-3), even to postcolonial theory (Chapter 4), across to the philosophy of culture (Chapter 5) and religion (Chapters 6-7), transiting to theology (Chapters 8-9) and concluding with bioethics (Chapter 10), which may of course have been the ultimate catalyzing factor for Jürgen Habermas's own *turn to the post-secular*.

Although the term „post-secular" carries no univocal connotation, this ambiguity does not make its application impossible or baseless, and not merely because the definition of *secularization* in itself has long been the subject of debate. To discourse (on) the post-secular permits its divergent layers of meaning – each of which equally belong to the very complexity of a situation whose contours are fluid – gradually to unfold itself. Generally speaking, we can detect three layers of meaning in the overall application of this term: (1) to the multiform manifestations of the *phenomena* pertaining to the permanent presence – according to certain interpretations, the growth – of religious influence within the contemporary cultural and socio-political context, in its traditional and new forms alike; (2) to those *questions* that are in any way related to these occurrences; and, (3) to the *discourse(s)* constituted by this situation on a wide scale of disciplines like philosophy, theology, social theory, theory of culture, literary theory and other branches of science. Adopting Connolly's terminology, we may describe as post-secular that *multidimensional pluralism*[1] which characterizes the present-day cultural and political situation in which religion plays an undeniable role, on the one hand, and also the complex interrelation that exists between the secular and the religious segments of the contemporary social situation. Despite the debateable exactness of this term and the nature of the contemporary resurgence of „religion" or of the „religious", certain recent developments can be even interpreted as reactions to this multiform process. Even the recent recovery of a virulent atheist (or a-theist) discourse animated by the works of Dawkins, Hitchens, Sam Harris and others is, according to Stephen Long, attributable to this unforeseen return and conjoined with that as a parasitic consequence.[2]

Evidently, one's position in this debate over the applicability of the concept of the „post-secular" is highly dependent on how inclusive a framework we set when speaking of the problems of secularization / religion / absence / resurgence. An empirical sociological approach may find the term vague and its application highly questionable, even if it is presented by a non-devotee of the secularization thesis.[3] However, it is itself a basic question whether the method applied by empirical sociology can even be credited to pronounce the final word in this regard, or instead whether we need to develop a cultural hermeneutical complementary to this empirical study[4] or whether a theologically-sensitive revision of the methods of sociology is necessary.[5] Jürgen Habermas, about whose most current writings we painstakingly devote each essay of this book, has characterized the post-secular situation as one wherein we are obligated to take into account not exclusively the predominant secular tendencies but inclusively the persistent presence of religious influences, and moreover wherein we are called to cultivate conditions whereby the constructive co-existence of these elements may occur within a public and political context. The Habermasian theses are formulated with dominant social scientific and political theoretical tones. However, we think that the many complexities of the questions regarding the post-secular condition are implicitly or explicitly represented by or reflected on by Habermas himself in a more essential and diverse manner. This set of

[1] William E. Connolly, *Why I am not a Secularist* (Minneapolis (Minn.): University of Minnesotta, 1999) 4.

[2] D. Stephen Long, „Foreword: Atheism's Resurgence and Christian Responses," in: A. David, C.J. Keller, J. Stanley (eds.), *„God is Dead" and I Don't Feel So Good Myself* (Eugene, Or.: Cascade Books, 2010) xiii-xxi, xiv.

[3] See for example, José Casanova, „Are We Still Secular? Exploring the Post-Secular: Three Meanings of 'the Secular' and their possible transcendence". (Draft presented at the Workshop with Jürgen Habermas at the Institute for Public Knowledge, New York University, October 22-24, 2009).

[4] Thomas Banchoff, „Introduction,", in: T. Banchoff (ed.), *Democracy and the New Religious Pluralism* (Oxford: Oxford University Press, 2007) 3-16, 7.

[5] James Sweeney S.J, „Revising Secularization Theory," in: G. Ward & M. Holezl (eds.), The New Visibility of Religion: Studies in Religion and Cultural Hermeneutics (London: Continuum, 2008) 15-29.

questions embrace the theory of culture, philosophy, theology, ethics, the theory of religion and several other issues. These are but mere hints on the context(s) within which Habermas' recent work reverberates, elides; thus, hints on the growing multifaceted discourse of the post-secular growing through and among the discourses. The papers in this volume aim at representing this fact and their task is therefore more than merely presenting a critical or sympathetic evaluation of Habermas' respective writings.

The first chapter by *John Rundell* well exemplifies the resurgent impact of the question of religion within contemporary social theory. Indeed, Rundell argues that even beyond a direct, challenging thematic for the social sciences, 'religion' functions as a catch-all category for myriad other issues and concerns generally indicative of the ever deepening pluralist situation within which we find ourselves today. While attempting to uncover why and how religion operates as a stand-in category, Rundell engages with Habermas' turn to religious concerns within the broader framework of the social imaginary, the construction of social meaning.

From social theory we move to political theory, where in chapter two *Devrim Kabasakal* ties together the radical plural environment evoked in the previous chapter by Rundell, the situation within which we now find ourselves, with Habermas' considerable interest in toleration and its significance in politics in his later works. Kabasakal analyzes the notion of a 'post-secular age' with a focus on its relevance and limits in what she sketches as Habermas's theory of toleration. Particularly, she argues that the notion of a 'post-secular age' serves the idea of toleration only on a descriptive basis by explicating the conditions of a pluralist world-society. Thus, while it provides a descriptive foundation by constituting a 'circumstance' for toleration, it is far from supplying a moral ground for toleration on its own. Consequently, Kabasakal claims that it is the idea of 'equal respect' in the work of Habermas that offers a moral justification for the necessity and significance of toleration. Only with the idea of 'equal respect' can the positive demands of toleration that Habermas envisions be possible in the post-secular era.

These very themes of tolerance within post-secular society are picked up and examined in the co-authored chapter three by *Patrick Loobuyck* and *Stefan Rummens*, a both wide and deep overview of the Habermasian post-secular turn and some fundamental political-philosophical problems by which it is beset. Although Habermas has recently launched the concept of the post-secular society, he continues to acknowledge that the sociological data still provides support for the secularization thesis. However, this does not mean that the political and public relevance of religion will definitely wane. For Habermas, this insight has some normative implications for political and public interactions between religious and nonreligious citizens. He insists on a complementary learning process. On the one hand, religion has to become reflective and has to agree with scientific knowledge, the neutrality of the state, the idea of religious tolerance, religious freedom and other constitutional basic values. On the other hand, Habermas asks the religiously tone-deaf citizen to give religious convictions a real epistemic status.

After a short presentation of Habermas's position along the lines mentioned just above, Loobuyck and Rummens analyze the specificity of Habermas's account of the post-secular public sphere, especially in discussion with the position of John Rawls. They are led to conclude that the post-secular 'burdens of tolerance' that secular and religious citizens have to shoulder, are less symmetric than Habermas has suggested in his writings. Moreover it is not clear whether these burdens are reasonable and feasible in the eyes of the secular and the religious citizens. Therefore, it seems that Habermas underestimates the presumably inevitable tension between public reason, secularization and religion.

The fourth chapter by one of the co-editors of the volume, *Aakash Singh*, still keeps a foothold within the political-philosophical methods, concerns and considerations of Loobuyck and Rummens's previous chapter, but also takes steps toward other inherently related disciplines like international relations and culture studies – *inherently* related, that is, within the context of globalization. Here in chapter four, Singh points out that Habermas' recent work attempts to find 'inspiring energy' in the religious traditions, but without disturbing the rationality and freedoms of enlightenment modernity. Rather, the secular would assimilate the religious like a blood infusion, becoming more vibrant and stronger, but not losing its hard-won advantage. For Habermas, the postsecular problem lies in how best to preserve the secular democratic institutions and keep them from being 'violated' through religiously motivated politics. Habermas criticizes Nicholas Wolterstorff, who would allow the religious to overrun the political, potentially violating vulnerable democratic institutions like the parliament. As Loobuyck and Rummens has already indicated, Habermas suggests use of an 'institutional filter' to protect parliament from violation. Singh maintains, however, that throughout his postsecular writings, Habermas persistently employs Victorian-like innuendo bestowing masculine 'inspiring energy', 'vitality', and danger onto religion, which runs the risk of 'violating' effeminate democratic institutions symbolized by the parliament; thus the prophylactic devise, the 'filter' which protects her virtue. In this vein, Singh attempts to demonstrate how in Habermas' dialectics of (post)secularism, the religious enters solely on terms set by the secular, and plurality solely on terms set by stability/security. He then explores whether it is merely a coincidence that the immigration rhetoric of every recent election in Europe evokes notions of preventing the swarthy barbarians at the gate from flooding in, of strengthening the institutional filter to prevent the others from violating our vulnerable order?

Habermas' recent work and his possible motivations behind it receives far gentler treatment in chapter five, which provides a comparative view of Habermas vis-à-vis Emmanuel Levinas. In this chapter, the co-editor *Péter Losonczi* focuses especially on Habermas's conception about the *linguistification of the sacred*, on the one hand, and on Levinas's criticism of the *sacred as idolatry*, on the other. Viewed from the specific perspective of this comparison – namely, the questions concerning „the sacred" and political idolatry – the differences between Habermas and Levinas turn out to be as relevant as the evident similarities. While in Habermas, a residuum of the sacred persist in the form of the linguistically approached consensus of autonomous and rational agents, Levinas's critique of the sacred disqualifies even this residual form of the sacred as the ultimate referent of political deliberation. Levinas declares that „human autonomy rests on a supreme heteronomy and that the force [...] which institutes force, the civilizing force, is called God," with this implication that deliberation is preceded by the doubly enigmatic events of the *elective* moment of the face of the other and the *graced* element of justice.[6] Furthermore, this supreme heteronomy continuously calls into question every form of self-enclosed autonomy addressing it with a *paradox*. In view of Levinas's criticism of the sacred and mythology, even Habermas's therapeutically conceived political religion risks functioning as mere repetition of the ambiguous and violent religion of immanence and egology.

The sixth chapter by *Mathias Riedl* also is a comparative one, and functions simultaneously to draw out specific differences of the approaches of Gianni Vattimo and Habermas, as well as to illuminate other corners of the post-secular milieu that we had indicated in the earlier part of this Introduction. Vattimo was among the first philosophers who (re-)turned to religion. His turn results from a religious experience, namely the sudden and surprising insight that his postmodern ontology of the weakening of Being coincides with the Christian idea of the incarnation of God, the *kenosis*. According to Vattimo, the process of divine self-revelation has not brought about the universality of Christian faith but precisely the opposite, a plurality of mutually interacting regional truths. Consequently, the daily encounters with otherness will gradually destroy the dominant religious truths and bring about the hermeneutic age, where no experience is given, which is not an interpretive act. Riedl thus provides a critical analysis of Vattimo's recent writings and confronts them with Jürgen Habermas' analysis of the post-secular situation.

The prior two comparative chapters straddling the philosophy of culture and religion have indicated a tendency increasingly toward the latter (religion), and the seventh chapter continues this trend. Interestingly, the two problems that *Nicholas Adams* addresses through the philosophy of religion in chapter seven – that of (1) discursive extraterritoriality and (2) the notion of appropriating religious 'contents' or their 'semantic heritage' – have already been approached earlier in this volume from the vantage point of other discourses, such as social and political theory, and will also later in the volume be addressed from a theological perspective. By running these themes through several reference points across socio-political sciences and humanities, a multi-dimensional or polyphonic approach is initiated, which, as we have above suggested, is essential for adequately addressing the multivalent phenomena of the post-secular situation.

Adams specifically dialogues with Habermas from the point of view of a religious believer or practitioner, and one who reflects upon the form and content of that belief/practise philosophically. He thus picks up on one of the relevant features of Habermas' recent works, which is his way of distinguishing between

[6] Cf. For justice and grace Bettina Bergo, *Levinas Between Ethics and Politcs: For the Beauty that Adores the Earth* (Dordrecht: Martinus Nijhoff, 1999) 183.

faith and reason. Despite having moved beyond some of the limitations of the Durkheimian approach so central to his earlier writings on the subject, even for late Habermas, the binaries are maintained: 'certainties of faith' are contrasted with 'fallible convictions of a secular nature'; an 'inviolable core of infallible revealed truths' is contrasted with the 'unreserved discursive examination' that secular conceptions may receive. The upshot of the binary is that faith is accorded a state of 'discursive extraterritoriality,' whereby matters of faith are non-negotiable. For Adams, this transmits four unfortunate effects into the domain of religious life and the self-understanding of ones own religion and its tradition(s): it makes it difficult to make sense of argumentation within a religious tradition, such as a church council (which, moreover, ought to be conceived as public in some sense); it makes it difficult to make sense of argumentation between two traditions that share a significant belief, such as monotheism; it makes it impossible to make sense of the evolution of any tradition, insofar as there are probably no 'certainties of faith' or 'infallibly revealed truths' that have not at some time provoked debate (so how did they suddenly become 'discursively extraterritorial'?); and, it makes it easy for ideologues on the religious right to claim immunity from criticism when appealing to 'matters of faith' (how can they ever be wrong?).

If Adams has identified some collateral damage to religion and religious *belief* arising out of the binaries still present in Habermas' post-secular thought, in his second main topic he raises the potential damage done to the religious *practitioner's* self-understanding. Habermas suggests that philosophy should appropriate the 'possible truth contents' or 'semantic heritage' of religious traditions, a suggestion which insinuates that the 'contents' or 'heritage' of religious life and practice is separable from the religious traditions. Adams evokes the imagery of the religious tradition as a shell and its truth-content as an oyster within that may be shucked out from it. This is a seriously problematic and clearly externalist conception of what is more properly experienced as the performative generation of truth through religious practice, ritual, and so on.

Adams, of course, is narrating one aspect of a story that is multifaceted, and it is enlightening to observe that despite of his (surely well-grounded) scepticism on the contribution of late Habermas to religious praxis, we find in the next chapter the articulation of a theology inspired by and grounded in earlier works of Habermas, when he was supposed to be even less open to the role of religion in public life. In chapter eight, *Edmund Arens* unfolds his conception of religion as simultaneously communication and action. This involves a portrait of religion as a practice, just as Adams had insisted in the previous chapter, but in Arens' understanding, it is a practice coping with contingency. Also remaining sensitive to related concerns raised by Adams, Arens discusses positions that comprehend religion as essentially ritual practice. Arens also devotes a good deal of chapter eight to examining the relationship of religion and communicative action in conversation with the work of Habermas, both the earlier work on communicative action, as well as the recent work on the status of religion in post-secular society. Building on these discussions, Arens addresses perspectives towards a communicative theological understanding of religion and takes steps to develop significant forms of religious-communicative practice. He concludes with pointing out five guidelines for communicative theology.

Although Arens has to some extent provided a Habermasian answer to the challenges thrown up by Adams, in chapter nine, *Michael Hoelzl* would seek to turn the tables once again by posing the question as to whether a critical theology à la Arens is at all consistent with the post-metaphysical paradigm under which contemporary communicative action is supposed to play out. How is a Catholic theology rooted in a sacramental worldview possible without metaphysics? Hoelzl's doubts regarding the non-negotiability of the post-metaphysical era arise as a consequence of his interest in rescuing a 'thicker' conception of transcendence than Habermas' thought allows. As Hoelzl insightfully captures through a quotation of Habermas on the theme of the linguistification of the sacred from his pre-, if you will, post-secular work, secularization can be read as a process of thinning out the understanding of transcendence:

> The disenchantment and disempowering of the sacred sphere will happen by a transformation into language [Versprachlichung] of the ritually secured normative common sense. This also means that the potential of rationality, of communicative action is set free. The aura of enchantment and fright caused by the sacred, the capturing power of the holy is transformed to the binding force of a validity clause that can be criticised and the holy is at the same time sublimated [sublimiert] and turned into an everyday experience [veralltäglicht].[7]

Although Hoelzl is underlining a unity of thought in Habermas over time, he is also positing the post-secular, against the grain, as a window of opportunity, a chance to move not in the direction of the sublimation of the sacred into the everyday, but contrarily, toward a thicker and more adequate notion of transcendence.

Or, to put it in another way, not necessarily Hoelzl's position, the new discourse(s) of the post-secular may allow for reversing that process of 'disenchantment' about which Habermas spoke. It is, of course, precisely the enchanted or disenchanted nature of the every day[8] that remains open to plurivocal dissensus: the secular has morphed to the post-secular partly because the assumption (by secularists) that the every day experience was an inevitably and increasingly disenchanted one has been shown the lie in and through a panoply of contemporary discourses.

One such, of no meagre contemporary relevance, is bioethics. In chapter ten, *Gábor Viktor Orosz* pushes our multidisciplinary approach to the Habermasian post-secular turn forward with a return to its possible beginnings, at least its catalyzing experience.[9] Consonant with the theological positions presented in

[7] J. Habermas, *Theorie des Kommunikativen Handelns*, Vol 2 (Frankfurt: Suhrkamp, 1987 [4th ed] 119. [Translation by Michael Hoelzl.]

[8] On the centrality of the notion of 'enchantment' at play in early modernity, see Akeel Bilgrami's „Gandhi, Newton, and the Enlightenment," in: A. Singh & R. Mohapatra (eds), *Indian Political Thought* (London: Routledge, 2010).

[9] This point is argued specifically by Mathias Riedl in Chapter Six.

the chapters preceding it, the final chapter of the volume deals with a particular aspect of Habermas' *The Future of Human Nature*, reading the bioethics sketched therein alongside the Christian theological tradition. Accordingly, Orosz pegs Habermasian bioethics to his ideas on solidarity, and pegs the Christian theological position on human genetic engineering and enhancement to its strong definition of human dignity. Orosz in the end does not merely carry out a comparison or show the dependence and relation of Habermasian bioethics on or against the Christian theological tradition, but out of a mediated conception informed by both sources, offers positive suggestions, such as regarding in the case of genetic enhancement the use of human dignity as a *regulative principle.* In this respect, Orosz's chapter previews what might take shape as a coming post-secular bioethical discourse.

Now, besides the analytic discussions executed in each of the chapters of this volume focusing with such concentration on the Habermasian post-secular discourse, as well as the several optional directions for relating his initiative to a larger milieu – i.e. the manifold (re)appearance of the religious in the socio-cultural and political environment – we may, finally, hint here at one other interesting dilemma, albeit one which steps well beyond strict scholarly interest. This has to do with Habermas' *persona*, with the man 'behind' the scholar's mindset. Of course, it is a deeply ambiguous task to speculate over such psychological or biographical issues. However, by sheer coincidence – or is it? – it is exactly in *Between Naturalism and Religion* where Habermas himself serves us with a narrative of his personal life and enlightens the readers as to how the elements of this narrative may have been influential in the framing of his theoretical attitudes.[10] Witnessing the complexities of the Habermasian works on religion, as well as the specific developments during the last phase of Habermas's intellectual endeavour, one may wonder if this new relatedness to issues regarding religion and the resulting dilemmas *themselves belong to a new phase of that narrative.* Might it be the case that Habermas's opinions regarding religious semantic potentials and their existential relevance, or his approach to the problems of faith and reason, are, beyond their undeniable theoretical relevance, providing a certain testimony about the dilemmas of a late modern intellectual about the (im)possibilities of his age?

[10] Jürgen Habermas, „Public Space and Political Public Sphere – The Biographical Roots of Two Motifs in My Thought," in: *Between Naturalism and Religion: Philosophical Essays* (Cambridge: Polity, 2008 [2005]) 11-23.

MULTIPLE MODERNITIES, SACREDNESS, AND THE DEMOCRATIC IMAGINARY: RELIGION AS A STAND IN CATEGORY

John Rundell

Introduction

Often when religion is discussed the topic is not about religion, as such. Religion becomes a catch-all category for other issues, topics and concerns. This essay aims to tease out what some of these concerns may be if religion is viewed as a stand-in category. From the vantage point of modern multi-faith and multicultural societies religion becomes a topic that concerns the *recognition* of religious pluralism and of cultural differences, and hence cultural encounters between groups, especially in the context of the complexity of the modern world. When one speaks of „the modern world" it is also less than a straightforward concept. In the history of concept formation it has often been referred to as secularization, modernization, and historical progress. In more recent social theory the concept of 'multiple modernities' has emerged as a way of capturing both the regional diversity of modernizing impulses, and the modern reality of living with its multiple dimensions, often in long term historical contexts.

One can critically draw on Habermas' engagement with the term post-secular as a way of looking at the problem of encounters and co-existences of multiple modernities and religiously constituted forms of belief and ways of life. It is here that religion can also be a signal for the way in which such intersections and co-existences may be articulated, ignored, or dogmatically or fundamentalistically „resolved". This essay is concerned with the way in which this intersection may be articulated democratically.

Moreover, the intersection itself opens onto the way in which the social meaning, which is imbedded in the intersections between religion and modernity, is socially produced or created. In other words it opens onto the nature of socially produced meaning itself, and religion has also often become a stand-in category through which the problem of the creation of meaning has been articulated. This issue of the social creation of meaning has often been conceptualized in terms of a great divide between the pre- or non-modern and the modern.

Within the classical traditions of the social sciences, of which Sociology and Anthropology are its handmaidens, Durkheim's work more than any other, asks whether the distinction between religious and modern societies that besets the founding tradition is a robust distinction. In summary, then, religion may become a stand-in category for the topics of modernity, encounters between it and religiosity, and the production of social meaning. In order to, first, explore the topic of the production of social meaning, our analysis will begin with Durkheim's notion of the sacred, before turning to the problem of religion and modernity.

I. Durkheim and the Problem of the Sacred

It can be argued that the Durkheimian problem of the sacred is a way of suggesting that no society can „live" without a sense of its sacredness irrespective of whether this is couched in either 'religious' or 'secular' terms. In the context of theorizing the „great divide" between the so-called pre-modern and the secular modern, Durkheim's work is a restful point of orientation because in his hands this „divide" is thrown into relief and problematized. Durkheim's work is important because he theorizes the social from the vantage-point of an ontologically posited idea of a social creation or socially created meaning that cannot be divided into a neat distinction between the religious and the secular.

In a summary here that draws on a discussion undertaken elsewhere, Durkheim posits his version of the sacred through his notion of collective representation.[1] What stands behind his particular notion of collective representation is a complex formulation through which Durkheim presents his social ontology.[2] For

[1] I have discussed Durkheim's work in relation to sacred and collective representations in „Durkheim and the Reflexive Condition of Modernity", in *Recognition, Work, Politics. New Directions in French Critical Theory*, edited by Jean-Philippe Deranty, Danielle Petherbridge, John Rundell and Robert Sinnerbrink, Leiden, Brill, 2007, pp. 203-230.

[2] In Durkheim's mature, 1914 position of the *homo duplex*, the exploration of the primordial conflict that it represents is both subtle and complex. He argues that this dualism has been expressed, in an intellectual register, by Pascal in his famous formulation that „'man is both angel and beast' and not exclusively one or the other", E. Durkheim, „The Dualism of Human Nature and its Social Conditions" in *Essays in Sociology and Philosophy*, edited by Kurt Wolff, 1960, New York, Harper and Row, p. 329. Moreover, this dualism entails a constant inner restlessness and disharmony that produces both misery and grandeur. Culturally, Durkheim argues, this dualism has been most articulately expressed in the great religions - principally Judaism and Christianity, for him, although all of the religions of the so-called Axial Age could be included here – Budhism, Shintoism, Islam and Confucianism, in as much as the latter can be thought of as a religion. These great axial religions have insisted on this contradiction and the struggles that it gives rise to. „These continue to depict us as tormented and suffering, while only the crude cults of inferior societies breathe forth and inspire a joyful confidence", Durkheim, „The

Durkheim, collective representations indicate the project of the humanization of the human being from a pre-social being to a social one, that is, one who opens outward towards social life by being disrupted by it. Collective representations represent two ways of viewing the social condition of the human being – one that is simultaneously caught or enclosed within the profane world of everyday life where values are particularistically viewed. It is a world of meaning, but one that is enclosed and limited in scope. The second world, which Durkheim terms the sacred, stands from the position of opening the social individual outward to a larger context of meaning, and thus meaning-filled social interactions. Its horizon expands outward beyond social individuals and thus is the socially universal point of orientation. Nonetheless, the next step of considering openness as a characteristic of the sacred world more generally cannot be taken immediately. For Durkheim, openness at the level of the sacred, that is, of collective representations themselves, requires specific social conditions in order for this specific type of social opening – otherwise termed reflexivity - to occur.

In his earlier formulation of the *conscience collective*, in *The Division of Labour in Society*, the sacred was posited as beliefs and sentiments; yet in the context of his later work, of which T*he Elementary Forms of Religious Life* is the most representative, beliefs and sentiments are but one aspect of the self-representation of society to itself and its membership, which, for Durkheim, is their core feature. In the light of Lukes' seminal suggestion sacred collective representations are reflexive „forms of interpretations", rather than functional and integrative mechanisms or causal structures.[3] In Lukes' view, the concept of (sacred) collective representations is Durkheim's way of saying that human beings construct an interpretation of the world through constituted beliefs and practices, and by so doing render the world, and their own place in it, intelligible. In this version, the sacred, as Durkheim himself states, is „a system of ideas with which the individuals represent to themselves the society of which they are members, and the obscure but intimate relations which they have with it".[4]

In this way, collective representations are cosmological, in that they are symbolic forms through which the natural and social environments, which, for Durkheim, constitute the totality of human existence, are interpreted in a comprehensive way.[5] For Durkheim, the comprehensiveness of a collective cosmology is two-fold. In *Primitive Classification* Durkheim argues that collective representations are the symbolic forms through which the natural and social worlds

Dualism of Human Nature and its Social Conditions", p. 331-332. It should be noted though that Durkheim does not limit his discussion of the anthropological dimension of the *homo duplex* to these Axial religions alone. The *homo duplex* belongs as much to so-called primitive religions, as it does to the modern ones of democracy and nationalism.

[3] Steven Lukes, *Emile Durkheim His Life and Work: A Historical and Critical Study*, 1987, Harmondsworth, Penguin, pp. 465-467.

[4] Emile Durkheim, *The Elementary Forms of Religious Life,* trans. Joseph Ward Swain, Introduction by Robert Nisbet, 1976, London, George Allen and Unwin, 1976, p. 225.

[5] Durkheim, *The Elementary Forms of religious Life,* p. 9.

are interpreted as intellectual and moral endeavours. To be sure, the Kantian universalism of the categories of time, space and morality are seen as social creations by Durkheim, but nonetheless, ones that have a synthetic character. As he states in *Primitive Classification* written in 1903 with Mauss, „society was not simply a model which classificatory thought followed; it was its own divisions which served as divisions for a system of classification. The first logical categories were social categories; the first classes of things were classes of men; into which these things were integrated".[6]

Intellectually, collective representations „translate" the natural world into an intelligible language through concepts that provide a unitary and cohesive interpretive field. Concepts, so Durkheim argues, depersonalize and objectify reality, and enable it to be classified in terms that demarcate and delineate it spatially, temporally and hierarchically.[7] In other words, they enable humankind to more effectively mobilize its relation to nature, and in this sense, they become „instruments of action". Concepts, and the systems of knowledge that are formed through them are epistemological in the sense that they have a truth content in relation to the reality that they describe. Moreso, and more importantly, for him, though, they are technico-pragmatic in the sense that they are a more efficient means than effects or sentiments, for example, through which external reality can be harnessed and controlled.[8]

As importantly, though, for Durkheim, collective representations are also the forms through which the force of social-moral life takes shape in a way that is collectively binding and coherent.[9] In this process of interaction within the realm of the sacred social actors are not so much integrated into collective representa-

[6] Emile Durkheim and Marcel Mauss, *Primitive Classification*, translated with an Introduction by Rodney Needham, 1963, Chicago, Chicago University Press, p. 82.

[7] Durkheim, *The Elementary Form of religious Life*, p. 429; Durkheim and Mauss, *Primitive Classification*, pp. 4-5, pp. 85-87.

[8] Emile Durkheim, *Pragmatism and Sociology*, translated by J.C Whitehouse, edited and Introduced by John B. Allcock with a preface by Amand Cuvillier, 1983, Cambridge, Cambridge University Press, 45-49.

[9] Durkheim reiterates his argument already posited in *The Division of Labour in Society* that morality is a basic dimension of collective life, and that the individual only becomes moral by being a member of a group. See Emile Durkheim, *Sociology and Philosophy*, translated by D.F. Pocock, with an Introduction by J.G. Peristiany, Glencoe, Ill., Free Press, 1953, p. 37. As Durkheim's discussion of *mana* in *The Elementary Forms of Religious Life* makes clear, whilst social-moral life may have a sanction that can be wielded physically, its force lies in an authority which transcends its physical presence. Coercion, fear and violence, although important aspects of collective representations, especially of the „mechanical" type, nonetheless, are secondary to a moral power that requires not so much an emotional economy of fear, but moreso one in which obligation, respect and exhaltation are operative. These dimensions give a collective representation - as social-moral authority - substance and longevity (Durkheim, *The Elementary Forms of religious Life*, pp.206-223. In this, and unlike intellectual collective representations, they are beyond „deliberation or calculation", ibid.p.207. When taken together -

tions, but opened by them. This entails, for Durkheim, that the tonality for intersubjectivity is found in the *rituals* of the sacred and not in the *minutia* of everyday life or the profane.[10] Intersubjectivity and meaning are combined in the rituals of the sacred in what might be termed „*creative-ritual action*" that both opens the individual to the world of sacredness, and ties him/her to it. Collective representations are part and parcel of the way through which social individuals understand themselves and others, and represent this understanding in symbolic forms. As such, for Durkheim, collective representations are not disconnected from the lives of social actors for they are acted out, re-made and re-affirmed in the rites and rituals „in which individuals represent to themselves the society of which they are members".[11] In this sense, they are the primary media through which creativity and individual self-expression can be articulated.

In Durkheim's view, then, sacred collective representations tie individual and social creativity together; they are the forms through which a singular individual transforms his or her own creative life into one that is simultaneously individual and social. In Durkheim's view sacred collective representations become meaningful for the individuals concerned. As such, the social creations that the social subject either participates in or creates, take the form of interpretations within existing collective representations, or in specific circumstances, the creation of new ones. In other words, for Durkheim, the sacred provides both the external-objective „fact" of social life and the context of intersubjectively shared meaningful existence. In this sense, all societies are sacred and social actors constitute their intersubjectivity meaningfully by not only drawing on them, but also by creating them.

This account of Durkheim's notion of sacred collective representations draws out an ontologically constituted dimension of the formation of all societies, that is, of their dimension of meaning, irrespective of whether this is formed wholly through language or symbols. Durkheim, though, seems to suggest that social thought and social action is constituted either linguistically through socially produced categories, or through symbols, which become their shorthand, even if emotion and ritual are imbedded in each. In comparison, for Cornelius Castoriadis, meaning cannot be so constituted – there is always a creative, inarticulable and inexhaustible dimension that cannot be rendered through language, symbols, materiality or culture. He terms this inarticulable dimension social imaginaries, and this term will be deployed here along with the Durkheimian notion of collective representations in order to emphasize the

that is, as both intellectual and moral forces - collective representations dominate and constitute the totality of the sacred world that humans inhabit, and are opened by.

[10] This distinction need not be accepted. Rather, as will be explored below, the sacred collective representations, or what can be termed social imaginaries, following Castoriadis' work, are not necessarily separate from everyday life in the institutional sense. We can articulate and practice social imaginaries in any setting.

[11] Durkheim, *The Elementary Forms of religious Life*, p.225.

ontologically creative and inarticulable dimension of the production of social meaning.[12]

For Castoriadis meaning is not exhausted by the linguisticality of the human universe. In his view, meaning comes about and refers to three forms of human activity and interaction: perception with its eye on the empirical, thought with its eye on the rational, and the imagination. It is imagination, or what Castoriadis prefers to call imaginary creation that „cannot be accounted for by reality, by rationality, or by the laws of symbolism".[13] It provides the centre of interpretation and explanation, which gives the symbolic orders of all societies, their unique unified meaning. Castoriadis puts it this way: „[There is] a system of imaginary significations that value or devalue, structure and hierarchize an intersecting ensemble of objects and corresponding lacks; and it is here that one can read, more easily than elsewhere, what just is as uncertain as it is uncontestable - the *orientation* of a society".[14] Elsewhere, he refers to imaginary significations as the invisible cement or glue that binds societies together.[15] In other words, according to him all societies refer to horizons of imaginary significations from which are generated and constituted symbolic and linguistic systems as systems. The social imaginary is the creative centre of the social - it originates new forms of imaginary significations and produces new horizons of meaning. Moreover, because society is inconceivable without reference to a core of imaginary significations the nature and notion of institutions is also transformed to embrace both its functional-institutional complex as well its imaginary one. In this way, „an institution is a socially sanctioned symbolic network in which a functional component and an imaginary component are combined in variable proportions and relations".[16]

If collective representations or social imaginaries are constitutive of any given society, this means that they are historically formed, changeable and multivarious. The inexhaustibility of meaning and the multivarious and changeable nature of collective representations or imaginary significations are the two background concerns against which the issue of the relation between religion and modernity can be contextualized.

[12] Cornelius Castoriadis, *The Imaginary Institution of Society*, 1987, Oxford, Polity Press. Castoriadis also terms this concealed constitutive internality „the immanent unperceivable". „The immanent unperceivable" is an *ideality*, which indicates that the signification is not rigidly attached to a material support, but that it goes beyond it without ever being able to do without it. It is this dimension of the immanent unperceived or social imaginary significations that create language and institutions, and without which the social human being cannot do without. See „The Imaginary: Creation in the Social Historical Domain" in *The World in Fragments*, Edited and translated by David Ames Curtis, 1997, Stanford, Stanford University Press, pp. 3-18.

[13] Castoriadis, *The Imaginary Institution of Society*. p.141.

[14] Ibid. p. 150.

[15] Ibid. p.142.

[16] Ibid. p. 132.

2. Religiosity at the Intersection of Multiple Modernities

In a discussion on the psyche and education Cornelius Castoriadis is asked by one of the discussants:

> Florence Guist-Despairie: „Couldn't the fact that growing numbers of people look to spiritual experience be seen as a protest against an increasingly atomised, fragmented, unbearable world?"
> C.C: „I definitely think so. What has been abusively, exaggeratedly called the revival of religion is of that order, but so is the [popular] Zenith music hall... These are all things on which to lean, through which to return to a sublation that seems to achieve a total meaning and at the same time precedes any articulated meaning".[17]

Two lines of thought emerge from Castoriadis' comment which can be taken up and developed in order to respond to a putative crisis of religiosity in modernity. On the one hand, Castoriadis' response of religiosity as a symptom of a crisis of meaning opens onto the direction explored above by way of Durkheim's work as well as his own, that is, the ontological formation of meaning. For Castoriadis, religion is viewed as only one dimension, one horizon or social imaginary through which meaning may be constructed, interpreted and conveyed. On the other hand, for Castoriadis, this crisis of meaning cannot be responded to in religious terms.[18] Rather, Castoriadis is making a critique of modernity in which religiosity is symptomatic of a crisis of meaning *within* modernity, and a crisis of meaning *per se*. However, from a different and more lateral view this double problem could be viewed as one of encounters and intersections between modernity, religiosity and the forms of meaning creation, rather than thinking of it in terms of a crisis.

Let's open onto this second line of thought regarding meaning and crisis before returning to the first. The idea of the crisis of religion stems from the classical sociological division between pre-modern religious traditional societies and modern secular ones. In conventional or classically inspired sociological theories, modernization and secularization includes industrialization, capitalization

17 „Psyche and Education " in *Figures of the Unthinkable*, trans Helen Arnold, Stanford University Press, 2007, p. 170.

18 This is because Castoriadis makes a categorial distinction within his own social ontology between heteronomy and autonomy. Notwithstanding Castoriadis' problematic distinction his formulation of social imaginaries provides an alternative path to Habermas' reading of modernity to the one laid down in *A Theory of Communicative Action*, where he also discusses Durkheim's work from a position of what he terms the „de-linguistification of the sacred". I have discussed Habermas' reading of Durkheim as well as Castoriadis' work in „From the Shores of Reason to the Horizon of Meaning: Some Remarks on Habermas' and Castoriadis' Theories of Culture", in *Thesis Eleven*, Number 22, 1989, pp. 5-24. See also, Johann P. Arnason, „Culture and Imaginary Significations" in the same issue, pp. 25-45.

and economic growth, urbanization, secularity (the separation of church and state), the rise of science and technology, and bureaucratization. In addition, this definition, inherited as much from Ferdinand Tönnies and Max Weber as Durkheim, is stabilized around a 'great' divide between religious belief, which is viewed as being synonymous with meaning per se, and non-religious secular forms of thought and patterns of purposively or instrumentally rationalized action that are disenchanted or de-magified and less than meaningful. Secularization becomes a stand-in category for modernization, more generally, thus, forging a synonymous relation between the two terms.[19] Modernization and secularization are conceptualized in terms of a linear historical movement from the pre-modern religious world(s) of transcendence to the modern secular age.

However, this assumption of a „great divide" between the religious and secular ages has been viewed as controversial or even false on both theoretical and empirical grounds. In the context of contemporary social formations the situation looks quite different. In his critique of the secularization thesis, Peter L. Berger, for example, argues a strongly counter position – that the modern world did not lead to a decline in religious belief or practice. In his terms, „modernization has had some secularizing effects, more in some places than in others. But it also provoked powerful movements of counter-secularization….Certain religious institutions have lost power and influence in many societies, but both old and new religious beliefs and practices have nevertheless continued in the lives of individuals, sometimes taking new institutional forms and sometimes leading to great explosions of religious fervour".[20] Moreover, Berger argues, that historically, secularization has been the exception rather than the rule, with respect to both the empirical and theoretical topographies and narratives of modernity. There are two exceptions, for him. One is Western Europe with its „massive secular Euro-culture", which for example, has, resulted in declining church

[19] See Max Weber, „Author's Introduction to *The Protestant Ethic and the Spirit of Capitalism*"; „Religious Rejections of the World and their Directions", in *From Max Weber*, edited by H.H. Gerth and C.Wright. Mills, Routledge and Kegan Paul, London, 1970, pp. 323-359; *The Sociology of Religion*, translated by Ephraim Fischoff with an Introduction by Talcott Parsons, Boston, 1960, Beacon Press. See also Bryan S. Turner, „Religion" in *Theory, Culture and Society*, Vol. 23, (2-3), 2006, pp. 437-455 for an overview.

[20] Peter, L. Berger, „The Deseculization of the World: A Global Overview", in *The Desecularization of the World: Resurgent Religion and World Politics*, edited by Peter L. Berger, 1999, Grand Rapids, Michigan, William B. Eerdmans Publishing Co, p. 3. See also Thomas Luckman, „Secularization – A Contemporary Myth", in *Life-World and Social Realities*, London, Heinemann Educational Books, pp. 124-132. Liliane Voye, „Secularization in the Context of Advanced Modernity", *Sociology of Religion*", Vol. 60, Number 3, (Autumn, 1999), pp. 275-288; Yves Lambert, „Religion in Modernity as a New Axial Age: Secularization or New Religious Forms?", *Sociology of Religion*, Vol. 60, Number 3, (Autumn, 1999), pp. 303-333; Edward A. Tiryakian, „Dialectics of Modernity. Reenchantments and Differentiation of Counterprocesses", in *Social Change and Modernity*, edited by Hans Haferkamp and Neil J Smelser, 1992, Berkeley, University of California Press, pp. 78-94.

attendance, and more importantly the decline in „the adherence of church directed codes for personal behaviour (especially with regard to sexuality, reproduction, and marriage)". The other exception is the growth of an international sub-culture of people who have been educated in the manner of Western higher education, especially in the humanities and social sciences, and who are bearers of the beliefs and values of the Enlightenment.[21] Berger's analysis can be put slightly differently in that two different trends are being noted, and these trends are the extension of particular versions of secularization, especially in terms of secular education, as well as the continuity *and* re-interpretation of religious forms in many societies, which it has been argued are responding to globalised modernity. However, Berger's point is that these religious forms are not merely responsive. They are constitutive of the articulation of social groups and societies, whether they take the form of continuity, disputes, or „revivals", for example, within Islam, Catholic or Protestant Christianity, or Buddhism, within or across particular national settings in the Middle East and Persian Gulf, South Asia, the Americas, South East Asia or the Pacific.[22]

Notwithstanding these continuous and „new" social formations, there is, nonetheless, also a presupposition by way of the secularization thesis that modernity not only disenchants but also empties and shallows out meaning. This presupposition assumes that it is only religion that can address and maintain depth of meaning, and this position has been articulated strongly by Thomas Luckmann, as well as Charles Taylor, at least in his recent work.[23] Luckmann makes a claim for the special dimension of social life that Durkheim reserves for the term „the sacred". For Luckmann, though, this term is, and can only be synonymous with religion. For him, religion is an „ontological fact" of human existence.

Moreover, for Luckmann we can only acquire our moral universe from a religious framework. For him, they go hand in hand. Because of this connection, for him, „religion is *not* a passing phase in the evolution of mankind but a universal aspect of the *condition humana* ... [It] remains a constitutive element of human life, bonding the individual human being, most particularly its experiences of

[21] Ibid, pp. 9-10.

[22] See Bryan S. Turner, ibid; Liliane Voye, „Secularization in the Context of Advanced Modernity", *Sociology of Religion*", Vol. 60, Number 3, (Autumn, 1999), pp. 275-288; Yves Lambert, „Religion in Modernity as a New Axial Age: Secularization or New Religious Forms?", *Sociology of Religion*, Vol. 60, Number 3, (Autumn, 1999), pp. 303-333; Robert W Hefner, „Public Islam and the Problem of Democratization"; *Sociology of Religion*, Vol. 62, No. 4, (Winter 2001), pp. 491-514; „Multiple Modernities: Christianity, Islam, and Hinduism in a Globalizing Age", *Annual Review of Anthropology*, 1998, Number 27, pp. 83-104.

[23] See Thomas Luckmann, „Transformations of Religion and Morality in Modern Europe", *Social Compass*, Volume 50, Number 3, 2003, pp. 275-285; Peter L. Berger and Thomas Luckmann, *Modernity, Pluralism and the Crisis of Meaning*, 1995, Gütersloh, Bertelsmann. This problem of modernity and its assumed crisis of meaning has also been explored by Charles Taylor in his *A Secular Age*.

transcendence, to a collective view of the good life".[24] Whilst everyday life shapes and limits experience, sacredness, for Luckmann is encountered, in a way similar to Durkheim's account, *beyond* it, and, notwithstanding the way this encounter is socially structured, it is for him the penultimate source of meaning and morality.

Whilst not drawing on Luckmann's work, Taylor makes a similar argument that further stratifies the relation between the sacred-religious and the modern world, which for him can also only be profane, notwithstanding a Romantic counter-current. In his critique of modernity as a secular age Taylor posits two contrasting images of selfhood to underpin his critique of modernity: a non-modern porous self, and a modern buffered one. The porous self is contextualized and constituted by a porosity between the mundane and enchanted worlds, whilst the buffered self establishes boundary conditions which limits the self. Taylor interprets these two worlds on the basis of the supremacy and sovereignty of the enchanted one with its cosmology, vertical and eternal sense of time, theogeny and miracles. This enchanted world is an exceptional and transcendent one, which the human world finds ultimately indeterminate, mysterious and unknowable, even though there is a porous relation between the two.[25]

Religion becomes the stand-in category for meaning, depth, morality, value, and the subjective experience of transcendence. It becomes an anthropological projection of the indeterminate nature of the human condition, one which may be ultimately unfathomable and uncontrollable. This anthropological projection, though, makes religion an umbrella concept under which is gathered not only the so-called „limit" experiences that occur on the edge of experience and perception, such as violence, suffering, mortality, and the expected or unexpected death of loved ones, but also those experiences that break through perception, often dissolving it and making the world inexplicable.

In other words, one can view the issue of religion, generally, in contemporary modernity as a stand-in category that addresses both the problem of meaning and the uncertain contingency of the human condition, and a set of problems that are related to specialization, differentiation, and complexity. Together, these two problem complexes of meaning and modernity appear as if there are ongoing crises on both fronts. However, it may be more illuminating to speak of intersections between the formation of new interpretations of religiosity in the context of the complexity of modernity *and* the complexity of meaning formation, itself. Put this way, and in the light of the discussions of Durkheim's and Castoriadis' works above, the relation between religion and modernity is not so much suggestive of historical linearity but of intersections

[24] Thomas Luckmann, „Transformations of Religion and Morality in Modern Europe", p. 276.

[25] Charles Taylor, *A Secular Age*. I have discussed Taylor's work in a review essay on *A Secular Age* in *Critical Horizons*, 11.1, 2010. It is beyond the scope of this essay to further explore Taylor's work. See also Habermas' critique of the priority of religiously conceived transcendence, which can also be read as an implicit critique of Taylor's position, in „Transcendence Within, Transcendence in this World", in *Religion and Rationality. Essays on Reason, God and Modernity*, edited with an Introduction by Eduardo Mendietta, 2002, Oxford, Polity, pp. 67-94.

and encounters between multiple modernities, and religions, and thus multiple „sacreds" or social imaginaries.

These intersections and encounters could be termed, following the work of Johann P. Arnason, 'intercivilisational ones', in which the notion of civilisation can be deployed in order to open onto the diversity of religious imaginaries, their long historical development and reach as well as their geographical breadth. As Arnason states intercivilizational encounters should not be viewed as either symmetrical or „dialogic" ones. Rather, for him, „they tend to be asymmetric in the sense that neither initiatives nor effects are evenly distributed ... They can, but not always do, involve high levels of violence and destruction – there is definitely no reason to invest the concept of intercivilizational encounters with the romantic aura that tends to accompany the notion of 'a dialogue between civilizations'. On the other hand they can be productive, in the sense of giving rise to new socio-cultural patterns and opening up new historical horizons, and there is no obvious pattern of direct or indirect relations between the productive and destructive aspects".[26] To put it slightly differently, a civilizational encounter is a moment, even a historically long one, in which power and cultural resources and interpretations are mobilized in ways where both spatial and symbolic or interpretative boundaries become porous, are opened and are often re-made.[27]

[26] Johann P. Arnason, „Understanding Civilizational Encounters", in *Thesis Eleven*, Number 86, August 2006, p. 44. It should be noted here that I am not equating civilisations with religions even though what are taken as 'civilisations' often have a central religious dimension through which they can be defined. Religions does not exhaust what a civilisation is, even in its more objectivistic definitions. Rather, this perspective of intersections between civilizations and modernities is typified by contemporary work that deploys images of tension between conflict and integration *within* modernity itself, *between* all of its different dimensions, and *between* these dimensions and the civilisational backdrops against which modernities can develop. In this way, credence is given to the specific characteristics of regional and civilisational identities and geographies, and the way in which tensions and conflicts are constitutive of these. In this way, too, civilization becomes an umbrella concept for the coalescence of cultural forms, or in Durkheimian-Castoriadian terms, rich complexes of meaning, as well as forms of power that mark the particularities of boundary formation. See S.M. Eisenstadt, „The Civilisational Dimension of Modernity: Modernity as a Distinct Civilisation"; „Multiple Modernities in an Age of Globalisation"; „Multiple Modernities"; and „Barbarism and Modernity: The Destructive Components of Modernity" all in *Comparative Civilisations and Multiple Modernities*, Vols 2, Brill, Lieden, 2003, chaps 20-23. Johnn P. Arnason, „The Multiplication of Modernity", in *Identity, Culture and Globalisation*, edited by Eliezer Ben-Rafael, with Yitzhak Sternberg, Brill, Leiden, 2002; Johann P.Arnason, „Questioning the West: The Uses and Abuses of Anti-Eurocentrism", in *Civilisations in Dispute*, Brill Leiden, 2003, pp. 323-359. For a more recent articulation of Arnason's positions see „Domains and Perspectives of Civilizational Analysis", and 'The Cultural Turn and the Civilizational Approach", both in *European Journal of Social Theory*, Vol. 13, Number 1, pp. 5-13, and 67-82, respectively.

[27] See John Rundell, „From Indigenous Civilization to Indigenous Modernities", in *Rethinking Civilizational Analysis*, edited by Saïd Arjomand and Edward A Tiryakian, 2004, London, Sage Publishers, especially p. 209.

The results of these intersections and encounters have been combinations of the long histories of regions and cultures, the specificity of modernising impulses, and conflicts at junctures of both of these forces, the focal point of which are the social imaginaries and their world pictures and programs. S.N. Eisenstadt, for one, argues that the best way to understand these intercivilizational encounters, which include the history of modernity, is to see these as stories „of continual constitution and reconstitution of a multiplicity of cultural programs. These ongoing reconstructions of a multiple institutional and ideological patterns are carried forward by specific social actors in close connection with social, political and intellectual activists, and also by social movements pursuing different programs of modernity, holding very different views on what makes societies modern".[28] For Eisenstadt, modernity, too, is a civilization. However, because of the multiplicity of modern forms, its dynamism and „unevenness" it might be better to conceive it as constituted by open indeterminate forms in the context of intercivilizational encounters.

However, the notion of multiple modernities is not merely a regional concept, that is, of building geographical and social specificity into the idea of modernity, itself. It is also a concept that pluralises the notion and experience of modernity into a series of competing dimensions that are irreducible to one another even though they may intersect. These multiple forms of modernity include the long histories of globalized markets, nation states and inter-state environments, democratization and public opinion, industrialization and the re-organization of work, and expressivist aesthetics, each of which swings between creations and interpretations of control and creations and interpretations of autonomization. In other words, multiple modernities is both a regional concept and one that multi-dimensionalises the concept of modernity itself. One can speak of multiple modernities in the context of intercivilizational encounters, the result of which are co-existences and shared social spaces.

The notion of multiple modernities create perspectives both in terms of its geographies and the ways in which its features are conceptually mobilized and prioritized. The intersections and the tensions that are so created entail that the appropriation of modern institutional patterns, ways of thinking and acting and the human self-images, that is, of the modern „sacreds" or social imaginaries that constitute these - for example, of being rational, free, a national, a capitalist, a democrat or an étatist – has neither been immediate nor straightforward. For example, a particular juncture for these competing modernities and religious imaginaries has often been the continuing (re-) formation of nations against a civilizational backdrop in which wars of independence gives way to often violently articulated competing claims. These claims include participating

[28] S.N. Eisenstadt, *Comparative Civilizations and Multiple Modernities, Part II*, p. 536. See also 'The Civilizational Dimension of Modernity. Modernity as a Distinct Civilization", in in *Rethinking Civilizational Analysis*, edited by Saïd Arjomand and Edward A Tiryakian, 2004, London, Sage Publishers, pp. 48-66. See Agnes Heller, *A Theory of Modernity*, 1997, Oxford, Blackwell, for an alternative way of theorizing the plurality of the modern condition.

in, shaping, or contesting their particular cultural and organizational models of modernity, including the secular or religious adherence that is being pursued by the predominant elite, and hence the relation between religiosity and the nation-state. It becomes an open question as to whether or not democracy is within the vocabulary of many of these participants, and within the orbit of the conflicts in which they are embroiled.[29]

In other words, a continuous selection, re-interpretation, and re-formulation of these imaginaries, including religious ones, has occurred that has given rise to new political and institutional arrangements and cultural programs that have their own antinomies and tensions, in which conceptions of collective identity, including negative and positive conceptions of others are constantly reconstructed in both religious and 'secular', or more properly *multiple modern* terms. This also entails that the singular points of reference that purportedly gave meaning its depth and morality its voice are also pluralized. If the depth of meaning is not synonymous with religion or transcendence (Taylor) *per se*, then the issue becomes the pluralisation of its possible sites, and not the absence or vacuity of meaning itself.

3. Multiple Modernities and the Democratic Imaginary: Religion as a Stand-in Category

In the wake of controversies and observations put forward by such writers as Berger, Luckmann and Taylor it has been argued that the current situation has been termed a post-secular one, rather than one simply of crisis. However, in the light of the above remarks, one can speak of intersections between the continuity of religious forms of belief, the formation of new interpretations of religiosity, the complexity of modernity and the complexity of meaning formation. In other words, it may be analytically more helpful to speak of civilizational encounters and multiple modernities than the post-secular condition. It is in this context that religion, again, becomes a stand-in category that denotes an intersection where modernities and religiosity meet. It is here that social actors, who may be either religious or secular, forge or navigate an increasingly complex environment that includes multi-faith and multicultural politics, transnational

29 Ibrahim Kaya, *Social Theory and Later Modernities The Turkish Experience,* Liverpool University Press, 2004; Augustus Richard Norton (Ed), Civil Society in the Middle East, Vols 1&2, Leiden, Brill Academic Publishers, 1995; Ibrahim Kaya, 'Modernity, openness, interpretation: a perspective on multiple modernities', *Theory and Methods*, Vol. 43, No 1, 2004, pp. 35-57; Luis Roniger, and Carlos H. Waisman, (eds), *Globality and Multiple Modernities*, Sussex Academic Press, 2002; Cihan Tuğal, „Islamism in Turkey: beyond instrument and meaning", *Economy and Society*, Volume 31, Number 1, February 2002, pp. 85-111; „Civilizing Islam, Islamist Civilizing? Turkey's Islamist Movement and the Problem of Ethnic Difference", *Thesis Eleven*, Number 58, August 1999, pp. 83-98.

demois and nation states in an age of uncertainty and contingent open-endedness. These complex environments might be described as „new world" societies for which „old" Europe is no longer the template. The „new world" societies include not only the Americas, Australia and contemporary Europe, but also societies of the Middle East, including Israel, notwithstanding profound differences between them.[30]

It is here that Jürgen Habermas' essays on religious tolerance helps to throw the problem of navigation into relief. Habermas, to be sure from his strong interpretive position of communicative action, shows *how* „new world" societies *could* function democratically in the context of opposing points of view, cultural programs and social imaginaries or sacreds (to use a language other than Habermas'). For Habermas, religion is a stand-in category for thinking through *the relation* between democratic politics and a constitutional patriotism to it and difference or multicultural contexts and experiences. It is not Habermas' more positive point of view that is of interest here. Rather it is the way that he discusses religious pluralism from the vantage point of the mutual recognition of their competing „styles of life", and the way in which this potentially agonistic situation opens onto the complexity of modernity – a complexity that should be modulated and mediated by modernity's democratic impulse rather than its darker tones.[31] Whilst this is not surprising given Habermas' „philosophical

[30] Habermas takes up the notion of the „post-secular" to also describe those societies that are or were secular, and this context also experience a vibrancy of religious communities. Apart from the essays mentioned he also critically discusses this term in „Notes on a post-secular society" in *sightandsound.com* (http://sightandsound.com/features. Accessed on 18.7/2008) Multiculturalism can also be viewed as a stand-in category for intersections between national, democratic, and particular identities. For the complexity of „new world" societies see *Comparing Modernities Pluralism versus Homogeneity*, edited by Eliezer Ben-Rafael and Yitzak Sternberg, 2005, Leiden, Brill, especially the essays by Danièle Hervieu-Léger and Eliezer Ben-Rafael, „Multiple Religious Modernities: A new approach to contemporary modernities", and „From Religion to Nationalism: The Transformation of Jewish Identity", respectively. See also Augustus Richard Norton (Ed), Civil Society in the Middle East, Vols 1&2, Leiden, Brill Academic Publishers, 1995; James Bohman, *Democracy Across Borders From Dêmos to Dêmois*, 2007, Cambridge, Mass, The MIT Press.

[31] In this context, fundamentalism will be viewed as a separate and different issue, one that is ultimately a non-religious response to modernity, a response that is a totalizing redemptive reduction of complexity and contingency. Fundamentalist movements or anti-movements (Wieviorka) are movements ultimately about the direction and cultural model of their respective nation states of origins, irrespective of their geographical locations-in-exile and their civilizational fantasises. See Michel Wieviorka, *The Making of Terrorism*, translated by David Gordon White, 1988, Chicago, University of Chicago Press. Ferenc Feher discusses the redemptive paradigm in „Redemptive and Democratic Paradigms in Radical Politics" (Ferenc Feher, „Redemptive and Democratic Paradigms in Radical Politics", *Eastern Left, Western Left*, 1987, Oxford, Basil Blackwell, pp. 61-76). Feher argues that modern redemptive politics is born at the end of the eighteenth century, and is first personified by Napolean. According to Feher the main features of the redemptive paradigm are, firstly, an over-reduction in the inherent

discourse of modernity", what is interesting about his later interventions in *Between Naturalism and Religion* and *Religion and Rationality* is that religion begins to emerge as a stand-in category for the dual issues of political will formation and meaning formation.

In his more recent work Habermas argues that a new double-sided learning process should occur on the side of the so-called secular constitutional democratic state and those religious communities who belong to it. He begins from the social and historical „facts" of cultural or civilizational pluralism. For Habermas, a culture (or civilization) „furnishes those who grow up in it not only the elementary linguistic, practical and cognitive capacities, but also the grammatically prestructured worldviews and semantically accumulated stores of knowledge ... [T]raditions preserve their vitality by insinuating themselves into the ramified and interlinked channels of individual life histories and, in the process, passing the critical threshold of the autonomous endorsement of every single potential participant ... The test of the vitality of a cultural tradition ultimately lies in the fact that challenges can be transformed into solvable problems for those who grow up within this tradition."[32] In other words, a culture provides depth and robustness, and can either be relatively closed or relatively open.

For Habermas, the contemporary challenge for religiously constituted cultures or civilizations is to learn one of modernity's own multiplicities - its democratic one. This is especially the case for those religions which stand outside the

complexity of modernity, which attempts to dissolve the inevitable conflicts and tensions between subsystems, and that this dissolution also comes through or is directed through a single medium – the irrational authority of the redeemer, who claims the highest form of rationality which cannot be questioned. Secondly, a homogenization of the plurality of groups, classes and organizations of civil society, accompanies this reduction of complexity. Political pluralism is subject to a homogenizing political state. In the context of the above two dynamics, Feher goes onto argue that, thirdly, no set of predictable institutions can emerge as these are reduced to the personality and strategy of the redeemer. Hence, they vary from redeemer to redeemer. The redemptive paradigm not only homogenizes the relation between society and the state. It also, Feher continues, a substitute for traditional religious cohesion in the domains of society and culture, which have been incompletely uncoupled from religious forms of meaning, and hence incompletely secularized. This is especially in the context of the inability of modern scientific spirit to fulfil all needs, and where democracy becomes legalistic and procedural and cannot supply directions for ethical and moral conduct. The logic of the redemptive paradigm is that it is the politics of ultimate ends. In more recent political history the redemptive paradigm has been recycled in unexpected places, for example, in Islamist fundamentalist politics where forms of potential or real terrorism can emerge from a negative, one-dimensionalizing critique of modernity coupled with, in this case, an imputed collective representation or social imaginary that needs to be saved. However, the form of terror carries the same aesthetic load as it it did with other terrorisms– it is stylized, ritualized and symbolic, and in a way that homogenizes and disregards both the complexity of the target group that has been constructed as the enemy, and the host civilization from which it originated.

32 Jürgen Habermas „Equal Treatment of Cultures", in *Between Naturalism and Religion: Philosophical Essays*, translated by Ciaran Cronin, 2008, Oxford, Polity, p. 302.

long history of the formation of European states and polities in which religious conflict and its resolution through a language of „tolerance" became one of its cultural learning processes. In other words, Habermas' implicit use of religion as a stand-in category contains a significant insight. The debate about religion is not about religion or even secularization as such, but about the democratization of religious horizons and „multicultural" co-existences.[33]

According to Habermas, because of the legacy of its own religious wars European democratic modernity has an already pre-existing burden of tolerance that should continue to be learnt, re-learnt or opened to new horizons and understandings in both European and non-European „new world" societies. The contemporary situation, is a case in point, where, as he states, „the inclusion of religious minorities in the political community awakens and promotes the sensitivity to the claims of other groups that suffer discrimination… From the perspective of equal inclusion all citizens [ ] religious discrimination takes place in the long list of cultural, linguistic, ethnic and racial, sexual and physical discrimination".[34] Habermas goes onto argue that the inclusivist dynamic that underlies tolerance occurs along two paths – one concerned with distributive justice and the other with full membership of the national-political state as a *political* sovereign within it. Although these paths have been practiced and applied individualistically Habermas argues that this can be extended to encompass group or cultural rights. Because, for him, cultures have a robustness and depth, the notion of individual right can be extended to the cultural group so that access by individuals „to the contents of experience, communication, and recognition in which people can articulate their self-understanding and develop and maintain identities" is guaranteed.[35] For Habermas group rights are the current litmus test and pacesetter for the modern democratic state, along with civil disobedience. Moreover, and importantly for Habermas, group rights ensure that „the polyphonic complexity of public voices" in the public sphere is not reduced.[36]

The burden of tolerance is in this context shared between the religious group *and* „secular new world" civil societies and their democratic constitutional states. On the one side, according to Habermas, groups that suffer discrimination do not „benefit from a morality of equal rights on inclusion without making this morality their own in turn".[37] From the other side, the burden of tolerance also

[33] Jürgen Habermas, „Religion in the Public Sphere", in *Between Naturalism and Religion*, p. 138. See also Jan Rath, Rinux Penninx, Kees Groenendijk, and Astrid Meyer, *Western Europe and its Islam*, 2001, Leiden, Brill, for responses that address the relation between Europe, including the UK, its Islamic citizens and non-citizens from democratic perspectives that attempt to build in the plurality of ways of life in both institutional and cultural ways.

[34] Jürgen Habermas, „Religious Tolerance as Pacemaker", in *Between Naturalism and Religion*, p. 267.

[35] Ibid, p. 269.

[36] Jürgen Habermas, „Religion in the Public Sphere", in *Between Naturalism and Religion*, p. 131.

[37] Jürgen Habermas, „Religious Tolerance as Pacemaker", in *Between Naturalism and Religion*, p. 269.

„demands that 'strong' secular communities should establish cognitive links between their internal ethos and the morality of human rights that prevails in their social and political environments".[38] In this way, Habermas implicitly proposes a type of quasi-corporatistic integrationist model so favoured by Durkheim in his own solution to the crisis of modernity, and more recently practiced by many „new world" societies such as Australia and Canada, especially in the areas of multiculturalism and indigenous politics.

Yet, for Habermas, this integrationist model requires a „ground" upon which it can rest. In his critical discussion of Rawl's proposal that the cognitive burden for tolerance and social inclusion falls upon religious believers-citizens themselves to subsume their belief to the liberal constitutional state, Habermas' argument goes in two different directions – one towards his theory of learning processes, and another towards an idea reminiscent of Durkheim's notion of collective representations. From one side, the liberal state should be agnostic and „must not transform the necessary *institutional* separation between religion and politics into an unreasonable *mental and psychological* burden for its religious citizens".[39] This burden is lightened, so to speak, when there is a shared and uniting bond between believers and secularists of a legally unenforceable civic solidarity".[40] This means that, as Habermas notes, there is a more-than-cognitive dimension. In other words, conflicts among religious groups, and between them and secularists cannot be solved cognitively. They require a hermeneutic self-reflection, which, for Habermas involves a reflection „concerning the normative premises of the constitutional state and of a democratic civic ethos".[41]

For Habermas, this hermeneutic self-reflection is the result of learning processes in which norms become open to discursive and argumentative reasoning about their universalizable validity. This insight regarding mutual learning processes can only be developed from his dual vantage point of *evolutionary* learning processes and his post-metaphysically posited, yet, quasi-transcendental claims to normative validity. According to Habermas, the learning processes themselves are tied to what he has termed, following his own reconstruction of Durkheim's work, „the linguistification of the sacred", that is, the internal differentiation of cultures into claims for truth, normative rightness, or authenticity. And it is this internal differentiation that is the operative condition that informs his idea of the double warrant. Religious social actors should be able to undertake a „double transcendence" – one towards an other-worldly form of belief, and another towards the claims to normativity that are imbedded in the speech acts themselves.

For Habermas, speech act theory or universal pragmatics also solves the problem of the constitution of meaning – meaning is intersubjectively constituted

[38] Ibid, . p. 270. It is beyond the scope of this essay to discuss the issue of group rights.

[39] Jürgen Habermas, „Religion in the Public Sphere", in *Between Naturalism and Religion*, p. 130.

[40] Ibid, p. 135.

[41] Ibid, p. 139.

through speech acts, and is neither grounded in cultures or traditions in Gadamer's sense, nor ontically concealed (Heidegger), nor deferred in „playful" slippages (Derrida). Habermas makes a counterfactual distinction between irrationality and rationality. According to Habermas, we do not decide to be rational beings – we *are* rational beings. Habermas attempts to re-claim the Enlightenment's claim to reason by locating it within speech acts, which by their very nature contain the validity claims of truth, legitimacy, or truthfulness which become exposed through argumentation. Habermas moves the democratic imperative of modernity to the intersubjective-linguistic constitution of the species in order to establish a post-metaphysical reflective foundationalism. As such, we are not simply linguistic animals, but argumentative ones, for it is through argument that the rightness of a norm is questioned. Consensus, at this level, means for Habermas at least in the context of political modernity, that there is an implicit agreement to argue, deliberate and understand. This implicit agreement to argue and to understand is imbedded in the law or collective representation of the modern constitutional state as a democratic deliberative proceduralism.[42] Distorted communication occurs when argument does not occur, and is replaced, for example with violence.

However, one needs to step outside the framework of learning processes and the theory of communicative action to develop Habermas' insight in a more open-ended dynamic and indeterminate way that does not pre-suppose progress or decline. Habermas thinks that „inter-civilizational" encounters, which include judgments from both sides, is resolved through learning process and universal pragmatics. However, there is a moment of disquiet for Habermas, even in this strong post-metaphysical position, which could lead in a different direction. This disquiet refers neither to the problem of pseudo-corporatist integration, not to the learning processes themselves. Rather, it belongs to the issue of the limits of both the learning processes and „new world" democratic constitutional states. Habermas admits that it remains an open question whether the relation between faith and democratic will formation can be pursued through epistemic means or argumentation.[43] Perhaps this issue is neither epistemic nor normative-argumentative, but ontological in the Durkheimian sense. Perhaps it refers to the shared bond between believers and non-believers that, as Habermas himself has noted, is ultimately legally unenforceable. If it is unenforceable, then this relation and its social power originate elsewhere, apart from language use and learning processes. This leaves open the suggestion that openness to learning is based on a prior value or imaginary, and that the arguments that this evinces are of a second order.

Agnes Heller, for one, acknowledges the complexity of the modern world and works with a differentiated model. Where Habermas places the public

[42] See Jürgen Habermas, *Between Facts and Norms Contributions to a Discourse Theory of Law and Democracy*, translated by William Rehg, 1997, Oxford, Polity Press.

[43] Jürgen Habermas, „Religion in the Public Sphere", in *Between Naturalism and Religion*, pp. 144-145.

sphere at the centre of his model, which is the result of his theory of communicative rationality, Heller does not equate democratization with an increase in argumentation. To be sure, Heller's project is located in the same arena as Habermas', and yet she is especially critical of his theory of communicative rationality. Heller argues instead that people do not move to reflexive action through argumentation. Rather they are motivated to argue from a prior condition. Crucially for her the agreement to argue originates from a prior and concealed value. It is not built-in, so to speak. Rather, according to Heller, the right to argue is something that has to be argued for, to convince others of, on the basis of a value perspective. It is here that Heller's argument has an affinity with the Durkheimian one outlined above. Values function homologously in the same way that collective representations do for Durkheim, or social imaginaries do for Castoriadis, notwithstanding the differences between these three thinkers – they are an „invisible cement". Values provide the bridge between the inner world of desires, interests and hopes, and the social world including the socially located activity of critical evaluation and judgment. They provide the focus around which the inner and outer life of the subject, and thus social action. For her, there is no „great divide" between reason and emotion, the profane and the transcendent.[44]

Modern reflexive culture is dynamic in the sense that, for Heller, not only can everyday life be evaluated, but also the values themselves – they are no longer ultimate. To be sure, different values are historically created and interpreted and have become embedded in modern culture. However, for her this does not mean that they become relative. Some become universalizable and universalizing points of orientation, and as such become the points of orientation from which one critiques other values and patterns of action.

The universalizable and universalizing modern value, according to Heller, is freedom. However, this freedom is paradoxical in that it is the ground of modernity which, itself, cannot be grounded. As she states, „*the moderns are sitting on a paradox.* This is the constellation of the modern world: it is grounded by a principle which, in principle, does not ground anything; it is founded on a universal value or idea, which in principle negates foundation".[45] It is also empty in the sense that it is created through its very actions and interpretations. What is unique about the modern condition are the arguments about its meaning

[44] Heller's concentration on values is linked to her anthropology where she states that „readiness for rational argumentation […] presupposes the involvement of the human being as a whole, as a needing, wanting, feeling being" (Agnes Heller, „Habermas and Marxism", in *The Grandeur and Twilight of Radical Universalism*, p. 463). To be sure, argumentation is certainly about raising claims as an action; but as an action it is also an activity that connects with and articulates needs, feelings, and values that acting subjects bring to the permanent context of intersubjectively constituted social life. See also *Theory of Feelings*, Second Edition, 2009, New York, Rowman and Littlefield; „The Role of Emotions in the Reception of Art Works" in in *Pathos, Affect, Gefühl. Die Emotionen in den Künsten* edited by Klaus Herding and Bernard Stumpflaus, Walter de Gruyter, Berlin, 2004, pp. 244-259.

[45] Agnes Heller, *A Theory of Modernity*, 1999, Oxford, Blackwell, p. 15.

and its reference points, but arguments that once gave the appearance of metaphysical certainty, an appearance that has been abandoned. It is a freedom without illusions of grandeur, of redemption, of the restoration of lost hopes and dreams. In this sense, for her, it is not only post-foundational, but also utopic. Nonetheless, this „empty" concept of freedom did not come out of nowhere. According to her, freedom functions as a shared cultural 'arche' to which cultural memory returns. Because of its function as a central cultural concept or social imaginary, Heller argues that the narrative of freedom, or the myths, stories and fictions that embody it has a long history that pre-dates modernity, even as modernity reinterprets these and creates new stories of freedom for itself.[46]

Because freedom is a groundless value or social imaginary, it co-constitutes the different and competing modern fields and inter-civilizational encounters as one of their possible interpretations. For example, modernity and religion might meet in the play of historical contingency, and thus in the competition and dissonance of values or imaginaries, one of which is freedom.[47]

The value or imaginary of freedom interpreted from the perspective of politics almost presumes intersubjectivity, but does not build this as an anthropological constituent. For Heller, politics could almost be seen as an empty space, in a similar way to Lefort's description of the political. In Lefort's view, and following de Toqueville's lead, democracy presumes not individualism, but interdependence, and it is this interdependence that provides a limit to the conduct of others, or more properly, in Lefort's terms, enables conduct to remain *political*.[48] In this sense, for Lefort, democracy or the political, and for him, they are co-terminus, is open and empty: it is an open-ended form of society, open to the circulation of power, the creation of forms of association and the making of politics, and open to forms of interpretation, all of which give it substance.

For Heller, and notwithstanding an initial asymmetricality of encounters, including civilizational and cultural ones, the political space should be transposed as recognition of the other *qua* other, or as a dynamic of symmetrical reciprocity on the basis of the circulation of the imaginary of freedom. It is here that freedom becomes an intersubjectively orientated concept and style of action, rather than one which is particularistic or ego-centered. Symmetrical reciprocity is

[46] See Agnes Heller, „European Master-Narratives About Freedom", in *Handbook of Contemporary European Social Theory*, edited by Gerard Delanty, 2005, London, Routledge, pp. 257-265. Heller also argues that life is the other universalizable value or imaginary of modernity. The value of life can be interpreted as the right to *be*, to exist, and instituted from the vantage point of justice as it pertains to the just distribution of life chances and the retribution of injustices against this right in both national and international contexts. Freedom is the value *beyond* justice and informs it.

[47] Agnes Heller, *A Theory of Modernity*, 1999, Oxford, Blackwell, especially p. 14, 54-55.

[48] Ibid; see also Lefort, *Democracy and Political Theory*, especially pp. 9-20. To be sure, Lefort has had a long engagement with de Toqueville's work in the context of his critiques of the Jacobin paradigm. See, for example his essays on de Tocqueville in *Democracy and Political Theory*, pp. 165-209, and *Writing the Political Test*, pp. 35-66.

constituted through the recognition of the person *qua* person, that is, men and women who „recognize each other's autonomy and have respect for each other's personality".[49] Symmetrical reciprocity assumes not only recognition, but also a relationship and reciprocity. As Heller notes a *relationship* of symmetrical reciprocity only occurs when each party gives and receives. It does not occur when one party gives and the other does not receive. In addition, there is no *reciprocity* when only one party gives and the other only receives, even though there may be a relationship.[50] Symmetrical reciprocity, along with argumentation, is, thus, a particular form of intersubjectivity – a second order one - through which both secular and religious social actors comport their relations with one another as mutual movements back and forth.[51]

Modernity is ecumenical or heterodox, which means that it was constitutively plural or multi-dimensional, even in the face of power and domination. In the face of this multi-dimensionality there is a burden, but it is the burden of value responsibility. Modernity, in fact, generates a double paradox for this burden – freedom is an imaginary that cannot provide a foundation, which itself produces another paradox, the irresolvability of inevitable clashes of cultures, religions and civilizations that cannot be removed. Nor can it simply be managed. However, for Heller, „in practice ... every culture makes a decisive choice. This is just as much of a leap as are many of our other choices ... The decision that one normally makes – that is, the leap – is not theoretically founded but contextual. In any given context, where the paradox appears and choice (in action and judgment) is unavoidable, one chooses either the one statement of the paradox or the other as the foundation of one's decision. This is not a logical but an ethico-political choice in each case. And this means that the man or the woman who so chooses is taking responsibility for his or her choice".[52] A person or a culture can leap out of the hermeneutical circle of freedom, or remain within in and accept the limit that is implied within the political notion of freedom, that is, the circulation of interpretations, power and symmetrical reciprocity.

If symmetrical reciprocity and argumentation are not a possibility, disentanglement and depoliticisation is an option. Mutual indifference and a self-conscious lack of reciprocity is a Stoic option rather than mere tolerance. Mutual indifference may here be viewed as keeping the circle of *possible* understandings and interpretations open, of keeping the possible discussions alive for another time. The issue of burden becomes an existential issue of living 'well' towards oneself and others in the context of the intersections of modernity, the tensions that these create, and the burden of ethical responsibility that is required to form a life lived more or less without causing damage.

49 Agnes Heller, 1990, 67.
50 Ibid, 1990: 53.
51 Ibid, 1990: 56.
52 Agnes Heller, *A Theory of Modernity*, p. 140. See also pp. 17-172.

THE RELEVANCE AND THE LIMITS OF THE NOTION OF A POST-SECULAR AGE IN JURGEN HABERMAS'S THEORY OF TOLERATION

Devrim Kabasakal

1. Introduction

Habermas developed a considerable interest in the issue of religion and its role in the contemporary world in his later writings. Especially after the event of September 11, he began to reflect on the 'public' role of religion rather than considering religion predominantly within the boundaries of the private realm.[1] Along with this interest in religion and its role in public political life, toleration comes to the fore as a central theme in his later writings in which he explicitly raises the issue within the context of contemporary democratic societies. This is because, on his view, toleration is a necessary condition to live together in peace, stability and justice as free and equal citizens of a democratic community who hold various worldviews and beliefs. Moreover, toleration is a relevant and significant issue also in his writings that deal with the question of religion and secularism in the global realm. In his international theory, he still considers toleration as a necessary condition to live together in peace and stability in a just world-society divided by various faiths and worldviews.

There is one central idea that is worth investigating in Habermas's later work that inspires his thought on toleration and its requirements in the contemporary world; that is his idea of a post-secular age. In this paper, I will analyze Habermas's understanding of the post-secular age with a focus on its relevance and limits as far as Habermas's conception of toleration is concerned. I will argue that the notion of a post-secular age is significant for the toleration argument of Habermas since it provides a descriptive foundation by qualifying as a circumstance of

[1] For an account and critic of Habermas's thought on religion in his earlier writings, see *Habermas, Modernity and Public Theology*, Don. S. Browning and Francis Schussler Fiorenza, eds (New York: Crossroad, 1992) and Michele Dillon, „The Authority of the Holy Revisited: Habermas, Religion and Emancipatory Possibilities", *Sociological Theory*, 17, No. 3 (Nov., 1999).

toleration. However, this descriptive foundation has a limited potential on its own to claim for the necessity and importance of toleration. The diagnosis that we live in a post-secular age does not provide enough reasons for the justification of toleration. Thus, we need a moral substantive reason and that is the idea of *equal respect* in the theory of Habermas which gives a moral reason for toleration. This might be argued both regarding his domestic and international conceptions of toleration.

First, I will begin the analysis by outlining the significance and place of toleration in the theory of Habermas. Secondly, I will examine his notion of a post-secular age with a focus on its relevance for Habermas's theory of toleration. This examination will also reveal the limits of the notion as far as Habermas's account of toleration is considered. Thirdly, I will bring in the idea of equal respect as a justification for toleration that provides the moral foundation for Habermas's toleration argument. Finally in the last section, I will outline the demands of toleration in a post-secular age in the theory of Habermas to demonstrate that it is not possible to argue the demands that Habermas envisions only by relying on the notion of a post-secular age. Throughout the whole analysis, I will be referring to Habermas's both domestic and international conceptions of toleration as two parallel and compatible conceptions that constitute a unified theory of toleration.

2. The Significance and Centrality of Toleration in the Theory of Jurgen Habermas

First of all, we need to consider the meaning and centrality of toleration in the political theory of Jurgen Habermas before dealing with his notion of a post-secular age and its relevance for his toleration argument. We might say that toleration for Habermas is a requirement of his understanding of political liberalism and thus, of justice.

The idea of toleration is embedded in Habermas's political theory due to his understanding of the justification of the secular constitutional state. He says: „political liberalism (which I defend in the specific form of a Kantian republicanism) understands itself as a nonreligious and postmetaphysical justification of the normative bases of the democratic constitutional state."[2] For him, the constitution of a liberal state derives its legitimacy in a self-sufficient manner on the basis of arguments that are independent of religious and metaphysical traditions. We could observe the independent legitimacy in the democratic will formation of people which gives justification to the law and authority in the

[2] Jurgen Habermas, and Joseph Cardinal Ratzinger (Pope Benedict XVI), *Dialectics of Secularization- On Reason and Religion*, Florian Schuller (ed.) (San Francisco: Ignatius Press, 2006), 24. For his defense of a Kantian Republican political liberalism, see his *Inclusion of the Other Studies in Political Theory*, Ciaran Cronin and Pablo De Greiff, eds (MIT, 1998).

political theory of Habermas. In a postmetaphysical age, the state does not refer to any religious and metaphysical worldview to claim its legitimate authority. Instead, the justification of political authority rests on a principle of toleration because it does not impose any religion or metaphysics on people.

In line with the above-mentioned claim, for Habermas, toleration comes to the fore as a requirement of justice as well. He says: „the theory of a discourse ethics criticizes traditional attempts to base conceptions of justice upon religious conceptions or conceptions of the good life."[3] Thus, in Habermas's theory, the concept of toleration justifies the principles of justice because justice requires its principles to be derived from an independent (autonomous) ground. Indeed it seems this is valid for any conception of justice in contemporary societies that claim legitimacy in a post-metaphysical age.

The significance and the centrality of toleration becomes evident in the theory of Habermas especially if we consider that tolerance arises as a question of both enacting and applying laws as well as a question of everyday practice.[4] Since tolerance is a principle rooted in the legitimacy of a constitutional state, no citizen should try to impose her own view on others or try to use the state power to apply her own ethos on other citizens. In this respect, he says:

> Tolerance means that believers of one faith and another and nonbelievers must mutually concede one another the right to those convictions, practices and ways of living that they themselves reject. This concession must be supported by a shared basis of mutual recognition from which repugnant dissonances can be overcome... The basis of recognition is not the esteem for this or that property or achievement, but the awareness of the fact that the other is a member of an inclusive community of citizens with equal rights, in which each is accountable to everybody else for her political contributions.[5]

Thus, the procedural democratic will formation of citizens underlines the significance of the principle of toleration. This principle has to be respected by citizens so that they should tolerate each other's worldviews in line with the independent legitimacy they themselves give to the state power. Each citizen, as a member of a democratic constitutional society, should recognize each other as free and equal and grant the right to be different to each other even though they disapprove of each others' world-views.

Habermas does not address toleration as an international issue as explicitly as in the case of the domestic context. Nevertheless, the necessity and significance of toleration is rooted in his writings that aim to focus on the question of religion and

[3] Francis Schussler Fiorenza, „The Church as a Community of Interpretation: Political Theology between Discourse Ethics and Hermeneutical Reconstruction" in *Habermas, Modernity and Public Theology*, Don S. Browning and Francis Schussler Fiorenza, eds (New York: Crossroad Publishing, 1992), 73.

[4] Jurgen Habermas, „A „post-secular" society- what does that mean?", paper presented at *Istanbul Seminars East and West* (2-8 June 2008), 6.

[5] Ibid.

secularism in the global realm because he still deals with the question of how it is possible to live together in peace in a world-society divided by various faiths, world-views and beliefs. As he says: „the conflict of cultures take place today in the framework of a world society in which the collective actors must, regardless of their different cultural traditions, agree for better or worse on norms of coexistence."[6] His awareness of diversity in the global realm motivates him to consider the possible answers for the question at stake and he considers toleration as a normative answer which is consistent with his considerations regarding the domestic toleration.

For Habermas, international toleration is a requirement of justice. He believes that a multicultural world-society which is peaceful and just can be possible with the endorsement of the principle of toleration. According to him, toleration is a cognitive presupposition „which must be satisfied if intercultural discourse on principles of political justice for a multicultural world society is to be successful."[7] In line with a tolerant disposition, as a requirement of intercultural discourse, „all parties, irrespective of their cultural backgrounds, had to consider controversial issues simultaneously from their own perspective and from those of the various other participants. Moreover they had to learn to restrict themselves to arguments that could in principle convince anyone irrespective of their underlying metaphysical or religious commitments."[8] Thus, for Habermas, the principle of toleration should be reflected in the attitude of the participants of an intercultural discourse on principles of a political justice for a multicultural world-society. In this way, a Habermasian conception of international toleration might be regarded as a requirement of international justice.

3. The Post-Secular Age as a Circumstance of Toleration and its Limits

It is usually accepted in the contemporary literature on toleration that for toleration to be possible, it is necessary to have the condition of diversity which is the source of disapproval or dislike.[9] Thus for toleration to be possible, what

[6] Jurgen Habermas, *Postnational Constellations* (Cambridge, Massachusetts: MIT Press, 2001), 128.

[7] Habermas, The Resurgence of Religion- A Challenge for a Secular Self-Interpretation of Modernity?, 10.

[8] Ibid.

[9] See Susan Mendus and John Horton, eds., *Aspects of Toleration* (London, New York: Methuen, 1985), Susan Mendus, *Toleration and the Limits of Liberalism* (London:MacMillan,1989), Susan Mendus and David Edwards eds, *On Toleration* (Oxford: Clarendon Press, 1987), Susan Mendus, ed., *Justifying Toleration- Conceptual and Historical Perspectives* (Cambridge: Cambridge University Press, 1988), John Horton, ed., *Liberalism, Multiculturalism and Toleration* (London: MacMillan Press, 1993), John Horton and Peter Nicholson, *Toleration: Philosophy and Practice* (Aldershot: Averbury, 1992), Peter Jones,

is needed is not sheer diversity or any diversity; it is diversity that is the source of dislike, disapproval or disgust. Otherwise, if we are happy with the plurality and nothing bothers us, we cannot talk about toleration. Diversity coupled with disapproval constitutes one of the circumstances of toleration.

In this paper, it is argued that Habermas's notion of a post-secular age constitutes a circumstance of toleration: It provides both the condition of diversity and disapproval. In other words, Habermas's comprehension of contemporary world- society which is marked by diversity and conflict can be described with reference to the notion of a post-secular age and this provides the descriptive foundation for toleration to be necessary. In order to understand in which manner the post-secular age qualifies as a circumstance of toleration, we need to comprehend the connection between secularization and modernization, and the dynamics of this relation itself in Habermas's view. In the texts in which he mention those processes, Habermas does not explain the nature of the dynamics in detail. However, he gives us the opportunity, at least to see what is peculiar to the age of post-secularism.

In the paper delivered in Rome in September 2007, *The Resurgence of Religion – A Challenge for a Secular Self-interpretation of Modernity?*, he attempts to answer what the resurgence of religion means for a largely secularized society. In this respect, he starts with the mention of the infamous secularization thesis which claims that „there is a close interrelation between the advancing modernization of society and an expanding secularization of the consciousness of the population."[10] For Habermas, this conventional reading of secularization is flawed in considering secularization as a zero sum game between productivity of science and technology on the one hand and the ongoing powers of church and religion on the other hand.[11] Hence, for him, this image is inconsistent with a post-secular society which contends that religious communities continue to exist in the ongoing process of secularization. He also points out that: „the awareness of

„Making Sense of Political Toleration", *British Journal of Political Science*, 37.3 (July 2007),"Toleration, Recognition and Identity", *The Journal of Political Philosophy*, Vol. 14, Number 2, 2006, „International Toleration and the 'War on Terror'", *Globalizations*, Vol.6, No.1(March 2009), „Toleration and Neutrality: Compatible Ideals" in D. D. Castiglione and C. McKinnon(eds), *Toleration, Democracy and Neutrality* (Dordrecht, Kluwer, 2003), „Toleration, Supererogation and Rights" (forthcoming) in D. Edyvane and Susan Mendus, eds., *Toleration Re-Examined* (University Park, PA, Penn State university Press), Catriona McKinnon, *Toleration: A Critical Introduction* (London, New York: Routledge, 2006), Rainer Forst, „Toleration, Justice and Reason", *The Culture of Toleration in Diverse Societies*, Catriona McKinnon and Dario Castiglione, eds. (Manchester, New York: Manchester University Press, 2003), Andrew Jason Cohen, „What Toleration is?", *Ethics*, 115, October 2004.

10 Jurgen Habermas, *Paper for the Conference „Religione e politica nella societa post-secolare"*, *The Resurgence of Religion- A Challenge for a Secular Self-Interpretation of Modernity?* (Roma, 13-9-2007), 1.

11 Jurgen Habermas, „Faith and Knowledge" in *The Future of Human Nature* (Cambridge: Polity Press, 2003), 104.

a living secular society is no longer bound up with the certainty that the advancing modernization of society and culture can occur only at the cost of the public influence and personal relevance of religion."[12] Therefore, the basic feature of a post-secular age is the ongoing impact of religion on individual and public life. In this sense, we might say that he considers the secular and religious standpoints as two considerably rival parties among the variety of world views under the conditions of intense pluralism.

In line with the features mentioned above regarding the post-secular societies, he makes a significant remark concerning what he means by describing modern societies as post-secular. In his paper *A post-secular society- What does that mean?*, he says that post-secular society refers to a change in consciousness that he attributes to three phenomena.[13] First, there is an emerging „awareness of living in a secular society is no longer bound up with the certainty that cultural and social modernization can advance only at the cost of the public influence and personal relevance of religion."[14] For him, the second indicator of a post-secular age is that religion is gaining influence not only worldwide but also in national public spheres: churches and religious communities are increasingly assuming the role of „communities of interpretation"[15] in the public realm of secular societies. And thirdly, according to him, the immigration of guest-workers and refugees particularly from traditional communities is a stimulus for a change in consciousness in modern countries regarding religion and its role.[16]

In Habermas's eyes, post-secular society (pluralistic society) seems to be a global condition which marks an intense diversity in the global realm. In this sense, a post-secular age requires new ways to deal with the problems arising from diversity and specifically religion. Toleration here comes to the fore as part of the response (if not the whole response) that Habermas gives to the specific problems of a post-secular age. In other words, it is the world- society, with its tendency to become a post-secular society that, for Habermas, provides the diversity condition for toleration as an international issue. The conditions of the post-secular age which manifest cultural and religious conflict constitute a circumstance of toleration. However, the argument of a post-secular age is limited in its potential to provide a full moral justification for toleration. It gives a rich and plausible understanding of the state of pluralism along with conflict at the global level; yet, it does not follow directly from this that we should tolerate each other's differences. This is evident especially if we remember the meaning and

[12] Ibid, 106.

[13] „A post-secular Society- what does that mean?", presented at the conference Istanbul seminars, East and West (2-8 June 2008), 3.

[14] Ibid.

[15] For the idea of church as a community of interpretation, see Francis Schussler Fiorenza, „The Church as a Community of Interpretation: Political Theology between Discourse Ethics and Hermeneutical Reconstruction" in *Habermas, Modernity and Public Theology*, Don S. Browning and Francis Schussler Fiorenza (eds) (New York: Crossroad Publishing, 1992).

[16] Ibid. 3-4.

centrality of toleration in Habermas's theory. He considers toleration as a requirement of justice and the idea of a post-secular age seems not to provide enough moral reasons for why we should tolerate. We need a strong moral reason (justification) for toleration that would be complementary with the notion of a post-secular age in the theory of Habermas to sustain the central and significant role that he attributes to toleration.

4. Equal Respect as a Reason (Justification) for Toleration

Beside the notion of a post-secular age that provides a descriptive foundation for toleration, there is one other notion that constitutes a moral reason (justification) for toleration in Habermas's theory; that is his idea of equal respect. Below, I investigate in which way equal respect gives moral foundation to toleration in Habermas's theory.

Habermas considers respect as the basis for justification of toleration in a pluralistic society. It is significant that citizens understand themselves to be the citizens of one and the same political community.[17] „For all their ongoing dissent on questions of worldviews and religious doctrines, citizens are meant to respect one another as free and equal members of political community."[18] Here, we might say that respect gives us the normative principle which we should appeal as citizens of a democratic community under the conditions of disagreement. Citizens, by living in the same community regardless of their dispute and difference, respect each other's status as free and equal members. Therefore, respect and toleration imply each other and the former comes onto the scene as a reason to be tolerant of citizens who are not like us at all, with whom we disagree but at the same time with whom we have to share the same political community.

Habermas's ideal of civic solidarity provides a foundation to the idea of equal respect as a reason for toleration:

> In the absence of the uniting bond of a civic solidarity, which cannot be legally enforced, citizens do not perceive themselves as free and equal participants in the shared practices of democratic opinion and will formation wherein they owe one another reasons for their political statements and attitudes. This reciprocity of expectations among citizens is what distinguishes a community integrated by constitutional values from a community segmented along the dividing lines of competing worldviews. [19]

Only in the condition of civic solidarity, can citizens of a democratic pluralistic society come to see each other as equal and free participants in

[17] J. Habermas, „Equal Treatment of Cultures and the Limits of Postmodern Liberalism", 26.

[18] J. Habermas, „Role of Religion in the Public Sphere", *Philosophia Africana*, 8, No. 2, August 2005, 3.

[19] J. Habermas, „Role of Religion in the Public Sphere", *European Journal of Philosophy*, 14, Issue 1, Apr. 2006, 13.

public deliberation. Respecting each other as free and equal members of a community is the starting point for achieving that goal. Respect (together with civic solidarity) as a reason for toleration is part of the idea of the ethics of citizenship which is significant for the democratic and deliberative will formation in a pluralistic society.

In Habermas's theory, equal respect is a reason for his conception of international toleration too. We might say that different cultures, civilizations, communities of faith and persons in viewing each other as equal members of a reflective dialogue/discourse; grant respect to each other. The idea of respect as a reason for toleration can be considered as rooted in Habermas's notion of a 'hermeneutical self-reflective dialogue' in the global realm.

Habermas considers social acceptance as a condition for toleration and intercultural dialogue. Each culture, civilization and community should accept the fact that they have to share the same world-society even though they disapprove of each other's worldviews. In this sense, social acceptance seems to be a first requirement for respecting and (thus tolerating) the equal status of different cultures and civilizations in the international realm. Social acceptance in the international context means accepting that each culture and civilization has the equal right to be part of the same world-society with their distinctiveness and difference. Thus, no culture or society could have any claim to impose its own world-view on others by using either violence or state power since each party has to recognize the fact that each culture and civilization are equal in status in sharing the same world- society.[20]

For Habermas, respecting the equal status of each culture and civilization requires a reflexive consciousness in which each party views the other as equal in status. Here he thinks that this is possible on the condition that modern faith becomes reflexive. He says modern faith „can only stabilize itself through self-critical awareness of the status it assumes within a universe of discourse restricted by secular knowledge and shared with other religions."[21] Becoming aware of the diversity and equal status of all faiths, each culture or community grants respect to each other's status as equal and does not impose its own faith on others.

There is a significant difference between Habermas's conceptions of domestic and international toleration regarding the idea of equal respect as a reason for toleration. In the case of domestic toleration, respect appears as a requirement of ethics of citizenship in a political society in which citizens are viewed as equal

[20] Here I do not mean that in Habermas's theory, each culture and civilization etc. should tolerate each other without limits. It has to be noted that whenever we talk about toleration, we always refer to it within certain limits. It might be claimed that human rights (and conventions of international law) might constitute the limits of toleration as far as the outlook of Habermas is concerned since they have the potential to define a common global public discourse. However, it is always difficult to address substantive limits since these have to be defined within certain contexts in the sense of what we should tolerate and what we should not.

[21] J. Habermas, „A Conversation About the God and the world" in *Time of Transitions*, Ciaran Cronin and Max Pensky (eds.) (Cambridge: Polity, 2006), 152.

and free members of that community. They are bound by solidarity towards each other as members of the same political community. On the other hand, in the case of multicultural world -society, it is still not possible to find this solidarity and the ethics of citizenship of the sort that characterizes domestic democratic society. Hence, in the international realm, respect seems to come onto the scene as a result of the recognition of each other's differences and equal status as members of the same multicultural world- society. In this sense, on a Habermasian view, respect as a reason for international toleration does not presuppose a thick ethical idea of citizenship through which one could make demands on citizens. Rather, the ideas of cosmopolitan citizenship and solidarity support the idea of respect as a reason for toleration in its emphasis on viewing each other as equal members of the same world- society.

So far, I demonstrated that the notion of a post-secular age provides a descriptive foundation for Habermas's theory of toleration. Furthermore, I claimed that it is the idea of equal respect that constitutes the moral justification for toleration in the theory of Habermas. Thus, on a Habermasian view, we should tolerate the differences of each other since we should respect the equal status of each citizen and this gives a reason for toleration which is a requirement of justice in the theory of Habermas.

5. THE DEMANDS OF TOLERATION IN A POST-SECULAR AGE

In this part of the paper, I analyze the demands of toleration from citizens of a post-secular age who should respect the equal status of each other in Habermas's theory. My view is that they are the demands that are possible only by relying on the moral idea of equal respect. The notion of a post-secular age does great job in providing the conditions of a pluralist world-society, yet it is not enough on its own to claim for the demands of toleration. In other words, the demands of toleration that Habermas outlines do not directly follow from his post-secular age argument. Thus, we can only ascribe demands that Habermas describes on citizens only if we refer to a strong moral reason for toleration such as equal respect.

Perhaps the first demand of toleration in Habermas's theory is *social acceptance.* What basically comes to the fore as a demand of toleration is the acceptance of the practical consequences of being in the same political environment like all others who have different ethos/worldviews. Habermas asserts that one can only realize her ethos within the limits of what everyone is accorded.[22] For Habermas, this has asymmetrical consequences for believers and nonbelievers in the democratic society.[23] For secular citizens, it is easier to abide by this rule because of their familiarity with the embedded heritage of democratic attitude.

[22] J. Habermas, „Equal Treatment of Cultures and the Limits of Postmodern Liberalism", 27.
[23] Ibid.

On the other hand, the believer has a different mental set which does not easily allow her to step outside the commands of her religious ethos to see the other as equally eligible to the same set of rules. The result is that the believer might end up in the enclave of her own ethos without any means to see the other's point of view. Therefore, for Habermas, considering tolerance only as noninterference could possibly lead to a situation in which competing worldviews exist without understanding each other. Therefore, on a Habermasian view, we need a more demanding notion of toleration which not only implies noninterference but also understanding and recognition.

Habermas refers to two other significant requirements which can be considered as demands of toleration too: a *complementary learning process* and a *translation requirement.* According to him, post-secular society reflects a normative insight which has consequences for the political relation between believing and nonbeliving citizens:

> In postsecular societies, the insight prevails that the 'modernization of public consciousness captures religious and secular mentalities in different phases and reflexively alters them. If they conceive of secularization of society in common as a complementary learning process, both sides can then reciprocally take seriously, for cognitive reasons, their contributions to controversial topics in the public sphere. [24]

For Habermas, a learning process between religious and secular reasons is required in a post-secular age because religion is still present with its influence in the public and private life of citizens. This claim of Habermas that there needs to be a learning process might be regarded as a proposal that would allow each party -secular and religious- to open up to the other in a hermeneutical way. Put exactly, a „complementary learning process" requires a condition of awareness that is expected from secular and religious citizens to open up dialogue and interaction concerning the contributions that might come up in public debate. Here one might argue that Habermas, in assuming that religious consciousness can be open to dialogue with secularism, disregards the dogmatic aspects of religion. However, being aware of this risk, he mentions that, politically speaking, this process of self- reflection from within the religious traditions might work only in favor of those religions that have learned to acknowledge democracy, religious pluralism, and the secular authority of science.[25] In this way, a certain level of awareness- a consciousness acknowledges pluralism and democracy- of religious standpoints is necessary in order for them to engage in self-reflection which is backed up by learning from the other part. Moreover, for Habermas, a cognitive adaptation is also required from the secular citizen in

[24] J. Habermas, „On the Relation between the Secular Liberal State and Religion", *The Frankfurt School on Religion: Key Writings by the Major Thinkers* (New York: Routledge, 2004), 344-345.

[25] J. Habermas, „The Resurgence of Religion- A Challenge for a Secular Self-Interpretation of Modernity?", 19.

the sense of a „self-reflexive overcoming of a rigid and exclusive secularist self-understanding of modernity."[26]

Evidently, on a Habermasian view, the demands of toleration require a highly engaging and positive endeavor from the believing and non-believing citizens. I claim that all these requirements, which are seemingly over-demanding, cannot be argued only from the normative insight reflected in the conditions of a post-secular age as Habermas mentions. Being aware of pluralism and the presence of religion might not guarantee the justification of the positive demands such as 'complementary learning'. This can be evident especially if we think of the costs and burdens that these demands would put on the shoulders of secular and religious citizens. In my view, it is only noninterference that might follow from the notion of a post-secular age as a demand of toleration but demands that require positive engagement and action cannot be argued only from a descriptive foundation of the notion of a post-secular age.

As mentioned before, the second significant notion Habermas outlines is the requirement of translation. Reflecting on this notion will give us the opportunity to understand better what Habermas requires of the secular and religious parties in terms of attitudes that they should take when behaving in a tolerant way. Habermas claims that the boundaries between the secular and religious reasons are fluid and deciding on those disputed boundaries should be seen as a cooperative task which requires taking the perspective of the other party.[27] Accordingly, translation of religious content into a publicly accessible language which would not lead religions to be excluded from public sphere is a task to be undertaken by both sides. In doing this, „secular reason should insist on the difference between certainties of faith and publicly criticizable validity claims but refrain from evaluating the rationality or irrationality of religion as such."[28] The move Habermas makes with the notions of complementary leaning process and translation is significant in thinking of a more positive and demanding toleration.[29] As Richard Wolin observes, by acknowledging religion's specific place in public political debate, Habermas also made a significant move to theorize a notion of multicultural toleration.[30] In this sense, toleration demands the capacity to take the standpoint of the other. But as I claimed before, this is only

[26] J. Habermas, „Religion in the Public Sphere: Cognitive Presuppositions for the „Public Use of Reason" by Religious and Secular Citizens" in *Between Naturalism and Religion* (Polity Press, 2008), 138.

[27] J. Habermas, „Faith and Knowledge", 9.

[28] J. Habermas, „The Resurgence of Religion- A Challenge for a Secular Self-Interpretation of Modernity?", 19.

[29] For further reference on 'complementary learning process' and 'translation requirement', see also Jurgen Habermas and Joseph Cardinal Ratzinger (Pope Benedict XVI), *Dialectics of Secularization- On Reason and Religion,* Florian Schuller, ed. (San Francisco: Ignatius Press, 2006).

[30] Richard Wolin, „Jurgen Habermas and Post-Secular Societies", *Chronicle of Higher Education,* 9/23/2005, 52, Issue 5, p. 5.

possible with the endorsement of a principled moral reason to tolerate such as the idea of equal respect.

Moreover, concerning the demands of international toleration, we might also claim that on a Habermas's view, one could appeal to an ideal in terms of assuming a hermeneutical opening up towards the other and taking the position of the other in the global realm which should direct the action of citizens as well as states and international communities of faith. This sort of demand might follow from Habermas's notions of a complementary learning process and a translation requirement that he envisioned regarding domestic societies. In other words, as tolerant agents in a post-secular age, we could appeal to a sort of cosmopolitan ethics of citizenship which might guide our action and which might allow different agents of international toleration to engage in dialogue in the sense of intercultural, inter-civilizational hermeneutical reflection. We might find the sources of such a view esp. concerning Habermas's hope for a consensus on human rights:

> A hermeneutical reflection on the starting point of a human rights discourse among participants of different cultures draws out attention to normative contents that are present in the tacit presuppositions of any discourse whose goal is mutual understanding. That is, independently of their cultural backgrounds all the participants intuitively know quite well that a consensus based on conviction cannot come about as long as symmetrical relations do not exist among them- relations of mutual recognition, mutual role taking, a shared willingness to consider one's own tradition with the eyes of the stranger and to learn from one another, and so forth.[31]

Here, demands such as the complementary learning and the translation requirement among different communities of faith as well as secular viewpoints in the global realm might be viewed as ideals that one should aspire just as the presuppositions of ideal discourse whose goal is mutual understanding. In this manner, they could be considered as positive demands of international toleration from a Habermasian point of view.

Apparently, the demands such as social acceptance, complementary learning and translation requirement are all positive demands that go beyond mere noninterference. The awareness of living in a post-secular age might provide a normative insight to the citizens to realize that there must be a complementary learning as Habermas puts it, but it is still a weak argument so far as the justification of toleration is concerned. This awareness itself enables a context in which a specific tolerant attitude is needed but it does not answer the question why we should tolerate each other as secular and religious citizens by acting in a positive manner. Although it sustains some ground for a negative attitude of toleration as noninterference, it does not supply a strong moral ground for the positive attitude and action that Habermas expects from the religious and secular

[31] J. Habermas, „Remarks on Legitimation Through Human Rights" in *Postnational Constellations,* 129.

citizens. A demanding notion of toleration such as Habermas's requires a principled moral reason as a foundation for toleration and that is his idea of equal respect that enables him to refer to the positive demands of toleration.

Concluding Remarks

In this paper, I analyzed Habermas's notion of a post-secular age by focusing particularly on its role and limits in Habermas's theory of toleration. I demonstrated that the notion of a post-secular age provides a descriptive foundation to the toleration argument in Habermas's theory. It explicates the nature and necessities of pluralism in the contemporary world-society quite well. However, as I demonstrated, it does not provide a principled moral ground for toleration. For toleration to have a strong moral foundation, one should appeal to Habermas's idea of equal respect as a justification for toleration. This appeal can justify the positive demands of toleration that Habermas envisions too.

BEYOND SECULARIZATION? NOTES ON HABERMAS'S ACCOUNT OF THE POSTSECULAR SOCIETY

Patrick Loobuyck – Stefan Rummens

In recent years, Jürgen Habermas has joined the debate about the role of religion in current day societies.[1] Somewhat surprisingly for those familiar with his earlier work on the rationalization of modern society, Habermas advances a rather positive view of religion and its possible contributions in the public sphere. Rejecting the secularist and reductive view of religion as a disappearing relic of premodern times, he recognizes the ongoing presence and importance of religion in what he calls our postsecular society.

After situating Habermas's current views in the framework of his previous works, we briefly sketch some of the main characteristics of the postsecular society he envisages and the duties it imposes on both religious and secular citizens. Next, we focus on the debate about the acceptability of religious reasons and asses to what extent Habermas makes good on his claim to provide a middle-ground position between inclusionists and exclusionists. In the two final sections we investigate Habermas's claim that religious and secular citizens need to assume equal cognitive burdens as well as his view on the relation between religion and reason. Both sections reveal that Habermas's postsecular society remains, to a large extent, a secular one.

[1] J. Habermas, „Faith and Knowledge" [2001], in idem, *The Future of Human Nature* (Cambridge: Polity, 2003) 101-115; J. Habermas & J. Ratzinger, *The Dialectics of Secularization: On Reason and Religion* (San Francisco: Shambala, 2006 [2005]); J. Habermas, *Between Naturalism and Religion. Philosophical Essays* (Cambridge: Polity, 2008 [2005]); J. Habermas, „Replik auf Einwände, Reaktion auf Anregungen", in R. Langthaler & H. Nagl-Docekal, *Jürgen Habermas über Religion Glauben und Wissen. Ein Symposion mit Jürgen Habermas* (Wien/Berlin 2007) 366-414; J. Habermas, „Die Dialektik der Säkularisierung", *Blätter für deutsche und internationale Politik* 4 (2008) 33-46.

HABERMAS ON RELIGION AND THE PUBLIC SPHERE

That Habermas recently started writing about religion in the public sphere should not come as a real surprise since the two themes – religion and the public sphere – have been prominently present throughout his earlier work. Already in *The Structural Transformation of the Public Sphere* (1962)[2], Habermas argues that the legitimacy of democratic decisions is closely related to the reasonableness of public debate. This idea of discursive reasonableness is further elaborated in his concept of the ideal speech situation which advances the ideal of an inclusive deliberation in which all people concerned can participate as equals and in which the force of the better argument determines the outcome.[3] This idea of free communication undistorted by power relations later becomes the starting point for a far more encompassing theory of action in *The Theory of Communicative Action* (1981)[4] in which he argues that human actions should be coordinated on the basis of a reasonable agreement between all individuals concerned. This reasonable agreement not only functions as the condition of possibility of social integration, but is also constitutive of the normative validity of moral and political norms.

In *Between Facts and Norms* (1991)[5] Habermas elaborates the idea of communicative action in the context of political and legal theory into an elaborate model of deliberative democracy. Here, democratic legitimacy again depends on the ability of the informal deliberations in the public sphere to influence actual decision-making procedures in the formal institutions of government and parliament. Thereby, deliberations in the public sphere should be reasonable and inclusive. If the democratic legitimacy of political decisions depends on a reasonable agreement between all concerned, it is necessary that all citizens affected are effectively capable of participating in the democratic debate and to introduce their interests, arguments and concerns.

Although less prominent than the idea of public reason, religion has also been an ongoing concern in Habermas's works. In his *Theory of Communicative Action*, religion is mainly analyzed from a sociological point of view and portrayed as an outdated mode of social integration. Discussing the works of George Herbert Mead, Emile Durkheim and Max Weber, Habermas sees the religion as a transitional phenomenon in a linear process of rationalization and differentiation. Because the sacred nature of religion resists rationalization and because its worldview is based on encompassing truth claims which are incompatible

[2] J. Habermas, *The Structural Transformation of the Public Sphere. An Inquiry into a Category of Bourgeois Society* (Cambridge, MA: MIT, 1989 [1962]).

[3] J. Habermas, „Wahrheitstheorien" [1973] in idem, *Vorstudien und Ergänzungen zur Theorie des komunikativen Handelns* (Frankfurt am Main 1984) 127-183.

[4] J. Habermas, *The Theory of Communicative Action* (Cambridge, MA: MIT, 1987 [1981]).

[5] J. Habermas, *Between Facts and Norms: Contributions to a Discourse Theory of Law and Democracy* (Cambridge, MA: MIT, 1996 [1991]) Ch. 7-8.

with a differentiation between an objective, a social and a subjective world with each their own distinct validity claims (truth, rightness and authenticity), religion can only appear as a premodern and increasingly meaningless remnant of premodern times.

In his later works, however, Habermas's view of religion gradually changes and he is increasingly prepared to engage in a constructive dialogue with theologians and philosophers of religion.[6] Although the change is already remarkable, its impact remains limited. Where Habermas now recognizes the ongoing importance of religion, its role remains limited to the existential sphere as a provider of consolation and comfort. Habermas continues to deny the moral or political relevance of religion and it is therefore not surprising that the issue of religion does not even figure in his main work on political and legal philosophy, *Between Facts and Norms*.

Only in recent years has Habermas firmly changed his position and developed a much more appreciative view of religion. Ever since his speech *Glauben und Wissen* for the *Friedenspreis des deutschen Buchhandels* on 14 October 2001 (shortly after the attacks of 09-11), religion became one of the most important themes of his work. In this speech he already describes current European society as a postsecular society, an idea which he further elaborates in his well-known conversation with Cardinal Ratzinger (just before he became pope Benedictus XVI) on 19 January 2004 in Munich, and in his book *Between Naturalism and Religion*.[7] With the concept of a postsecular society, Habermas refers to the fact that modern consciousness has to adapt „to the fact that religious communities continue to exist in a context of ongoing secularization"[8]. He now no longer believes „that religious views will ultimately dissolve in the acid of scientific criticism and that religious communities will not be able to withstand the pressures of advancing cultural and social modernization."[9] He acknowledges that the sociological data still provide support for the secularization thesis, but he doubts if that means that the political and public relevance of religion will definitely wane.[10] Therefore, Habermas now attempts to describe the conditions necessary for an open society in which religious and non-religious traditions and worldviews can peacefully coexist in a mutually respectful manner. As we shall see, he thereby explicitly recognizes the legitimate role of religion in the public domain as well as its possible enriching contributions to the public debate.

[6] Cf. J. Habermas, *Religion and Rationality* (Cambridge, MA: MIT, 2002).

[7] This book contains Habermas's part of the discussion with Ratzinger (ch. 4: *Prepolitical foundations of the constitutional State*) and the article *Religion in the public sphere* (ch. 5; also in *European Journal of Philosophy* 14 (2006) 1, 1-25).

[8] Habermas, „Faith and Knowledge", 104.

[9] Habermas, *Between Naturalism*, 139.

[10] Habermas, „Die Dialektik".

Habermas's Postsecular Perspective

With his account of a postsecular perspective, Habermas tries to provide an answer to the increasing tension between two countervailing contemporary developments: the spread of *naturalistic worldviews* on the one hand, and the political *reawakening of religious consciousness* and the growing political influence of religious orthodoxies on the other hand. Habermas is aware that these conflicting intellectual trends „do not merely clash at the level of academic controversies. They also develop into powerful political forces both within the civil society of the leading Western nations and at the international level in the encounter between the major world religions and the dominant global culture."[11]

In order to find an adequate political answer to this increasing polarisation, neutrality of political decision-making should not be understood as a form of reductionist secularism which assumes that religion is an exclusively private matter and denies religion its place in society and public discussion. In order to go beyond this secularist reduction of religion Habermas argues that political solutions should be based on a *democratic common sense* which remains neutral towards both secularist and religious (truth-)claims. Of course, Habermas still emphasizes that democratic legitimacy depends on a reasonable agreement between all citizens and will therefore depend on „cognitive resources of a set of arguments that are independent of religious or metaphysical traditions."[12] This autonomous and immanent grounding of legitimacy is based on the rational dialogue and consensus between free and rational citizens.[13] Nevertheless, he argues that such a secular democratic common sense can and should remain at an *equal distance* from all traditions and worldviews and abstain from prejudging political decisions in favour of one side or the other. Habermas also insists on a willingness to learn from others in terms of their possible contributions concerning basis moral and political intuitions. This means that religious and secularist worldviews should take each other's contributions to controversial public debates seriously. Indifferent tolerance in the public sphere is not enough. Religious citizens have to translate their religious beliefs into secular language and secular citizens must remain sensitive to the force of articulation inherent in religious languages.[14]

More generally, from the postsecular perspective, the modernization of public consciousness requires *a complementary learning process* in terms of an adequate

[11] Habermas, *Between Naturalism*, 2.

[12] *Ibid.*, 104.

[13] In his *Between Facts and Norms*, he refers to the power of communicative reason as „innerworldly transcendence". This „transcendence from within" is the only legitimate justification of the secular state. (Habermas, *Between Facts*, 5; see also J. Habermas, „Transzendenz von innen, Transzendenz ins diesseits", in idem, *Texte und Kontexte* (Frankfurt am Main 1991) 127-156)

[14] Habermas, „Faith and Knowledge", 109.

transformation of both traditional orthodox religious traditions and the secular(ist) mentality.[15] On the side of religion, the modernization of religious consciousness consists of the development of a *reflexive religion.*[16] This development does not require religions to abandon their religious beliefs. Instead, it demands, first, that religious citizens accept and agree with the fact of pluralism and acknowledge freedom of religion as a universal right. Secondly, religious citizens must accept the independent validity of scientific knowledge. They must conceive the relationship of sacred and secular knowledge in such a way that the progress of scientific knowledge cannot contradict with faith. Finally, religious citizens must acknowledge the secular character of the constitutional state and give priority to secular over religious reasons in public debate. They have to accept that the exercise of political authority must be neutral towards competing worldviews and that, therefore, in the formal political sphere only neutral, secular reasons may count. This requires the epistemic ability to consider one's own faith reflexively from the outside and to relate it to secular views. This means that they have to connect the egalitarian individualism and universalism of modern law and morality with the premises of their own religious doctrine. Only when religions meet these three normative and epistemic expectations can they be taken seriously in the political sphere. In Western culture, the required processes of religious rationalization can be observed in the evolution of religious consciousness of Christianity since the reformation and Enlightenment. This ongoing process has not been easy and in the case of the Catholic Church we had to wait until the Second Vaticanum in 1965 for a real confirmation of the liberal political values of modern society. It seems fair to say that many Muslim communities still have a large part of this often painful learning process before them.[17]

On the secular side, the complementary learning process consists in the development of a *post-metaphysical thinking.*[18] Like religious citizens, secular citizens need to assume a cognitive burden which goes beyond the political virtue of mere tolerance as a *modus vivendi.* Something more is called for. What is expected of religiously tone-deaf citizens is a „self-reflexive overcoming of a rigid and exclusive secularist self-understanding of modernity" and, thus, the rejection of a form of secularism that is solely based on hard naturalism and radical scientism. This requires, first that these citizens accept the idea of a „multidimensional concept of reason" according to which reason is not simply reduced to scientific rationality but also applies to moral, legal and religious judgements. Secondly, secular citizens should accept that religions are not necessarily irrational relics of premodern times. Instead, they should accept that religious discourse might contain morally and politically relevant meanings which could perhaps be translated and introduced into secular political discourse. What is at stake

[15] Habermas, *Between Naturalism,* 111.

[16] Habermas, „Faith and Knowledge", 104; Idem, *Between Naturalism,* 136-7.

[17] Habermas, *Between Naturalism,* 136-7; Idem., "Die Dialektik".

[18] Habermas, *Between Naturalism,* 112-3, 138ff.

here is more than a respectful sensibility for the possible existential significance of religion for other persons. The postsecular perspective requires that religious contributions to contentious political issues can be taken seriously and that secular citizens in the public sphere must be able to speak with their religious fellow citizens as equals. „Secular citizens, in their role as citizens, may neither deny that religious worldviews are in principle capable of truth nor question the right of their devout fellow citizens to couch their contributions to public discussions in religious language."[19]

RELIGION AND THE NEUTRALITY OF PUBLIC REASON

This postsecular perspective provides the background for Habermas's take on the discussion about the place of religious arguments in public reason. Habermas aims to develop a middle-ground position between exclusionists like Robert Audi, who reject the use of religious reasons in political debate, and inclusionists like Nicholas Wolterstorff and Paul Weithman, who find religious reasons perfectly acceptable. This middle-ground position is characterized by what Habermas calls his *institutional translation proviso*. This proviso states that religious reasons can be introduced into the informal public debate in the public sphere, provided that, in the course of the debate, these religious reasons are adequately translated into secular reasons equally accessible to all. Importantly, this process of translation has to be completed before the debate crosses over into the formalized institutions of democratic decision-making such as parliament and government.[20] The proviso thus operates as a necessary filter between „the wild life" of the informal public sphere primarily concerned with opinion-formation on the one hand and the formal proceedings within the political bodies primarily concerned with will-formation and decision-making on the other.[21] Because legitimate democratic decisions should be based on a reasonable agreement between all citizens and because the particularity of religious reasons precludes such an agreement, these reasons are no longer acceptable in the more formal context of actual decision-making.

In order to further clarify and justify his own position, Habermas, like many authors in this debate, uses Rawls as his point of reference.[22] With Rawls, Habermas emphasizes that political decisions about fundamental issues are legitimate to the extent that they are based on a reasonable agreement between citizens. In the absence of such an agreement, political decisions are necessarily coercive for at least some groups of citizens.

[19] *Ibid.*, 113.

[20] *Ibid.*, 130-1.

[21] For this distinction see Habermas, *Between Facts*, 304-8.

[22] Habermas, *Between Naturalism*, 119-23.

> ... only those political decisions can count as legitimate that can be impartially justified in the light of generally accessible reasons, in other words, that can be justified equally toward religious and nonreligious citizens and citizens of different confessions.[23]

In this context, Rawls advocates a *duty of civility* according to which citizens should be prepared to provide reasons in support of the political positions and policy proposals they endorse. Thereby, the reasons used should be based on the political values of public reason, i.e. values acceptable to all reasonable and rational citizens and as such part of the overlapping consensus.[24] Rawls emphasizes that this duty is a moral duty, not a legal duty for in that case it would be incompatible with freedom of speech.

Regarding the use of religious arguments, the duty of civility gives rise to what is known as the Rawlsian *proviso.* This proviso states that „reasonable comprehensive doctrines, religious and nonreligious, may be introduced in public political discussion at any time, provided that in due course, proper political reasons – and not reasons given solely by comprehensive doctrines – are presented that are sufficient to support whatever the comprehensive doctrines are said to support."[25] So, religious reasons are not excluded from public debate but they can only be introduced on the condition that in the course of the debate adequate political reasons, i.e. reasons acceptable to *all* reasonable citizens, supporting the same proposals are also provided.

In order to understand the specificity of Habermas's position, a closer inspection of the relation between the Rawlsian and the Habermasian proviso is in order. In this regard, it seems, at first glance, that Rawls advocates the more inclusionist position and, thus, leaves more room for religious argumentation than Habermas. Here, two differences are of interest. First, Rawls indicates that his proviso „specifies public political culture as distinct from the background culture"[26], while for Habermas the proviso specifies the distinction between the formal sphere of political institutions and the informal public sphere. Importantly, what Rawls means by „the public political culture" is not the same as what Habermas means by the „formal sphere of political institutions". The public political culture of Rawls does not refer to all political questions indiscriminately, but refers only to political debate by judges, legislators, chief executives, and other government officials concerning „constitutional essentials and questions of basic justice". As a result, the limitations imposed by the proviso also seem to apply only to this limited – though essential – set of political questions. Secondly, Rawls applies his proviso to debate in public political

23 *Ibid.*, 122.

24 J. Rawls, *Political Liberalism* (New York: Columbia University Press, 1996) 127; J. Rawls, „The idea of public reason revisited", in idem, *The Law of Peoples* (Cambridge, MA: Harvard University Press, 2001) 135ff.

25 Rawls, *Political Liberalism,* ii-iii; Rawls, „The idea", 152, 144.

26 Rawls, *Political Liberalism,* I, 213-16, 220-3, 382; Rawls, „The idea", 152, 133-4.

culture, whereas Habermas applies his proviso to debate in the informal public sphere. This means that Rawls, unlike Habermas, imposes no restrictions whatsoever on discussion in the background culture (media, civil society, universities, churches)[27], whereas Habermas, unlike Rawls, completely rejects the use of religious reasons in the formal public sphere.[28] These differences also result in a different interpretation of the duty of civility. For Habermas the public discourse of citizens has to be translatable into neutral terms, always and everywhere, while for Rawls, the duty of civility only applies for discourse on essential constitutional issues by government officials and candidates for public offices. Although Rawls hopes that ideally citizens who are not government officials „are to think of themselves *as if* they were legislators", they already fulfil their duty of civility by doing what they can to hold government officials to the idea of public reason and „repudiate government officials and candidates for public office who violate public reason."[29]

In spite of his own seemingly more exclusionist stance, Habermas himself surprisingly criticizes Rawls for being too exclusionist. In order to assess this rather paradoxical critique, closer scrutiny of the arguments advanced by Habermas is in order.[30] His first argument is *sociological*: although there are examples to the contrary, religious movements and churches have, in the past, played an important role in advancing, stabilizing and reproducing a liberal political culture. In this regard, Habermas mentions Martin Luther King and the US civil rights movement, but also the civil religion which has developed in American society.[31] Therefore, if only for „functional reasons", it would be a bad idea to obstruct the democratic participation of religious citizens and groups.[32] However, as Habermas rightly mentions, this argument is not an objection against Rawls's position, because Rawls does not impose his own proviso on participants in the wider civil society. So, on his account, the religious groups or actors do not face any restrictions. In fact, Rawls cites Martin Luther King as a clear example of a religiously inspired contribution to the political process which is in line with the requirements of public reason.[33]

Habermas's second argument hinges on the idea that any 'ought' implies a 'can'. „A state cannot encumber its citizens, to whom it guarantees freedom of

[27] Rawls, „The idea", 153.

[28] Here, Habermas misreads Rawls's proviso when he wrongly claims that Rawls would not allow religious arguments in the formal public sphere of the „political institutions" (Habermas, *Between Naturalism*, 122-3). It should also be noted that the restrictions Habermas imposes in the informal public sphere are only institutional and do not strictly apply to individual citizens (cf. infra).

[29] Rawls, „The idea", 135-6.

[30] Habermas, *Between Naturalism*, 124-32.

[31] Cf. R. Bellah et. al., *Habits of the Heart* (New York: Harper and Row, 1985).

[32] Habermas, *Between Naturalism*, 125. See also P. Weithman, *Religion and the obligations of citizenship* (Cambridge: CUP, 2002) 91.

[33] Rawls, *Political Liberalism*, 249-51.

religion, with duties that are incompatible with pursuing a devout life – it cannot expect something impossible of them."[34] This is the case when citizens who take a stance on political issues from a religious perspective do not have enough knowledge or imagination to find independent secular justifications. Although possible lack of imagination or knowledge already provides sufficient reason not to impose certain duties on citizens, there is an even stronger, normative reason, since genuine faith is not merely a doctrine but also a source of energy that nurtures the whole life of the devout person.[35] Endorsing a similar claim by Wolterstorff, Habermas emphasizes that it may, from the perspective of religious citizens, be an *existential necessity* „to base their decisions concerning fundamental issues of justice *on* their religious convictions."[36] Habermas therefore concludes that a liberal state, which expressly protects religious ways of life, cannot expect religious citizens and organizations to justify their political positions independently of their religious worldview. This duty can only be imposed on all those who hold or aspire to hold public office.[37]

With this second argument, Habermas explicitly challenges the exclusionist account of Robert Audi who advocates two secular „principles of democratic citizenship".[38] His first principle – the *principle of secular rationale* – says „that one has a prima facie obligation not to advocate or support any law or public policy that restrict human conduct, unless one has, and is willing to offer, adequate secular reasons for this advocacy or support." The second principle – the *principle of secular motivation* – says that one has a prima facie obligation to „abstain from advocacy or support of a law or public policy that restricts human conduct, unless in advocating or supporting it one is sufficiently *motivated* by (normatively) adequate secular reasons".[39] For Habermas, it is unrealistic to hold these principles of secular justification and motivation, because some religious citizens may not be able to fulfil them. Against the second principle, Habermas argues that in terms of the secular justification of political decisions and, thus, in terms of their democratic legitimacy, the personal motivation of citizens is irrelevant. Moreover, we may not neglect that the civil society and all kinds of „pre-political sources" are important for the socialization and habituation of citizens in the practices and attitudes of a liberal political culture. The political

[34] Habermas, *Between Naturalism*, 126.

[35] *Ibid.*, 127.

[36] N. Wolterstorff, „The role of religion in decision and discussion of political issues", in R. Audi & N. Wolterstorff, *Religion in the Public Square* (London: Rowman and Littlefield, 1997) 67-120, 105.

[37] Habermas, *Between Naturalism*, 128.

[38] For a recent response by Audi to Habermas's challenges, see R. Audi, „Religion and the politics of science: Can evolutionary biology be religiously neutral", *Philosophy & Social Criticism* 35 (2009) 1-2, 23-50, 37-40.

[39] R. Audi, „The Separation of Church and State and the Obligations of Citizenship", *Philosophy and Public Affairs* 18 (1989) 259-296, 293; Idem, *Religious Commitment and Secular Reason* (New York: Cambridge University Press, 2000) 86, 96.

virtues essential for the survival of democracy are not independent of the worldviews and religious convictions of citizens. Instead, citizens's motives for participating in political opinion- and will-formation often draw their sustenance from cultural, ethical and religious forms of life.[40] Similarly, the requirement of secular justification is untenable because some religious persons are not able to make a division between their public and their private life and opinions. Along Habermas we have to take into account „the faithful who cannot abstain from the political use of 'private' reasons without compromising their religious way of life". For religious people whose existence is „*guided* by faith"[41], religion is relevant for all aspects of their life and is not „about *something other* than their social and political existence"[42]. Agreeing with Weithman that some religious persons are incapable of discerning „any 'pull' from any secular seasons"[43], Habermas argues that religious people should be able to make contributions to the political debate without having to provide adequate translations for their arguments themselves.[44] Instead, they are allowed to rely on the cooperative efforts of their fellow citizens to provide for these translations into reasons equally accessible to all.[45]

Although Habermas convincingly distances himself from Audi, it remains to be seen whether his arguments also mark a difference with Rawls. Here, it should be noted that Rawls would also reject the *principle of secular motivation.* If religious arguments comply with the proviso and if there exist, therefore, adequate political reasons supporting the same position, it is perfectly acceptable for this position to be religiously motivated.

All those who affirm the political conception start from within their own comprehensive view and draw on the religious, philosophical, and moral grounds it provides. The fact that people affirm the same political conception on those grounds does not make their affirming it any less religious, philosophical, or moral, as the case may be, since the grounds sincerely held determine the nature of their affirmation.[46]

Regarding the *principle of secular justification,* Rawls's position is more ambiguous. On the one hand he restricts the scope of the proviso to discourse of government officials only and imposes no restrictions whatsoever on public debate in the background culture. On the other hand, Rawls recognizes that, ideally, the full requirements of public reason also apply to „citizens who are not government officials":

[40] Habermas, *Between Naturalism*, 105.

[41] *Ibid.*, 131, 129.

[42] Wolterstorff, „The role of religion", 105.

[43] Weithman, *Religion*: 157.

[44] Habermas, *Between Naturalism*, 128.

[45] *Ibid.*, 130-2.

[46] Rawls, *Political Liberalism*, 147-8.

> We say that ideally citizens are to think of themselves as if they were legislators and ask themselves what statutes, supported by what reasons satisfying the criterion of reciprocity, they would think it most reasonable to enact.[47]
> Just as judges are to decide cases by legal grounds of precedent, recognized canons of statutory interpretation, and other relevant grounds, so citizens are to reason by public reason and to be guided by the criterion of reciprocity, whenever constitutional essentials and matters of basic justice are at stake. [...] if, when stand-offs occur, citizens simply invoke grounding reasons of their comprehensive views, the principle of reciprocity is violated.[48]

Along this interpretation, citizens are always under the moral duty to give neutral, political reasons in political debates where key issues affecting constitutional essentials are at stake.[49] This marks a clear contrast with Habermas's – at least in this case – more inclusionist position which allows the contribution to the informal public debate of monoglot religious citizens unable to translate their own religious contributions into secular language. Moreover, for Habermas, the Rawlsian distinction between different categories of political issues is moot because „virtually any controversial legal issue can be heightened into an issue of principle."[50] In our modern legal systems in which basic rights directly affect concrete legislation and adjudication, the domain of constitutional essentials is much broader than Rawls seems to suggest.

The third argument Habermas advances concerns the *semantic potential of religious arguments*. It is a core concern of Habermas's postsecular approach that religious contributions to the public debate should be taken seriously. This marks a contrast with Rawls's approach.[51] The specific Rawlsian proviso to provide political reasons supporting the same position implies that religious arguments do not perform any genuine semantic work and leave the content of public reason unaltered. Rawls argues that

> [...] the introduction into public political culture of religious and secular doctrines, provided the proviso is met, does not change the nature and content of justification in public reason itself.[52]

For Habermas, in contrast, religion can give expression to important human moral intuitions and „can also open the eyes of citizens to aspects that were hitherto neglected."[53] Crucial for Habermas but absent in Rawls, is the idea that the notion of translation implies that at least part of the original religious meaning

[47] Rawls, „The idea", 136.

[48] Rawls, „The idea", 168. also Rawls, *Political Liberalism*, 240-1.

[49] Cf. C. Lafont, „Religion in the public sphere: remarks on Habermas's conception of public deliberation in postsecular societies", *Constellations* 14 (2007) 2, 239-259, 240, 242, 256 nt. 20

[50] Habermas, *Between Naturalism*, 123 n. 18.

[51] S. Rummens, „The semantic potential of religious arguments. A deliberative model of the postsecular public sphere", *Social Theory & Practice* (forthcoming).

[52] Rawls, „The idea", 153.

[53] Habermas, *Between Naturalism*, 264, see also 2, 131, 139-40, 245.

of arguments can be preserved in the process of making arguments equally accessible to all.

Religious traditions have a special power to articulate moral intuitions, especially with regard to vulnerable forms of communal life. In corresponding political debates, this potentials makes religious speech into a serious vehicle for possible truth contents, which can then be translated from the vocabulary of a particular religious community into a generally acceptable language.[54]

With this third argument Habermas does not emphasize as much the right of religious citizens to take part in the discussion, but above all, the loss for society in his whole since the state cannot know in advance what might be contributed by religious arguments. The sociological and existential normative reasons for an inclusive point of view as to what concerns public reason, are being completed with „functional reasons for not overhastily reducing the polyphonic complexity of public voices."[55] It is important for all of us to conserve all cultural sources that nurture citizens's solidarity and their normative awareness.[56] Habermas argues that the constitutional state, democracy and the political dialogue themselves have an interest in the free expression of religious voices in the public arena and in the political participation of religious organisations

> ... for it cannot be sure that secular society would not otherwise cut itself off from key resources or the creation of meaning and identity. Secular citizens or those of other religious persuasions can also learn something from religious contributions under certain circumstances, for example, when they recognize buried intuitions of their own in the normative truth contents of a religious utterance.[57]

Although the recognition of the potential contribution of religious arguments to public debate marks a distinction between Habermas and the exclusionist positions of Audi and – partly – Rawls, this does not mean that Habermas would agree with the inclusionists who suggest that in terms of religious argumentation simply anything is allowed. Here, Habermas insists on the importance of his institutional translation proviso which is designed to filter out non-generalizable arguments and concerns before they can enter into the formal deliberations of parliament and the executive. He strongly criticizes inclusionist authors like Wolterstorff and Weithman, who wish to jettison even this proviso because „they thereby infringe against the principle that the state should remain neutral in line with liberal premises". Since no institutional filters are envisaged between the state and the public domain, there is a possibility that policies will be implemented solely on the basis of religious beliefs and this is a violation of the discursive nature of the deliberation preceding the vote.[58] The possible

[54] *Ibid.*, 131.
[55] *Ibid.*
[56] *Ibid.*, 111.
[57] *Ibid.*, 131.
[58] *Ibid.*, 132-3.

emergence of such religious majorities would thereby pose a real threat to the stability and integration of our modern, pluralistic society.

Although the need for some constraints on the kinds of arguments that can be used as a basis for democratic legislation is adequately argued for by Habermas, it remains unclear why the translation required should already be completed before the debate enters the formal decision-making institutions. He writes that we cannot make a split between political and religious identity of actors in the informal public sphere, but he still allows this split on the formal level of decision-making. It is not clear why this split here does not remain cause for concern and why Habermas cannot allow the inclusion of (non-authoritarian) religious and other metaphysical contributions on all levels of democratic deliberation.[59] Habermas insufficiently shows why the formal, institutional level cannot endure philosophical pluralism and inclusion. What is wrong with religious input, e.g. in parliament, if, in due course, this input is translatable in secular language accessible for all? Moreover, it is unclear whether the presupposed sharp distinction between the wild life of the public sphere and the formal institutional political sphere can actually be drawn.[60] Can a Muslim politician use religious arguments in an ethical committee commissioned by the government? Can politicians candidating for religious parties pronounce themselves on political issues using religious arguments?

Summarizing this comparison of the Rawlsian and the Habermasian proviso, we come to a balanced conclusion. On the one hand, Rawls is more inclusionist than Habermas because for Habermas the transformation of religious into political arguments already has to be completed in the informal sphere. Rawls, in contrast, leaves this informal sphere totally free and also allows religious arguments in the formal sphere provided political reasons supporting the same position can be found in due course. On the other hand, Habermas is more inclusionist in the sense that Rawls seems to impose the proviso on all individuals as far as they participate in discussions concerning constitutional essentials, reflect on public interest or decide on their preferred candidate during elections. Habermas regards such a demand as an unacceptable psychological burden on religious citizens who, in his opinion, are allowed to vote and to participate in public debate while, at the same time, remaining religious mono-glots. Concerning the semantic impact of the proviso, finally, Habermas distinctively claims the more inclusionist position. Where Rawls states that the proviso guarantees that the political content of public reason remains unaltered, Habermas points out that religious arguments can have a genuine semantic impact on the agreement at the end of the debate.[61]

[59] M. Cooke, „Salvaging and secularizing the semantic contents of religion: the limitations of Habermas's postmetaphysical proposal", *International Journal for Philosophy of Religion* 60 (2006) 187-207, 196ff.; M. Cooke, „A secular state for a postsecular society? Postmetaphysical political theory and the place of religion", *Constellations* 14 (2007) 2, 224-238.

[60] Lafont, „Religion in the public sphere", 255 nt. 11.

[61] James Boettcher provides an extensive comparison between Rawls's en Habermas's views on religion and concludes that the differences between them are, all things considered, very

SYMMETRICAL BURDENS?

In the final two sections we shall have a look at two issues which illustrate that Habermas's postsecular society still remains secular to a large extent in the sense that it still imposes asymmetrical burdens on religious as opposed to secular citizens and still fails to fully resolve the at times tragic tension between religious faith and public reason. These findings are not necessarily intended as a strong critique of the postsecular model. Indeed, we believe that in any pluralistic society this tension and this asymmetrical burden can never be fully eliminated. Nevertheless, the purpose of an open political as well as academic debate is best served if these facts are fully laid out and the true nature of the postsecular society is fully recognized.

In this section we focus on Habermas's claim that the postsecular society imposes cognitive burdens on religious as well as secular citizens in a symmetrical manner.[62] However, it should be clear from the start that this symmetry can only be formal, since the content of the respective learning processes imposed by Habermas are different. Religious citizens are required to translate their religious arguments into secular arguments equally accessible to all. By way of compensation, secular citizens are expected to keep an open mind and to take the potential semantic contribution of their religious peers seriously. Whether these requirements are equally burdensome and whether they somehow compensate each other remains to be seen.

If we look, first, at the burdens imposed on religious citizens it is obvious that secularization demands substantial concessions. Religious citizens must not only superficially adjust to the secular constitutional order, they are expected to appropriate the secular justification of constitutional principles under the premises of their own faith.[63] They have to accept that the postsecular society remains a secular society as far as it is essentially not religiously founded but innerworldly. The final source of political legitimacy does not lie in God, but in the democratic debate between all free and equal citizens. In this respect, Habermas has not changed his earlier views according to which the history of secularization and rationalization is the history of the gradually replacement of the authority of the holy by the authority of an achieved consensus.[64]

small. J. Boettcher, „Habermas, religion and the ethics of citizenship", *Philosophy & Social Criticism* 35 (2009) 1-2, 215-238. His analysis fails, however, to consider the differences between both authors in terms of the potential semantic impact of religious arguments on public reason. As indicated, it is precisely here that the main differences between them are located. See Rummens „The semantic potential of religious arguments".

[62] Habermas, *Between Naturalism*, 143.

[63] *Ibid.*, 112; Habermas, „Die Dialektik".

[64] Habermas, *The Theory*, vol. 2: 77; Habermas, *Between Facts*, 145ff. See also S. Rummens, „Deliberation interrupted. Confronting Jürgen Habermas with Claude Lefort", *Philosophy & Social Criticism* 34 (2008) 4, 383-408.

As far as religion has to do with the experience of a transcendent authority which gives moral guidance in personal *as well as* in social and political life, it is fundamentally at odds with the secular conception of politics. Therefore, the development of a reflexive religion is a cumbersome process and Habermas does not really analyze its feasibility, but simply notes that a big part of the Christian community has *de facto* met these demands. In the end, as Habermas writes, it are the participants and their religious organisations themselves which have to resolve the question whether a „modernized" faith that meets the (post)secular expectations is still the „true" faith.[65]

By emphasising the symmetry of the burdens, Habermas fails to take seriously the fundamental and permanent tension between the secular authority of the democratic process on the one hand and the religious authority of God on the other. This tension, it should be noticed, is not only confronted by more fundamentalist religious believers who wish to provide society once again with theocratic rather than democratic foundations.[66] This tension also remains relevant for modern religious believers who explicitly aim to adopt a reflexive attitude towards their religion. Even for them, the requirements imposed on them by the will of God and those imposed by the will of the people might contradict one another. In terms of the Habermasian approach, this means that not everything that people find compelling about their own religious doctrine will turn out to be translatable into a language generally accessible to all. Therefore, important and compelling parts of that religious belief, for instance concerning the acceptability of abortion or gay marriage, might get lost in translation. As the case of abortion illustrates, where many even modern reflexive religious citizens strongly feel that from their religious perspective abortion amounts to a form of legalized murder, this tension might be highly consequential and in this sense, tragic.

To the extent that secular or secularist citizens are not confronted with a potentially tragic tension between two different sources of legitimacy in social or political matters but can simply accept the people as the single source, they do not face cognitive or existential burdens similar to those of religious citizens. Of course, Habermas does impose on them another burden which is supposed to act as a kind of compensation. This burden consists in the requirement to be open for the semantic contents of religious discourses, to enter into a genuine dialogue with religious citizens and even to cooperate actively in translating their religious arguments into a generally accessible language. Here, however, it seems questionable, whether the one-sided imposition of this burden of cognitive openness on secular citizens can be adequately justified.

First of all, it is unclear why secular citizens are expected „to participate in a cooperative search for truth to determine whether the [religious contributions] may contain elements that can be expressed in a secular language and be justified by rational arguments" while religious citizens may be „monolingual" and

[65] Habermas, *Between Naturalism*, 145.

[66] Cf. L.A. Swaine, „How ought liberal democracies treat theocratic communities?", *Ethics* 111 (2001): 302-343.

„unable to discern any pull from any secular reasons."[67] This asymmetry seems to amount to a violation of the basic principle of political equality. Moreover, as Cristina Lafont points out, this privilege itself is highly problematic because it is non-generalizable. Without „the additional obligation to provide arguments and reasons that other citizens can reasonably accept [...] the practice of public deliberation in the informal public sphere would collapse." [68] If all citizens were to behave as mono-glots and make use of their prerogative to argue exclusively from their religious or otherwise comprehensive views, without any further justificatory obligation, it is totally unclear how the institutional translation proviso could ever be upheld. It seems, therefore, that Habermas should stick to his earlier statements, manifestly inconsistent with his statements regarding the possibility of mono-glot citizens, in which he imposes on *all* religious citizens the duty to engage in the translation of their own religious arguments.[69]

Secondly, even if we were to assume a more consistent requirement on *all* religious citizens to engage in translation and even if we (plausibly) assume that a similar requirement to argue in terms equally accessible to all should be imposed on secular citizens, it is not clear why the burdens imposed on secular citizens should go beyond that and also imply, as Habermas suggests, the need to take the semantic and cognitive content of religion seriously as a potential contribution to public debate.[70] This cognitive duty of openness seems hard to reconcile with the neutrality of the liberal rule of law. How could one deny secular citizens, in the light of that neutrality, the right to publicly express the view that religion is opium for the people and, therefore, a threat to humanity?[71] Moreover the requirement of cognitive openness seems only feasible if it concerns an open cognitive attitude regarding religions *in general* and does not necessarily have to apply to all possible particular discussions between religious and secular citizens. A secular citizen can, in line with Habermas, be prepared not to exclude beforehand that religions are, in general, bearers of relevant semantic content of interest to her, but at the same time feel strongly that this open attitude is inappropriate in the specific controversies concerning, e.g., the truth of creationism or the perverse nature of homosexuality.

The open cognitive attitude towards religion can thus not be considered an essential component of the civic duties of all citizens in all circumstances. It can at the most be part of a personal philosophy but not a duty imposed by liberal political theory. In fact, the open cognitive attitude seems unnecessary. As Lafont has convincingly argued, an inclusionist approach regarding public debate can also be defended without this cognitive requirement.[72] Taking reli-

[67] Habermas, *Between Naturalism*, 139, 130, 128.

[68] Lafont, „Religion in the public sphere", 251.

[69] Habermas, *Between Naturalism*, 137.

[70] *Ibid.*, 138-9.

[71] Lafont, „Religion in the public sphere", 249, 258.

[72] *Ibid.*; C. Lafont, „Religion and the public sphere: What are the deliberative obligations of democratic citizenship?", *Philosophy & Social Criticism* 35 (2009) 1-2, 127-150, 135-137.

gious and other contributions to public issues seriously only obliges citizens to engage with them in a serious manner. Secular citizens fulfil all their civic duties by their readiness to enter into an open discussion regarding religious arguments and convictions. It suffices to test these convictions deliberatively and argumentatively on their merits. And in case one believes that the religious convictions at stake are incorrect, arguments and evidence demonstrating their inadequacy have to be made public. And this is exactly what happens, e.g., in the debate concerning evolution and creationism.

Those defending evolution are certainly fulfilling their political obligations towards their fellow citizens by investing an incredible amount of work, energy, and human resources to provide counter evidence for every claim that defenders of creationism bring to the informal public sphere. More importantly, they are fulfilling their obligations of citizenship *regardless of what their personal cognitive stance towards the cognitive substance of religion may be.* [73]

Religious Faith and Public Reason

Habermas's claims concerning the *symmetrical* distribution of cognitive burdens have only emerged in his most recent writings on religion in the public sphere. In his earlier texts, he recognized that, even in a postsecular society, the burdens imposed on religious citizens are heavier.[74] Our analysis reveals that Habermas had better held on to his earlier position. The tension between the religious and the democratic sources of authority regarding political matters generates a heavy burden on some religious citizens which cannot simply be compensated by the open attitude of secular citizens. The cognitive openness of the secular citizens, as imposed by Habermas, insufficiently succeeds in restoring symmetry and introduces, moreover, an additional, unnecessary and unjustifiable asymmetry at the cost of the secular citizen.

It does not make sense to keep the burden of the religious citizens hidden, under the guise of the alleged symmetry of the postsecular perspective. Instead, it should be fully recognized that this asymmetry is in an important sense ineliminable and reflects the ineliminable tension between religious faith and public reason. This tension is nicely illustrated by the two different metaphors Habermas uses to describe the relation between a reflexive religion and secular public reason. Although Habermas uses both metaphors in an attempt to suggest that religion and reason can be easily reconciled, we contend that the religious reference to a divine source of authority, if taken seriously, entails that both metaphors remain problematic.

On the one hand, Habermas talks about the need to *decouple* religion from the social domain in order to avoid religious conflicts in the political sphere.

[73] Idem, „Religion in the public sphere", 249.

[74] Habermas, *Between Naturalism*, 112.

Although such a decoupling limits the practical effects of the religious doctrine, it supposedly leaves its doctrinal substance unaffected.

The imposition results not from relativizing one's own convictions, but from restricting their practical effects; it is an implication of being allowed to realize one's own ethos only within limits and having to accept the practical consequences of the ethos of the other.[75]

This metaphor, however, referring to the *privatization of religion*, seems to underestimate the claim to universality that is typical of most religions. As Habermas himself recognizes and as demonstrated by the debates on abortion, same-sex marriage or recent bio-ethical issues, religions rarely limit themselves to providing a conception of the good life for their own community.[76] They also express what they believe to be universally binding moral concerns. Precisely because divine authority necessarily claims to have universal scope, religions cannot remain 'unaffected' when they are privatized. The hope for a privatization without remainder of religion therefore seems spurious.

On the other hand, Habermas repeatedly describes the relation between religion and public reason with the use of Rawls' image of public reason as a *module* which fits into and is supported by various reasonable comprehensive doctrines.[77] This image emphasizes that there should be a *discursive continuity* between religion and public reason in the sense that it should be possible to reconstruct the principles of equality and liberty, as the basic principles of the modern democratic state, from truths contained in the religious doctrine. This second metaphor, referring to the full *rationalization of religion* in the modern era is, however, equally problematic. Although this view of the evolution of religion as a process of rationalization dovetails with Habermas's earlier views, in line with Durkheim, concerning the „linguistification of the sacred"[78], it seems at odds with some of his more recent views. Habermas now recognizes that religions are characterized by an opaque core which is not accessible to discursive reason.

At best, philosophy *circumscribes* the opaque core of religious experience when it reflects on the specific character of religious language and on the intrinsic meaning of faith. This core remains as profoundly alien to discursive thought as the hermetic core of aesthetic experience, which likewise can be at best circumscribed, but not penetrated, by philosophical reflection.[79]

Whereas the first metaphor is problematic because it fails to recognize that religion cannot be contained in the private sphere, the second one remains problematic because religion, as a presence in the public domain, will necessarily resist full discursive integration into modern public reason.

[75] *Ibid.*, 308-9.

[76] *Ibid.*, 309.

[77] *Ibid.*, 112, 262, 308.

[78] Habermas, *The Theory*, vol. 2: 77ff.

[79] Habermas, *Between Naturalism*, 143.

The problematic nature of both metaphors implies, we submit, that Habermas's rather optimistic picture of a postsecular society in which religious contributions to the public debate can be taken seriously should be somewhat qualified. Although we welcome Habermas's attempt to maximize the cognitive openness of the democratic process towards religious contributions and we believe that a full appreciation of the burdens necessarily imposed on religious citizens by the requirements resulting from the need to guarantee the legitimacy and stability of our pluralistic society shows that such openness might also reveal persistent and irreducible tensions. No theoretical attempt to devise a fully inclusive democratic process can 'resolve' the double bind resulting from the two sources of authority commanding the loyalty of the religious individual. The harmonious concordance of divine and popular will is never guaranteed and tragic conflicts between them, tragic from the point of view of the religious citizen, will always remain possible.

The fact that Habermas himself minimizes this tension might suggest that he is still more tied than he is willing to concede to the program of rationalization prominent in his earlier works. It is noteworthy that Habermas emphasizes that a careful reconstruction of the genesis of reason and philosophy makes clear that philosophy is a 'translation program' that did a lot of work by translating and recovering meaning from religion. In some respect, the history of philosophy is a history of liberating „cognitive contents from their dogmatic encapsulation" in the melting pot of rational discourse; a history of rescuing „the profane significance of interpersonal and existential experiences that have so far only been adequately articulated in religious language." Precisely because it would be unreasonable to reject out of hand the possibility that religions still bear semantic potentials, Habermas now beliefs that the cognitive substance of religions has not yet been exhausted.[80]

It is remarkable that, in this context, Habermas often uses here the formulations „so far", „not yet", „as long as" or „for the time being". This suggests that at a future time, philosophy might be able to translate *all* the morally and politically relevant meaning from religious discourse into secular language. The fact that this hasn't happened yet, is not necessarily the result of some human cognitive deficit, but could be the result of a cultural deficiency that might someday be overcome.[81] If this were the case, postsecular society would mark a temporary phase and could, in due time, evolve into a society where religion hardly plays a role anymore. However, regarding the potential transient nature of our postsecular society, Habermas remains ambiguous. There are also passages where he talks about „the limits of secular reason" and hopes that the secularist mindset can „overcome its limitations."[82] This suggests that religion has a semantic potential which will *always* exceed secular reason and philosophy. He remarks

80 *Ibid.*, 142; Idem, „Faith and Knowledge", 111; Idem, *Religion and Rationality*, 164.

81 S. Chambers, „How religion speaks to the agnostic: Habermas on the persistent value of religion", *Constellations* 14 (2007) 2, 210-223, 219.

82 Habermas, *Between Naturalism*, 140, 144.

that even post-metaphysical thinking will be able „neither to replace nor to repress religion, as long as religious language is the bearer of a semantic content that is inspiring and even indispensable."[83]

It remains unclear, therefore, whether 'reason' is limited 'in principle' or only 'provisionally' and in an interview Habermas's answer to the question how this ambiguity will evolve is „I don't know."[84] Is religion from the epistemological perspective just a Wittgensteinian ladder that can be discarded once one has found the desired secular terms? With a Hegelian movement, the original religious meaning would be transformed into something new.

Philosophy has no content other than religion, but inasmuch as it transforms this content into conceptual knowledge, 'nothing is [any longer] justified by faith'.[85]

Or does religion have a semantic potential which can never be entirely captured in secular philosophical terms and will continue to challenge secular reason? In that case, the postsecular society and the burdens it imposes on religious citizens are here to stay.

[83] J. Habermas, *Postmetaphysical Thinking* (Cambridge: Polity, 1992) 51.

[84] Habermas, *Religion and Rationality*, 163.

[85] J. Habermas, *The Philosophical Discourse of Modernity* (Cambridge: Polity, 1987), 36. The quote is from Hegel.

HABERMAS'S POSTSECULARISM: THE PENETRATION / PRESERVATION OF THE (EUROPEAN) POLITICAL PUBLIC SPHERE

Aakash Singh

I. Habermas' Postsecular Turn as a Conservative Revivalism

The recent work[1] of Juergen Habermas, exemplifying the so-called postsecular turn, harnesses a great number of voices – from the left, the right, even the apolitical – drawing attention to the failure of the secularist paradigm to expel religion from the public realm, and indeed, quite the opposite, perceiving what can be called 'the new visibility of religion.'[2] According to many,[3] the Gordian

[1] J. Habermas (2003) *The Future of Human Nature* (Cambridge: Polity Press); J. Habermas and J. Ratzinger (2005) *Dialektik der Säkularisierung: Über Vernunft und Religion* (Freiburg: Herder); J. Habermas (2006) Religion in the Public Sphere. *European Journal of Philosophy* 14(1), 1–20; J. Habermas (2008) Die Dialektik der Säkularisierung. *Blätter für deutsche und internationale Politik*, 4, 33-46; J. Habermas (2008) *Between Naturalism and Religion* (Cambridge, MA: MIT Press); J. Habermas (2008) A 'post-secular' society — what does that mean? *Reset DOC.* Source: http://www.resetdoc.org/EN/Habermas-Istanbul.php; J. Habermas (2009) 'The Political': The Rational Sense of a Questionable Inheritance of Political Theology. http://blogs.ssrc.org/tif/2009/11/02/rethinking-secularism-audio; J. Habermas (2010) A Postsecular World Society? On the Philosophical Significance of Postsecular Consciousness and the Multicultural World Society. An Interview with Jürgen Habermas by Eduardo Mendieta. Source: http://blogs.ssrc.org/tif/wp-content/uploads/2010/02/A-Postsecular-World-Society-TIF.pdf.

[2] M. Hoelzl and G. Ward (eds) (2008) *The New Visibility of Religion: Studies in Religion and Cultural Hermeneutics* (London: Continuum). Also see: T. Banchoff (2007) *Democracy and the New Religious Pluralism* (Oxford: Oxford University Press).

[3] P. Losonczi and A. Singh (eds) (2010) *From Political Theory to Political Theology: Religious Challenges and the Prospects of Democracy* (London: Continuum).

knot binding religion and politics was not meticulously unknotted in late modernity, but magisterially sword-sliced in Alexandrine fashion, and thus the resurgence of public religion is the inevitable consequence, possibly even in a polemical stance, against secularizing powers.[4] Within this context, Habermas' postsecular turn appears as an attempt to take up both sides and make amends.[5] Habermas attempts to find new life, 'inspiring energy', in the religious traditions, in order to counter-balance decadent tendencies and aid us in questions of value arising in late modernity (our age), but he does not want the fundamental rationality and freedoms of modernity disturbed thereby. Rather, in his account, the secular would assimilate the religious like a blood infusion, becoming more vibrant and stronger thereby, but not losing its advantage:

> We cannot at any rate exclude the thought that [religious tradition]…unleashes an *inspiring energy* for all of society….In short, postmetaphysical thought is prepared to learn from religion, but remains agnostic in the process. It insists on the difference between the certainties of faith, on the one hand, and validity claims that can be publicly criticized, on the other…[6]

In Habermas, the postsecular problem lies in how best to preserve the secular democratic institutions and keep them from being 'violated' through religiously motivated politics:

> Religious *traditions* have a *special power* to articulate moral intuitions, especially with regard to vulnerable forms of communal life. In the event of the corresponding political debates, this potential makes religious speech a serious candidate to transporting possible truth contents, which can then be translated from the vocabulary of a particular religious community into a generally accessible language. However, the institutional thresholds between the 'wild life' of the political public sphere and the formal proceedings within political bodies are also a *filter* that from the Babel of voices in the informal flows of public communication allows only secular contributions to pass through. In parliament, for example, the standing rules of procedure of the house must empower the house leader to have religious statements or justifications *expunged* from the minutes.[7]

This rich paragraph is replete with suggestion; let us draw out just three: (a) religious traditions have a 'special power'; (b) translation from particular

[4] R. Ingelhart and P. Norris (2004) *Sacred and Secular: Religion and Politics Worldwide.* (Cambridge: Cambridge University Press).

[5] This new development of Habermas' thought is reflected in several of the articles in this volume. It is also succinctly sketched in A. Harrington (2007) Habermas and the 'Post-Secular Society'. *European Journal of Social Theory*, 10, 543-560. Also see A. Braeckman (2009) Habermas and Gauchet on religion in postsecular society. A critical assessment. *Continental Philosophy Review*, 42, 279-296.

[6] J. Habermas (2008) *Religion in the Public Sphere. European Journal of Philosophy* 14 (1), 17.

[7] Ibid., 10.

(i.e. the language of religion) to general (i.e. secular language) serves the 'threshold' protecting institutions like parliament from the public Babel exterior to it; (c) the leader of the house in parliament should be empowered to expunge religious language from the minutes.

Regarding (a), we see here what we might call a romanticization, not to say fetishization, of religion's relevance – 'religious traditions have a *special power.*'[8] It is also interesting to notice the emphasis on 'traditions'; does this include the Hare Krishnas and Scientologists, neither of which is granted the tax-free status of religious organizations in Germany? However we understand it, the 'special power' is part of what constitutes that vitality injected by religion which Habermas hopes to harness. But, of course, to harness on his own terms.

Thus we get (b), the 'threshold', and the protection of institutions like parliament from the Babel surrounding it – what peripety: Habermas de-scripturalizes 'Babel' here, in relation to insulating and protecting a wholly profane institution like parliament.

And speaking of 'special power', (c) provides the speaker with a rather unprecedented one: the threshold filtration or prophylactic, if compromised during parliamentary discourse with a religious seed planted in the minds of the debaters, would have a second level of protection in the abortion of that seed, expunging the religious statement from the minutes.

Habermas is attempting to situate himself as a mean between two extremes. On the one side, he criticizes John Rawls because he finds that Rawls' logic excludes too rigorously the religious, not allowing it to be infused into the blood of the body politic. This reading of Rawls of course recapitulates one of the fundamental disagreements articulated in the Habermas-Rawls debate, treating of the dilation / contraction of the political public sphere.[9] Rawls contracts what Habermas hopes to dilate.

On the other extreme, Habermas criticizes Nicholas Wolterstorff, who errs on the side of excess as much as Rawls errs on the side of miserliness. According to Habermas, Wolterstorff would overrun the political by the religious, thus violating vulnerable democratic institutions like the parliament:

> Since no *institutional filter* is envisaged between the state and the public domain, this version does not exclude the possibility that policies and legal programs will be implemented solely on the basis of the religious or confessional beliefs of a ruling majority. This is the conclusion explicitly drawn by Nicholas Wolterstorff, who does not wish to subject the political use of religious reasons to any restraints whatsoever. At any rate, he allows for a political legislature making use of religious arguments. If one thus opens the parliaments to the battle on religious beliefs, governmental authority can evidently become the agent of a religious majority that asserts its will and thus *violates* the democratic procedure.[10]

[8] Habermas often employs the phrase, *Die Vitalität des Religiösen*

[9] For this debate, see *The Journal of Philosophy* 92 (March 1995), and Rawls' subsequent reply.

[10] J. Habermas (2008) *Religion in the Public Sphere.*, 10.

Habermas' 'institutional filter' which protects the parliament from its violation allows the state to preserve its earlier legitimacy – preserve state sovereignty – while opening it to the life-affirming but politically destabilizing domain of religious vitality. Throughout his important recent writings, above all *Religion in the Public Sphere*, Habermas persistently, unwittingly employs Victorian innuendo bestowing masculine 'inspiring energy', 'vitality',[11] and also danger, onto religion, which runs the risk of 'violating' effeminate democratic institutions symbolized by the parliament, were it not for some prophylactic devise, the oft-mentioned 'filter', which serves to protect her virtue. In the event she, the parliament, is violated by some premature ejaculation or expression by a religious parliamentarian, Habermas' proposed mechanism of expunging religious terms stands by ready to abort the product. Habermas will only countenance a refined or immaculate conception of effete democracy by vitalizing, energetic religion.

This revivalist endeavor seems, moreover, a rather conservative one: first, as Ungureanu has pointed out, Habermas fails to negotiate and draw out the consequences of his ostensible openness to religious traditions, and 'not infrequently, there is an empirical correlation between right-wing and conservative politics and religious affiliation'.[12] Moreover, Habermas has also insufficiently addressed his prioritization of religious 'traditions' over religious movements, sects of various sorts, hybrids, and the panoply of other new religious expressions in public spaces. Finally, in a not unrelated set of issues, about which more below, since 2003, in respect to the debates on the EU – the European Constitution, the need for a common identity, foreign policy, etc – Habermas has seemingly reversed his earlier position for critically self-reflective and rational identities and tends toward a glorification of the European model, conceived in terms of superiority to the American hegemonic model. In so doing, he has slipped into the populist talk of 'values' as opposed to principles; that is, as in Article I-2 of the European Constitution, 'The Union is founded on the values of respect for human dignity, freedom…' – obviously, these could have been termed 'principles' or 'norms' rather than the conservative choice of 'values'.[13] Habermas' post-metaphysical thought, if it had a vocabulary, ought certainly to have preferred 'principle' rather than 'value' in this regard.

In, therefore, this conservative-leaning revivalist endeavor of Habermas' postsecular turn, then, it seems that everything would hang upon the effectiveness of the prophylactic, the 'institutional filter.' In short, how to let religious values into the political public sphere without impregnating democracy with the bastard child that

[11] Again, 'Some religious traditions would appear, even if they at times take the stage as the opaque Other of reason, to have remained present in a more vital manner than has metaphysics' (*Die Dialektik der Säkularisierung*).

[12] C. Ungureanu (2008) The Contested Relation between Democracy and Religion: Towards a Dialogical Perspective. *European Journal of Political Theory*, 7, 405-429.

[13] J. Lacroix (2009) Does Europe Need Common Values?: Habermas vs Habermas. *European Journal of Political Theory*, 8, 141-156. Also see: A. Baumeister (2007) Diversity and Unity: The Problem with 'Constitutional Patriotism'. *European Journal of Political Theory*, 6, 483-503.

goes by the name: *political theology*. Habermas' implicit preoccupation with political theology became explicit in late 2009, when he gave a talk in New York entitled, 'The Political: The Rational Sense of a Questionable Inheritance of Political Theology.'[14]

Political theology is dubious; religion is powerful – New York's Twin Towers stand, or do not stand, as a painful reminder of these facts. This is why Habermas requires the postsecular to be realized wholly upon the terms set by the secular. We open ourselves to the religious in good faith and wish not to be violated. Europe, as it is, is already suffering under pains of contraction and miscarriage, and thus vulnerable, according to Habermas. For, as he describes in the closing paragraph of his 'A Plea for a Common Foreign Policy, Beginning in the Core of Europe', to which Derrida inscrutably appended his signature:

> Each of the great European nations has experienced the *bloom* of its imperial power. And...each has had to work through the experience of the *loss* of its *empire*...with the *loss* of *colonial territories*. With the growing distance of imperial domination and the history of colonialism, the European powers also...could learn from the perspective of the defeated to perceive themselves in the dubious role of victors who are called to account for the violence of a forcible and uprooting process of modernization.[15]

This is an interesting thought: but poor Poland, Habermas would not include it among the 'great' European nations. Let the Poles take refuge in Donald Rumsfield's 'old Europe-new Europe' (di)vision.[16]

II. THE 'POSTIES': FROM POSTSECULAR TO POSTSOVEREIGN TO POSTMODERN...

The 'violence of a forcible and uprooting process of modernization' about which Habermas speaks in relation to imperial power and colonization, was a far more masculine era in European political history. Europe's position in a postcolonial world is as unsettling as the prospects of a postsecular one.

[14] J. Habermas (2010) A Postsecular World Society? On the Philosophical Significance of Postsecular Consciousness and the Multicultural World Society. An Interview with Jürgen Habermas by Eduardo Mendieta.

[15] J. Habermas, with J. Derrida (2003) February 15, or What Binds Europeans Together: A Plea for a Common Foreign Policy, Beginning in the Core of Europe. *Constellations*, 10(3), 3-15.

[16] See Charles Turner (2004) Jürgen Habermas: European and German?. *European Journal of Political Theory*, 3, 303: 'The idea that a common European identity might be based on „painful experiences" in common is hampered by the fact that many in Eastern Europe perceived the states of Western Europe and those of NATO as having accepted Europe's postwar division....The process undergone by countries such as Poland was painful, but the source of the pain was not „nationalist excess" alone but rather six years of Nazi occupation followed by forty years of Soviet domination.'

Modernization with its avatars as secularization (internally) and colonization (externally), though violent and uprooting, was contemporaneous with the era of the consolidation of the sovereign nation-state.

Not only in the work of Carl Schmitt[17] but even in that of his inspiration Thomas Hobbes,[18] secularity is at ground a question of sovereignty. In one reading of Schmitt, consistent with Habermas' position in his relatively early work *Legitimation Crisis* [LC], since political theology asserts a direct and inevitable connection between religion and politics, secularism has inevitably entailed a decline in political authority and, consequently, eroded sovereignty[19] (though various other techniques – which Foucault gathers under the idea of 'governmentality'[20] – have of course served to recuperate that sovereignty by other means). In the opposing reading, modern political authority, no longer sanctioned and legitimated by divinity, fosters what Habermas refers to as a polemical 'secularist' (as opposed to indifferent 'secular') attitude that ensures that religious orientations do not prevent citizens from 'rendering unto Caesar what is Caesar's'.[21] This is Habermas' orientation in the recent work 'Die Dialektik der Säkularisierung'. Whether we subscribe to Habermas' more radical position from LC or his more conservative position of today, the correlation between sovereignty and secularism remains established.

It is therefore tempting to correlate the secularity-sovereignty nexus with a postsecularity-postsovereignty one.[22] At the very least, given the current and

[17] C. Schmitt (2006) *Political Theology: Four Chapters on the Concept of Sovereignty* (Chicago: University of Chicago Press).

[18] As A.P. Martinich (2005) writes in his entry on the 'Ten Commandments': 'Hobbes casts his discussion of the Ten Commandments in such a way that it becomes part of his general design to secularize certain religious concepts. For example, he transfers various divine attributes to the sovereign. Just as God is omnipotent and the judge of all, the sovereign has overwhelming power and is the judge of all facts and events. Also, just as eternal salvation from the ravages of sin comes from God, worldly salvation from the wretchedness of the state of nature comes from the sovereign. Similarly, the Ten Commandments are reinterpreted within a secular, political framework. Hobbes interprets the first four commandments, which are usually thought of as applying distinctively to God, as analogous to what is required of any civil sovereign: „the first [table of stone] contains the law of sovereignty"'. *Hobbes Dictionary* (London: Blackwell).

[19] P. O. Espejo (2007) Does Political Theology Entail Decisionism? On the Relation of the concept of Sovereignty to different conceptions of God in Christianity. *Paper presented at the annual meeting of the American Political Science Association.* http://www.allacademic.com/meta/p210995_index.html.

[20] M. Foucault (2004) Naissance de la biopolitique: cours au Collège de France (1978-1979) (Paris: Gallimard).

[21] 'Unlike the indifferent stance of a secular or unbelieving person, who relates agnostically to religious validity claims, secularists tend to adopt a polemical stance toward religious doctrines that maintain a public influence' (*Between Naturalism and Religion*).

[22] 'Political theology might well become the discipline of studying and eventually mastering such „escalation", that is, the excesses of sovereignty and their violence, as well as the rhetorical overdrive with which they are accompanied, ideologically justified, and irresponsibly spiced up'

continued erosion of the nineteenth-century paradigm of univocal nation-state sovereignty (in spite of the success of governmentality) by means of regionalization and various currents of globalization, further research on the problematic of sovereignty post secularism would be urgently required if indeed we were being ushered into a postsecular environment. Hints of this have already arisen, with expected controversy, in the debate surrounding the Archbishop of Canterbury's remarks challenging the absolute authority of secular law:

> There is a position – not at all unfamiliar in contemporary discussion – which says that to be a citizen is essentially and simply to be under the rule of the uniform law of a sovereign state, in such a way that any other relations, commitments or protocols of behaviour belong exclusively to the realm of the private and of individual choice. As I have maintained in several other contexts, this is a very unsatisfactory account of political reality in modern societies.[23]

By 'modern societies' Williams implies highly and multiform pluralistic[24] societies, and it thus seems somewhat to overlap with what Habermas calls 'postsecular societies'. Both capture the current resurgence of interest in legal pluralism, which of course takes many forms.[25] One such is the widespread attention focusing on the dual-codes of countries like India (with one set of laws for Muslims and another for Hindus, and so on), and Pakistan.[26] Most of the furor around Williams' challenge centers on the point of dual codes, especially his remarks that the adoption of certain aspects of Sharia law in the UK 'seems unavoidable': 'There's a place for finding what would be a constructive accommodation with some aspects of Muslim law, as we already do with some other aspects of religious law.'[27]

Habermas' watershed essay *Religion in the Public Sphere* was also partly inspired by the fact that, to quote from his opening page, 'In several Muslim countries, and in Israel as well, religious family law is either an alternative or a substitute for secular civil law.' It is of course intriguing to try to reason out how Habermas envisioned parliamentary and legislative debate surrounding the framing and adopting of such laws, considering that religious statements and

(20). H. de Vries and L. E. Sullivan (eds) (2006) *Political Theologies: Public Religions in a Post-Secular World* (New York: Fordham University Press).

[23] R. Williams (2008) Civil and Religious Law in England: a Religious Perspective. http://www.archbishopofcanterbury.org/1575.

[24] 'Multiform pluralism' is a term used by W. E. Connolly (1999), in *Why I am not a Secularist?* (Minneapolis: University of Minnesota Press).

[25] See, e.g., The Birmingham Law School's *Journal of Legal Pluralism*, or Mark Tushnet's CLS and deconstructive experiments.

[26] The architecture and layout of the buildings on Islamabad's Constitution Avenue beautifully capture the parallel juridical system of Pakistan, where the Federal Supreme Court stands face to face from the Supreme Shariat Court across the street.

[27] BBC News (2008) 'Sharia law in UK is „unavoidable"'. http://news.bbc.co.uk/2/hi/uk_news/7232661.stm.

justifications should be expunged from the minutes. How could the Israeli *Knesset*, the Indian *Lok Sabha* or the Pakistani *Majlis-e-Shoora* – just to take a few examples of countries with plural legal systems – possibly function under the constant erasure of religious statements?

Of course, for Habermas, India and Pakistan fall outside the scope of his (post)secular dialectics; because not 'affluent', they are not entitled to the designation 'postsecular':

> A 'postsecular' society must at some point have been in a 'secular' state. The controversial term can therefore only be applied to the *affluent* societies of Europe or countries such as Canada, Australia and New Zealand, where people's religious ties have steadily or rather quite dramatically lapsed in the post-War period.[28]

This exclusion of South Asia does not prevent Habermas from speaking of Hinduism, Buddhism, and Islam over a dozen times in this same essay, nor does it dissuade him from opening his recent talk on Political Theology in New York with pithy remarks on China.[29] But why even speak of phenomena in these non-affluent areas if by definition they do not bear on the theme under consideration: postsecular societies? It is a vexing question as to why so much of the evidence of the resurgence of religion, which characterizes the postsecular condition Habermas apprehends, is drawn from regions lying outside the 'affluent societies of Europe' – it cannot be that Europe may develop into a postsecular society because Israel, India, Pakistan, Afghanistan, China, Russia, and other outliers fail to fit the framework of the secular paradigm; that is a *non sequitor*. The affluent societies were at one time secular, and they dialectically proceed to postsecular. India, for example, on the other hand, was never perfectly secularized, but remains static in it's a-secular condition. The echo of Hegel's *Philosophy of World History* and *Philosophy of Religion* come out crisp and clear in Habermas' dialectical account.[30]

How ironic, then, that Habermas explicitly defends and develops his conception of 'postmetaphysical' in contrast to Hegel's philosophy of history, the swansong of metaphysics.[31] Habermas' sixth section of *Religion in the Public Sphere* is devoted to unraveling how 'the secular awareness that one is living in a postsecular society takes the shape of postmetaphysical thought at the philosophical level.'[32] By 'postmetaphysical' Habermas is speaking of the current constellation of scientific and epistemic paradigms ostensibly neutral toward the metaphysical. Roughly defining the latter term, he states:

[28] J. Habermas (2008) *Religion in the Public Sphere.*, 4; J. Habermas (2008) *Between Naturalism and Religion.*

[29] Minute 13, SSRC website – 22 october 2009. He moves on from China to the September 11 attacks, then to Bush and Afghanistan.

[30] Cf. F. Dallmayr (1987) The Discourse of Modernity: Hegel and Habermas. *The Journal of Philosophy,* 84 (11), 682-692.

[31] J. Habermas (1994) *Postmetaphysical Thinking.*.

[32] J. Habermas (2008) *Religion in the Public Sphere.*, 16.

> I am using metaphysical to designate the thinking of a philosophical idealism that goes back to Plato, and extends by way of Plotinus and Neo-Platonism, Augustine and Thomas Aquinas, Cusanus and Pico de Mirandola, Descartes, Spinoza, and Leibniz, up to Kant, Fichte, Schelling, and Hegel.[33]

In this exposition of the passage from the metaphysical to the postmetaphysical, just as in the passage from the secular to postsecular, there is no room for the extra-European – and strangely the Arabic and Islamic *falsafa* are also missing – beyond of course the related affluent 'countries such as Canada, Australia, and New Zealand.' In the case of the postmetaphysical, unlike the postsecular, there are not even any sensational media events from outliers like China, India or Iran – to select countries with long traditions of metaphysical speculation – for Habermas to draw attention to in illustration of his argument.

In his book devoted to the subject, *Postmetaphysical Thinking*, Habermas enumerates 'four themes' or 'four movements of thought' which characterize the break with the tradition of enlightenment modernity / metaphysics: 'postmetaphysical thinking, the linguistic turn, situating reason, and reversing the primacy of theory over practice – or the overcoming of logocentrism.'[34] Just as he envisions his position on the postsecular scene as a mean between two extremes, he situates himself as a postmetaphysical thinker at the mean between the extreme of idealistic, rationalist, ego-centric metaphysics, on the one hand, and the radical form of postmodernism embodying the above-mentioned four movements of thought, such as deconstructionism.[35]

The Postmodern turn to religion has been coeval with the postsecular turn, and not merely coincidentally. Rodney Stark's 'Secularization, R.I.P.' appeared in the same year as Hent de Vries' *Philosophy and the Turn to Religion*. Peter Berger's 'Secularism in Retreat' appeared the same year as Graham Ward's book *The Postmodern God* and John D. Caputo's book *The Prayers and Tears of Jacques Derrida*.[36] Not to mention the against-the-grain writings on religion from Zizek, Badiou, Agamben.[37]

[33] J. Habermas (1994) *Postmetaphysical Thinking*, p. 29.

[34] J. Habermas (1994) *Postmetaphysical Thinking*, p. 6.

[35] This is not to say that Habermas equates the postmetaphysical and the postsecular; he clearly does not. As he laments in a recent interview, 'It seems I should have prevented the misleading equation of „postmetaphysical" with „postsecular"' (*A Postsecular World Society?*).

[36] R. Stark (1999) Secularization, R.I.P. *Sociology of Religion*, 60 (3), 249-273. H. de Vries (1999) *Philosophy and the Turn to Religion* (Baltimore: Johns Hopkins University Press). P. Berger (1996/7) Secularism in Retreat. *The National Interest*, Winter, 3-12. P. Blond and G. Ward (1997) *The Postmodern God* (London: Blackwell). J. D. Caputo (1997) *The Prayers and Tears of Jacques Derrida, Religion Without Religion* (Indianapolis: Indiana University Press).

[37] S. Zizek and J. Milbank (2009) *The Monstrosity of Christ: Paradox or Dialectic?* (Cambridge, MA: MIT Press). P. Badiou (2003) *Saint Paul: The Foundation of Universalism* (Stanford: Stanford University Press). Also worth mentioning are the influential works of M. Foucault (1999) *Religion and Culture* (Manchester: Manchester University Press), J. Derrida

In the early 1980s, Habermas spoke collectively of 'postenlightenment, postmodernity, even of posthistory'[38], and in the early 1990s he made reference to 'posties' while postulating the inevitability of postmetaphysical thought.[39] A decade later, Habermas begins attempting to balance the postmetaphysical with the postsecular, a precarious move seeking to appropriate both the critical energy of postmodernity and the 'special power' of religion simultaneously, without succumbing to the combined explosive defects he finds in postmodern religion, about which he writes with palpable contempt:

> Let us take the example of 'radical orthodoxy', an approach that takes up the intentions and fundamental ideas of the political theology of a Carl Schmitt and develops them with the tools of deconstruction. [T]heologians of this ilk deny Modernity any intrinsic right with the intention to once again give a nominalistically uprooted Modern world ontological anchors in the 'reality of God'....[40]

Remember, 'postmetaphysical thought is prepared to learn from religion, but remains agnostic in the process.' We mentioned that Derrida had appended his signature to Habermas' open letter on European Foreign Policy; is Habermas' postsecular turn not a sort of inadvertent appending of *his* signature to Derrida's *The Gift of Death* – naturally, of course, with the motivation of rewriting it?

In *The Philosophical Discourse of Modernity*, the prequel to *Postmetaphysical Thinking*, Habermas speaks explicitly of 'the destruction or overcoming of metaphysics by Nietzsche and Heidegger [which] meant something other than the sublation (*Aufhebung*) of metaphysics...'. He continues, 'and yet these attitudes point back to the break with tradition...'.[41] Habermas identifies the break with tradition, what he calls 'the entry into Postmodernity' as beginning with Nietzsche, and its project of 'the undermining of Western rationalism through the critique of metaphysics as beginning with Heidegger, and then sees Derridian Postmodernism as something of an inevitable offspring of the two, considering the *Sonderweg* of this subject-centered conception of reason which is basically begging to be deconstructed.[42] This sketch from the earlier book matches the later one, but with one noteworthy point: notice that Habermas appends the adjective 'Western' to 'rationalism' but not to 'metaphysics'. A far cry from the liberal multicultural, and now current, gesture of prefixing 'metaphysics' or 'philosophy' by 'Western' to exhibit awareness of the presence or vibrancy of philosophy elsewhere in the world, this is a counter-reformative

(2002) *Acts of Religion* (New York: Columbia University Press), and R. Rorty and G. Vattimo (2005) *The Future of Religion* (Cambridge: Polity Press).

[38] J. Habermas (1981) Modernity versus Postmodernity. *New German Critique* 22.

[39] J. Habermas (1994) *Postmetaphysical Thinking*, p. 6.

[40] J. Habermas (2008) *Religion in the Public Sphere.*, 19. Habermas refers to J. Milbank (1990) *Theology and Social Theory: Beyond Secular Reason* (London: Blackwell).

[41] J. Habermas (1987) *The Philosophical Discourse of Modernity*, p. 52.

[42] See Jürgen Habelated by William Rehg, 1997, Oxford, Polity Press.

maneuver staking exclusive claim to rationalism by the western world. While that rationalism is problematic in its logocentric avatar, it is precisely Western reason (reconceived intersubjectively) that Habermas seeks desperately to rescue and preserve from the excesses of postmodern critique. Habermas' account thus functions as a new chapter sewn into the Eurocentric paradigm of Hegel's *Philosophy of World History* and *Philosophy of Religion* – revised and updated – and fails daringly to introduce a new paradigm; it clings to the center-periphery epistemic bias that characterized colonialist modernity. Though Habermas would seek strongly to deny it, the transition from the metaphysical to the post-metaphysical in his own account is indeed a sublation (*Aufhebung*), which, as Hegel explained, picks up and preserves even as it cancels.[43]

Once again, Habermas believes he can bring the straying Postmodern flock back into the fold of (the as yet incomplete project of) modernity[44] by *inter alia* proposing an alternative way out of the philosophy of the subject – communicative reason as opposed to subject-centered. There is, then, an analogous if not identical dialectical process in Habermas' attempt to dictate terms, secular and modernist, to both the postsecularists and the postmodernists. Both scenarios are attempts to find a middle-ground, and above all a stable ground. What goes sadly unrecognized in all the secondary literature is that his solution is fundamentally not pluralist. It is, rather, the classical attempt to brace up the center all over again.

III. ...And from Postmodern to Postcolonial

Now, except in the thought of Peter Berger[45] and a few others,[46] most scholars agree that to speak of modernity is to speak of secularization, just as clearly as it is to speak of colonization. That modernity – whose requiem is being sung by

[43] A. Singh and R. Mohapatra (eds) (2008) *Reading Hegel: The Introductions* (Melbourne: Re.Press), pp. 6, 8, 35ff.

[44] J. Habermas (1997) 'Modernity: An Unfinished Project', in: M. Passerin d'Entreves and S. Benhabib (eds) (1997) *Habermas and the Unfinished Project of Modernity* (Cambridge, MA: MIT Press).

[45] 'I think what I and most other sociologists of religion wrote in the 1960s about secularization was a mistake. Our underlying argument was that secularization and modernity go hand in hand. With more modernization comes more secularization. It wasn't a crazy theory. There was some evidence for it. But I think it's basically wrong. Most of the world today is certainly not secular. It's very religious.' P.L. Berger (1997) Epistemological modesty: An interview with Peter Berger. *Christian Century*, 114, 974. Also see: P. L. Berger (1999) *The Desecularization of the World: Resurgent Religion and World Politics* (Grand Rapids: Eerdmans).

[46] Indeed, Habermas himself has begun to question the link between modernization and secularization (see 'The Political': The Rational Sense of a Questionable Inheritance of Political Theology; and, A Postsecular World Society?); however, we speak of *modernity* as an era, and not modernization in general. Berger conflates the two, as visible in the previous note. On the

postcolonial theorists like Ashis Nandy[47] – secular, rationalist, progressive-historical, the project which for Habermas remains incomplete,[48] seems now to complete itself only through its own sublation: postsecularity smacks of the violation of modernity by postmodernity, at least an attempt, however reluctantly, to accommodate the cacophony of postmodern complaints which occur in what Habermas calls 'the 'wild life' of the political public sphere.[49] The marriage of postsecularity and postmodernity's religious orientation is of course a reluctant and suspicious one. But as we begin to see, it is telling that they both immediately succeed a decade awash in the violation of Western academia by postcolonial theory, again typified by Nandy's requiem or funeral for modernity. As Hamlet explained to Horatio, 'The funeral baked meats / Did coldly furnish forth the marriage tables'.[50]

To speak of modernity is to speak of colonization, just as clearly as it is to speak of secularization. Are we justified in correlating the postsecular with the postcolonial, a direction Habermas himself seems to indicate in the passage cited from 'A Plea for a Common Foreign Policy' above? ('Each of the great European nations has experienced the bloom of its imperial power. And…each has had to work through the experience of the loss of its empire…with the loss of colonial territories.') More recently (in an interview from 2009), Habermas speaks of colonization in terms of an interruption of the 'linear development' of egalitarian universalism which constitutes the basis of the 'normative self-understanding' of European peoples. It appears that Habermas' earlier attempt to apply the Metzean framework of suffering in his quest for European identity-construction was short-lived, and he atavisticly reverted to the enlightenment notion of a (exclusively) European development toward universal freedom as the basis of self-understanding (i.e., identity):

> egalitarian universalism becomes more pointed in law and morality; and there is a progressive individualization. In any case, we still draw our normative self-understanding from this. Of course, we should not view this as a linear development, despite certain evolutionary thresholds. The postcolonial encounter with other cultures in the 20th century brought to

concept of 'modernity' vis-à-vis 'modernization', see S. Kaviraj (2010) 'Outline of a Revisionist Theory of Modernity', in: A. Singh and R. Mohapatra (eds) *Indian Political Thought* (London & New York: Routledge). The topic is also covered in John Rundell's Chapter One of this volume.

47 A. Nandy (1990) *Science, Hegemony and Violence: A Requiem for Modernity* (New Delhi: Oxford University Press).

48 See note 44. It is of course not necessary to rehash here the debate kindled by this notion between Habermas and Lyotard, who forcefully concluded his position, saying, 'My argument is that the modern project has not been abandoned or forgotten but destroyed, liquidated'. J.-F. Lyotard (1984) *The Postmodern Condition* (Manchester: Manchester University Press), p. 111.

49 J. Habermas (2008) *Religion in the Public Sphere.*, 10.

50 W. Shakespeare, *Hamlet*, Act 1, Scene 2, lines 179-180.

> our attention the wounds of colonization and the devastating consequences of decolonization, and thus also the shocking dialectic of higher-level reflexivity. Today we find ourselves in the transition to a multicultural world society and are wrestling with its future political constitution. The outcome is entirely open-ended.[51]

Nevertheless, Habermas admits to the relationship between the postcolonial and the postsecular a few paragraphs later in the same interview:

> There certainly is a connection between the emergence of postsecular consciousness and the new migration flows that fundamentally pose two problems for nation-states. First, the naturalized immigrants from a different culture must be integrated socially and economically, and they must be given space for the assertion of their collective identity….Classical immigrant societies cope better with the first problem than European societies that either opened themselves primarily to immigrants from their own colonies (like Great Britain and France) or to foreign workers (like Germany).[52]

Then what about the next step, linking the postcolonial with the postmodern? According to the narrative of Robert Young's *White Mythologies* and *Postcolonialism, An Historical Introduction*, postmodernity arose preponderantly as a postcolonial discourse, at least in certain 'foundational' authors whose work arise out of their experiences *as* Algerians. Specifically, Young asserts that poststructuralism is a Franco-Maghrebian theory, born out of the experience of the Algerian War of Independence (1954–1962).[53] He focuses on those writings of Jacques Derrida, Hélène Cixous and Jean-François Lyotard, which are autobiographical, such as Cixous' *Reveries of the Wild Woman. Primal Scenes* and 'My Algeriance, in other words: to depart not to arrive from Algeria', Derrida's *Monolingualism of the Other* and Lyotard's *Political Writings.*[54]

Habermas, on the other hand, does not entertain this exogamous possibility in *The Philosophical Discourse of Modernity*, where, instead, he sees poststructuralist and postmodernist currents as arising endogamously, internally from the tradition that, though they break with, they nevertheless reflect. Perhaps Algeria was not affluent enough to enter Habermas' dialectics of (post)modernity.

But while Habermas nevertheless accedes to the notion of postmodernity as a rupture with modernity, as an anti-Enlightenment, others – especially Marxists

51 J. Habermas (2010) A Postsecular World Society

52 Ibid.

53 R. Young (2001) *Postcolonialism: An Historical Introduction* (London: Blackwell), pp. 411-28.

54 However, Lyotard makes it clear that his political writings on Algeria were made possible only by his stay in the Algerian city of Constantine, between 1950 and 1952, where he worked as a teacher. A. Sajed (2008) Nativizing Discipline(s) and Disciplining Natives: Post-Structuralism and the Postcolonial in IR Theory. *Paper presented at the annual meeting of the ISA's 49th ANNUAL CONVENTION, BRIDGING MULTIPLE DIVIDES.* http://www.allacademic.com/meta/p252874_index.html

and post-Marxists – understand postmodernity as a seamless and continuous process of reflection upon modernity. Habermas captured this possibility in asking, 'Is 'postmodern' a slogan which unobtrusively inherits the affective attitudes which cultural modernity has provoked in reaction to itself…?'[55]

Frederic Jameson's comprehension of postmodernity as no more than an expression of late capitalism (i.e. late modernity), and consequently his critique of postmodernist tendencies within postcolonial critique as evidence of the latter being hardly more than the commoditization and purveying of third-world thought, is another example of the tendency to reject exogamous elements in the philosophical discourse of postmodernity.[56] With Terry Eagleton as with Jameson, postcolonial thought is assimilated into the self-reflexivity of late Western modernity itself[57] – a dialectic that mediates all otherness and, consequently, closes off the possibility of an openness to otherness on terms set by the other rather than by oneself.

Even if we reject – as Habermas, Jameson and Eagleton do – Robert Young's revisionist inversion of standard critiques of postcolonial theory as being neo-orientalist and even Eurocentric, due to its reliance on postmodern motifs (with postmodernity conceived as a purely endogamous development), in either direction, the link between postmodernity and postcoloniality is sufficiently established, even celebrated by the likes of Derrida's most famous translator and architect of postcolonial theory, Gayatri Spivak.[58] That is, we can be confident of Habermas' awareness of the correlation of the postmodern and the postcolonial, just as he himself drew attention to the correlation of the modern and colonial, just as he did the postcolonial and the postsecular.

But so much for these diverse declensions, from postsecular to postsovereign to postmodern to postcolonial, and back again, associations made in each case, such as through the notion of postmetaphysical, by Habermas himself. What we seek to uncover is that in each case the strategy is parallel, and indeed reactionary: the danger is identified, and the center is then fortified against it.

Against all these abhorrent threats from without and from within, our fundamental democratic institutions such as parliament seem far too vulnerable. No wonder Habermas is desperate to strengthen that 'institutional filter', that protective barrier separating the sanctity of the interior of parliament from the exterior wild and unruly din of a postsovereign, postmodern, postcolonial clamor. He is protecting effete democracy from both the right and the left, from within and without…perhaps we should have Christo re-wrap the Reichstag!

[55] J. Habermas (1987) *The Philosophical Discourse of Modernity*, p. 38-39.

[56] F. Jameson (1991) *Postmodernism, or, the Cultural Logic of Late Capitalism* (Durham: Duke University Press).

[57] See Terry Eagleton's review of Gayatri Spivak's book *Critique of Post-Colonial Reason* entitled, 'In the Gaudy Supermarket', *London Review of Books* (13 May 1999).

[58] As Spivak stated in an interview: 'My position is generally a reactive one. I am viewed by Marxists as too codic, by feminists as too male-identified, by indigenous theorists as too committed to Western Theory. I am uneasily pleased about this.' S. Harasym (ed) (1990) *The Post-Colonial Critic: Interviews, Strategies, Dialogues* (London: Routledge).

IV. The 'violence of a forcible and uprooting process of modernization'

And so we have this deep context of threats, fear, uncertainty ('the outcome is entirely open-ended'[59]). In this vein, Habermas speaks frequently of September 11 whenever he lectures on religion in the public sphere, postsecularism, and/or political theology.[60] It seems that Habermas believes that September 11 did a great deal to bring concrete challenges of a postsecular dispensation into the daylight. (I would add that it also served to transform numerous philosophers into political theorists and numerous political theorists into pseudo-theologians.)

And indeed, Habermas' recurrently articulated fear, that religion will violate the parliament, was violently realized in New Delhi, India, only two months after September 11: on 13 December 2001, the Indian parliament building was stormed by a group of five heavily armed Islamic terrorists of the Jaish-e-Mohammed outfit, one of which was wearing the now-fashionable explosive suicide vest.[61]

But this attribution of danger and power to religion, the politics of fear, is not fed only by these spectacular images, threats coming from the wild periphery to the passive center, from the far-flung caves of Tora Bora flown into the financial district of Manhattan, from the terrorist training camp of Moridke boated in to the shore of Mumbai's financial district. The immigration rhetoric of every recent election in Europe and beyond[62] – not to mention the rise of the far right in the recent European elections[63] – evokes these violative notions, the urgent need to prevent the swarthy barbarians at the gate from flooding in, of strengthening the institutional filter in order to prevent them from penetrating our vulnerable order:

> We find ourselves, once more, in that paradoxical *vulnerability* that our forebears suffered for more than 20 centuries. The old menace, long vanquished, has returned in new guise. We are threatened again by an enemy whose weaknesses in peace become strengths in war.

[59] J. Habermas (2010) A Postsecular World Society?

[60] J. Habermas (2006) Religion in the Public Sphere; J. Habermas (2008) Die Dialektik der Säkularisierung; J. Habermas (2008) A 'post-secular' society – what does that mean?; J. Habermas (2009) 'The Political': The Rational Sense of a Questionable Inheritance of Political Theology; J. Habermas (2010) A Postsecular World Society?

[61] 'Storming of Parliament', *Dawn*, 15 December 2001.

[62] M. Kiraly (2010) Immigration Issues in National and State Elections: A comparative analysis. *Paper presented at the annual meeting of the Southern Political Science Association.* http://www.allacademic.com/meta/p395966_index.html

[63] For a comprehensive analysis – opening with the ominous sentence, 'The recent European elections saw all sorts of far-right parties making gains across the continent' – see *The Red Pepper* (31 August 2009): http://www.redpepper.org.uk/Europe-s-far-right-rises.

> Our civilization is exposed to ruin by the very sources of its greatness. After a long respite, the barbarians are at the gate again. [64]

This penetration/preservation discourse colours and captures the imagination of contemporary Europe and its related 'affluent' societies.[65]

But as Habermas himself acknowledged in his European Foreign Policy article, speaking of the 'violence of a forcible and uprooting process of modernization', as well as in his more recent interview, the decolonization processes have uncovered that the threat had been long present in the opposite direction: from the center to the periphery, and from the top down. From the so-called secular democratic institutions, such as the parliament, the secularized sanctum sanctorum of the liberal democracy, down against those who were violated within the state under its leviathanic sovereignty. These include cults labeled criminal, aborigines and tribes labeled inassimilable or unmodernizable, and swathes of postcolonial peoples, subject peoples at one moment, and free-and-equal citizens of a liberal-democratic nation-state at the next moment.[66]

In India, where the hyper-plurality of religious traditions, cults, castes, languages, classes, colonies, cultures, tribes, and so on lends itself to an impossibly complex 'society', a nation of heterogeneous rather than homogenous temporality (following Partha Chatterjee[67]), 'impossible to discipline' (i.e. homogenize, at the level of 'civil' society),[68] the assumption is that discipline, the triumph of governance over anomie, calculative rationalism (in its highest social expression as enlightened self-interest), would descend upon the land as it finally, grudgingly entered fully into modernity. On the contrary, it is now beginning to seem as though *that* modernity will be finished before India finishes its entry into it.

[64] B. Lindsey (2002) At the Gates, Again: A New Barbarism. *National Review*, November 19. http://www.nationalreview.com/comment/comment-lindsey111902.asp

[65] P. Johnson (2004) Are Our Utopian Energies Exhausted?: Habermas's Radical Reformism. *European Journal of Political Theory*, 3, 267-291.

[66] The latter, for example, allegedly occurred at the stroke of midnight on 15th August 1947, where India's 'tryst with destiny' miraculously transubstantiated a hundred million oppressed illiterates into liberated citizens – there is of course a reason Prime Minister Nehru's historic speech was broadcast in English. Although the formerly unfree were now formally free, substantially and socially they remained, in Frantz Fanon's words, *Les Damnés de la Terre* (the wretched of the earth).

[67] P. Chatterjee (2004) 'The Nation in Heterogeneous Time' in: *The Politics of the Governed: Reflections on Popular Politics in Most of the World* (New York: Columbia University Press).

[68] D. Arnold (1994) 'The Colonial Prison: Power, Knowledge and Penology in Nineteenth-Century India', in: D. Arnold and D. Hardiman (eds) *Subaltern Studies VIII* (New Delhi: Oxford University Press).

This is precisely what Habermas intends by his reference to a Gestalt-switch:

> In this way, the Occident's own image of modernity seems, as in a psychological experiment, to undergo a switchover: *the normal model for the future of all other cultures* suddenly becomes a special-case scenario.[69]

Is this intuition of a Nandy or a Chatterjee, that modernity shall *forever* remain unfinished[70] – in Habermas framed explicitly in terms of the 'fact of pluralism' – implicitly reflected in Habermas' postsecular turn?

Rawls developed his 'Theory of Justice' into 'Political Liberalism' because he increasingly recognized the immeasurable relevance of the 'fact of pluralism'. He did posterity a great service in thinking at an early date about the political role of religion.[71]

But it must be repeated that Habermas rejects the validity of the Gestalt-switch – he says that it 'does not quite bear up to sociological scrutiny'[72] – and, I suppose, this means that the Occident continues, in his words, as 'the normal model for the future of all other cultures'. Habermasian postsecularism in this respect reeks of Fukuyamian posthistoricity: the 'men without chests'[73] at the end of history, the triumph of liberalism globally, gets a new vitality and inspiring energy (*thumos*) from religion in the public sphere – thus gets configured the 'political role of religion.' So what, then, of the 'immeasurable relevance' of the fact of pluralism? It may be 'immeasurable' but the supposedly immeasurable, in Habermas as always in Hegel, can still be subjected to dialectical self-mediation.[74]

It seems that Habermas, again like Fukuyama, would have the wolverine wilderness of plurality tamed into a faithful domestic dog. Although inspiring, energetic, nevertheless standing by *outside* the threshold of the parliament door, in eager expectation of its master's return. Master has entered the building of the parliament: the sign hanging outside reads, 'No Dogs or Jews allowed'.[75]

[69] J. Habermas (2006) Religion in the Public Sphere, p. 2.

[70] The echo with Derridean *differance* is clear.

[71] J. Habermas (2006) Religion in the Public Sphere, p. 20.

[72] J. Habermas (2006) Religion in the Public Sphere, p. 2.

[73] 'The typical citizen of a liberal democracy was a „last man" who, schooled by the founders of modern liberalism, gave up prideful belief in his or her own superior worth in favor of comfortable self-preservation. Liberal democracy produced „men without chests," composed of desire and reason but lacking *thymos*, clever at finding new ways to satisfy a host of petty wants through the calculation of long-term self-interest. The last man had no desire to be recognized as greater than others, and without such desire no excellence or achievement was possible. Content with his happiness and unable to feel any sense of shame for being unable to rise above those wants, the last man ceased to be human'. F. Fukuyama (1992) *The End of History and the Last Man* (Glencoe: Free Press).

[74] On 'dialectical self-mediation', see W. Desmond (1995) Being, Determination, and Dialectic: On the Sources of Metaphysical Thinking. *The Review of Metaphysics*, 48.

[75] The sign, 'No Dogs or Jews Allowed', has been extensively discussed in *Only In America:*

CONCLUSION:

In the dialectics of Habermas' postsecular turn, the religious enters solely on the terms set by the secular, plurality must enter solely on the terms set by stability and security, and in an unexpected but I think sufficiently documented sort of Leo Strauss *redivivus*,[76] for Habermas religion is meant to reinvigorate democracy so that the latter can rise up against the challenges of Europe's now vulnerable position in a postcolonial (externally) and postmodern (internally) environment.

When we reflect on religion in the public political sphere within this framing of the dialectics of the postsecular order, the challenges posed by resurgent political theologies within the hellbroth of postmodern, postcolonial, and postsovereign discourses are abundantly clear. They are, indeed, concretely apocalyptic in the form of Talibanism. But the masculinization of religions and spiritual revivalism in Habermas' postsecular discourse does nothing to remove us from this apocalyptic spiral. Habermas' attempt to dialectically mediate the so-called 'immeasurable relevance of the fact of pluralism' to which Rawls drew our attention leaves us precisely where we started: wrapped up, closed off, and drifting rightwards.[77]

Celebrating 350 Years of the American Jewish Experience; see the Episode entitled, 'No Dogs or Jews Allowed: The Story of Anti-Semitism in America', *American Public Radio*. To be clear, here 'Jews' is signifying all religious people, or more accurately, those religious language as appropriate in Parliament (Knesset, Majlis-e-shoora, Lok Shaba) – let no one mistake me for accusing Habermas of some latent anti-semitism. That would just be absurd and inappropriate.

[76] A. Singh (2005) *Eros Turannos: Leo Strauss and Alexandre Kojeve Debate on Tyranny* (University of America Press).

[77] Contrast Emmanuel Levinas, who takes the 'immeasurable' gravely, without the self-mediating dialectics of Habermas, capable of measuring the immeasurable. See P. Losonczi's Chapter Five of this volume.

HABERMAS, LEVINAS AND THE PROBLEM OF THE SACRED: POSTSECULAR STRATEGIES IN RESONATING DIVERGENCE*

Péter Losonczi

I. Intellectual Universes in Resonating Divergence: Habermas and Levinas

In the Preface of his book *From Communicative Action to the Face of the Other* Steven Hendley explains the dilemmas one faces when executing a combined study of Habermas and Levinas. Pointing to the significant differences between the two thinkers' respective intellectual positions and philosophical methods, he also asserts that this dilemma has to do with the general differences between their intellectual attitudes or frames of mind.[1] Hendley adds that notwithstanding these complications it is still possible to present a productive analysis of the works of these two philosophers. This kind of investigation, he argues, is rendered possible by certain points of convergence or common ground in their philosophies. On the one hand, he defines one such converging point as a fundamental concern for the restoration of the sources of morality among the conditions of the late-modern historical and intellectual circumstances. On the other hand, he finds a converging element in the specific place that the human capacity for language plays in the exploration of the morally driven philosophical programs of these two figures.[2]

Obviously, it is an important correspondence between them that the intellectual endeavours of both Levinas and Habermas are fuelled by, in the words

* I am indebted to Staff Hellemans, Michael Hoelzl, Peter Jonkers, John Rundell, Aakash Singh and Theo De Wit for their comments on earlier versions and parts of this paper.

[1] Steven Hendley, *From Communicative Action to the Face of the Other: Levinas and Habermas on Language, Obligation, and Community* (Lanham-Boulder-New York-Oxford: Lexington Books, 2000) ix.

[2] *Ibid.*

of Nicholas H. Smith, „some apprehension of a structural normative deficit in the forms of thought and practice that are believed to characterize modernity."[3] Arne Johan Vetlesen also detects this moral commitment as a unifying point.[4] It is also an important common feature how they attribute an elementary moral relevance to the use of language and the linguistic determinedness of the interpersonal sphere. However, it is a question whether these converging frames can annul those remarkable differences that according to other interpreters constitute the nature of their philosophies; whether they can be taken as anything more than some interesting complements.[5] Neither position can be easily refuted: there is certainly an important *resonance* between the intellectual worlds of Habermas and Levinas insofar as the basic perspectives of their philosophical works are really determined by worries about the moral deficit we referred to in the quotation drawn from Smith. Nevertheless, there are important strategic elements of their philosophical programs that seem to dissolve the direct relatedness of these two intellectual universes. Central themes of their works like autonomy, the contours of rationality, the problem of universalism, and so on – themes that at the same time are paradigmatic for the modern, as well as postmodern, philosophy – are treated in such radically divergent manners that imply profound differences that cannot be easily explained away. That is why I propose to describe the nexus between the two philosophers by inventing the somewhat paradoxical term *resonating divergence* that, in my view, aptly embraces the important relatedness of these two emblematic authors, but also expresses the vibrant differences between their thought.

In what follows I discuss a specific theme relevant for both Levinas and Habermas, and that implicitly or explicitly belongs to the basic terminological apparatus and problem-horizon of their theories. This question also implies essential theoretical and attitudinal questions belonging to the very core of their program, and in my view will explain how this resonating divergence works between them. The question I would like to focus on is their approach to the concept and the problem of *the sacred*. My view is that in the light of the Habermasian postsecular shift it is even more interesting to scrutiny their specific approaches to this issue. However, this investigation may also be taken as a preliminary investigation to a wider study concerning strategies for thinking over the modes of rethinking the relationship between religion and politics. In other words, their ideas can be interpreted as alternative ways of thinking about these questions in a postsecular scenario.

During the last decade the concepts of „postsecular" or „postsecularism" have rapidly come onto the scene and generated intensive debates in philo-

[3] Nicholas H. Smith: „Levinas, Habermas, and Modernity", in: *Philosophy and Social Criticism* 34 (2008) 643-664, 645.

[4] Arne Johan Vetlesen: „Worlds Apart? Habermas and Levinas", in: *Philosophy and Social Criticism* 23 (1997) 1-20.

[5] Cf. John Llewelyn, *Appositions of Jacques Derrida and Emmanuel Levinas* (Bloomington and Indianapolis: Indiana University Press, 2002) 2

sophical, social scientific, cultural theoretical and theological circles. Goenawan Mohamad analyses elements of the so-called postsecular era and defines as the two opposing poles of this scenario the postmodern turn to religion, on the one hand, and the rise of different forms of fundamentalism, on the other hand.[6] Interestingly enough he makes no mention of Habermas and other liberal theorists as contributors to the internally diverse postsecular discourse. In my interpretation, and also in the light of the emerging literature, this context implies a couple of questions pertaining not merely to sociology and political science, but also to philosophy, cultural theory, theology, literary criticism. It is enough to say that even Mohamad warns us of the dangers of oversimplification when diagnosing the trends of religious resurgence and secular decline, and *vice versa*, in declaring the triumph of secularism and the demise of the religious impetus. As he writes, „[l]ike religion, secularism too has nine lives [moreover, a] clear break never exists [and, in fact, what] is taking place is more open ended and tumultuous."[7]

2. The Problem of „the Sacred"

As I mentioned above, in this study I want to make a contribution to this tumultuous discourse in the form of an analysis regarding the respective Habermasian and Levinasian theories about the sacred. As it will be shown, both thinkers express certain ambiguities regarding the phenomena described by this concept and this critical attitude determines their particular proposals for defining the role that religion may play in the formation of the socio-political circumstances. So, the point of view of this paper can be located around philosophy and theory of religion and, in a certain sense, theology rather than political theory or sociology, but even so the findings of the present study can bear relevance for these latter disciplines too. From this follows the pertinence of this essay for the discourse on the postsecular in general and the Habermasian postsecular program in particular.

The concept of „the sacred" has played a dominant role in sociology, in late modern philosophy of religion, religious studies, and it gained a central position also in theology during the twentieth century. The once established distinction between the *sacred* and *profane* is an operational twin-category in the religious discourse today that extensively influences the method and the attitude of the scholarly work concerning religion. However, as Talal Asad convincingly argues, the term *the sacred*, as well as the twin-category, have a specific history

[6] Goenawan Mohamed: „Secularism, 'Revivalism', Mimicry", in: *The Future of Secularism* (ed. T.N. Srinivasan, New Delhi: Oxford University Press, 2007) 161-180, 161.

[7] *Ibid.*, 161.

[8] Talal Asad, *Formations of the Secular: Christianity, Islam, Modernity* (Stanford: Standford University Press, 2003) 33.

and genealogy. Drawing on other scholars he shows how Robertson Smith's notion of „taboo" as a distinctive element of primitive religion led to the introduction of a universalized concept of the sacred in Durkheim, and how it functions for determining a universal essence or quality „hidden in things and [functioning as] an objective limit to mundane action."[8] This use of the word gained a paradigmatic function in late modern religious discourse. It got to be conceived as a transcendent force that imposes itself on the subject and, at the same time, constitutes a space whose integrity cannot be violated – that is: profaned – without serious consequences.[9] However, it is exactly this latter element of the powerfulness of the sacred and the resultant biding character that makes it so problematic for both Habermas and Levinas, and fuels the formation of their – partly or completely – critical position with regard to this conception and the attitudes that are brought about by this binding quality.

My special focus here will be on Habermas's conception about the *linguistification of the sacred*, on the one hand, and on Levinas's criticism of the *sacred as idolatry*, on the other. It is especially interesting to consider this interpretative perspective because during the last years a radical change has occurred in Habermas's position regarding the political involvement of religion. His famous postsecular turn makes it possible to rethink the context of the rather sporadic reflections on the work of the two thinkers. As I intend to demonstrate in the course of the following investigations, an important constituent of this study can be executed with a special attention of the problem of the „sacred" and the related question of idolatry.

3. Habermas on the Linguistification of the Sacred and his „anti-idolatrous" Motivations

According to Habermas the topic of the sacred has an important role in the understanding of the evolution of the modern social and political discourse. In the second part of his *The Theory of Communicative Action* he discusses the question of religion with fundamental Durkhemian overtones. As is well-known, Durkheim's interpretation of religion is a *universalistic* and *anthropologically* driven theory with a special attention to the problem of sociability.[10] Another important aspect of Durkheim's theory of religion, and this is a central element for my study, is that while discussing the nature of religion he applies the aforementioned concepts of the sacred and profane. He defines religion as follows: „[a] religion is a unified system of beliefs and practices relative to sacred things, that is to say, things set apart and surrounded by prohibitions – beliefs and

[9] *Ibid.*

[10] „In reality [...] there are no false religions. All are true in their fashion: all respond, in different ways, to the given conditions of human existence." Émile Durkheim, *The Elementary Forms of Religious Life* (Oxford: Oxford University Press, 2001) 4.

practices that unite its adherents in a single moral community called a church."[11] In spite of certain differences, Habermas's conception of religion in the 1980s was fundamentally reliant on that of Durkheim's. This influence is evinced by the very fact of the terminological-theoretical representation of the question of „the sacred" in Habermas's discussion of the linguistification of the sacred.

As Nicholas Adams puts it, three themes are identifiable concerning the sacred as being operative in Habermas's account of religion in the *The Theory of Communicative Action*:

> (1) [t]he sacred is the source of motivation and 'being bound' to a community's values
> (2) the sacred is the source of an attitude towards an objective „truth"
> (3) the sacred is the 'original' form of what later comes to be the 'performative attitude' of partners in dialogue according to the Habermasian theory of secularization and social history.[12]

In this period Habermas is interested in a *formal structure* understandable by means of this theory, and not in the internal content of religious attitudes. As Adams argues, his concern was to describe the logic of how commitments to moral norms functioned in pre-modern societies. As we can read in Habermas, in this system of norms „[t]he moral is traced back to the sacred, and the sacred to collective representation of an entity that is itself supposed to consist of a system of binding norms."[13] In Habermas's reading of Durkheim, religion resides in „the experience of a collective, supra-individual consciousness"[14] whose intentional object is the community itself. This transcending consciousness is manifested through the *symbols* which constitute a conceptual and normative network of the religious community.[15]

According to Adams this interpretation of religion has a peculiar overtone. As he puts it „Habermas does not say so directly, but it seems reasonable to assume that, in his account, what members of a society are oriented to [...] is in fact *themselves as a collectivity* [which in theological terms is but] *idolatry*."[16] It is a question whether Habermas had the notion of idolatry in mind when he discussed the problem of the social aspects of religious symbolism and collective consciousness in the aforementioned way, or rather whether he was concerned with matters of *ideology* – as it would follow from his intellectual background. However, as Peter Scott convincingly argues, matters of idolatry and ideology are convertible problems from the perspective of theology,[17] so we can read

[11] *Ibid.*, 46.

[12] Nicholas Adams, *Habermas and Theology* (Cambridge: Cambridge University Press, 2006) 67.

[13] Jürgen Habermas, *The Theory of Communicative Action, Volume 2: The Critique of Functionalist Reason* (Cambridge: Polity Press, 1987) 50.

[14] *Ibid.*

[15] Cf. Adams, *Habermas and Theology*, 70.

[16] *Ibid.*, 72.

[17] Peter Scott, *Theology, Ideology and Liberation: Towards a Liberative Theology* (Cambridge: Cambridge University Press, 2008 [1994]) 71.

Adams's interpretation as a very important and interesting one – and not merely in view of Habermas's theory of religion and sociability. This direction of approaching the problem of the sacred may turn out to be relevant for the intensifying contemporary discourse on matters of political theology and public religion too. In Adams's view – and this opinion strengthens the just implemented link between idolatry and ideology – introducing the question of idolatry into the analysis of Habermas's work renders it possible to interpret this program as a reflection upon those phenomena that characterised „a form of ethics in the wake of German nationalism" and is meant for expressing an „urgent critique of idolatry."[18]

I propose to call this potentially idolatrous form of religiosity *ambiguous religion.* In the light of this specific dimension of the Habermasian understanding of archaic religion and its internal idolatrous challenge it is not surprising that the German thinker gives a specific attention to the normative, collective identity-constituting role of religion and its secular transformation in the wake of modernity. Taken from this perspective, the so-called linguistification would function as a protective tool against this political theological ambiguity stemming from idolatry.

In consequence of the linguistification the pre-modern form of the consensus – legitimised by the authoritative power of the sacred – transforms into the consent attained through a *mutual learning process* evolving within the *rational* discourse of the *autonomous* members of the community. The moral consensus is formed through argumentative process, through the Kantian-style free public use of reason, in which not the mysterious and tranquilising power of the sacred functions as the principle of normative persuasion but, in the words of Hent De Vries, it „is contingent upon an open and, in principle, unending discourse that permits not other force than the 'force of the better argument'."[19] In this way the community of believers gets to be secularized into a community of cooperation and, consequently, „only a universalistic morality can retain its obligatory character."[20] This model would prevent the members of the political community from the effects of any „idolatrous" inclination, as it disqualifies heteronomy as the context of sociability. This exclusion of the heteronymous is in a great extent attributable to the idolatrous ambiguity that follows from the effects of the functioning of the archaic form of the sacred as the principle of the social cohesion. That is why Habermas defines autonomy as the dogmatic core of critical social theory, dogmatic in a – at least, assumedly – harmless sense. The *rational* linguistification of the sacred and the formation of autonomy brought about that symmetrical pattern of sociability which constitutes the paradigmatic framework of the functioning of modern democratic societies. The transcendent character of the sacred is internalized in the form of a „transcendence from

[18] *Ibid.*, 72.

[19] Hent De Vries, *Minimal Theologies: Critiques of Secular Reason in Adorno and Levinas* (Baltimore: The Johns Hopkins University Press, 2005) 113.

[20] Habermas, *The Theory*, 90.

within," a *horizontal*[21] element. These principles are persistent in the subsequent periods of Habermas's thought too, and true for his thematization of the post-secular scenario as well.

In fact, it is exactly the thesis concerning the linguistification of the sacred that can be detected in his characterization of the postmetaphysical form of *religious language* as „the bearer of semantic content that is inspiring and even indispensable, for its content eludes [...] the explanatory force of philosophical language and continues to resist translation into reasoning discourses."[22] This description represents a remarkable shift in comparison with that of the ambiguous-archaic religion. At another occasion Habermas defines *consolation* as the moment which makes the most fundamental distinction between religion and post-metaphysical philosophy and which he finds important as religion's contribution to modern life.[23] In the domain of philosophy, he says, unconditionality appears as a moment of *truth*. This philosophical meaning of truth, nevertheless, is radically different from „an unconditional meaning that offers consolation."[24] This latter moment is significant as it shows that while earlier Habermas was interested only in the formal aspects of religious life here we can clearly see that he discusses questions concerning the *content* of religious traditions. He admits an important *existential* aspect, at least on the level of the private-individual life-worlds, and attributes an essentially *therapeutic* role to religion. That is why I think that in opposition to ambiguous religion the other important element of Habermas's theory of religion is *therapeutic religion*.

[21] For problem of horizontality cf.: Michael Hoelzl: „Recognizing the Sacrificial Victim: The Problem of Solidarity for Critical Social Theory," *Journal for Cutural and Religious Theory*, 6/1 (2004) 45-64.

[22] Italics added. The cited passage goes as follows: „In the wake of metaphysics, philosophy surrenders its extraordinary status. Explosive experiences of the extraordinary have migrated into an art that becomes autonomous. Of course, even after this deflation, ordinary life, now fully profane, by no means becomes immune to the shattering and subversive intrusion of extraordinary events. Viewed from without, religion, which has largely been deprived of its world-view functions, is still indispensable in ordinary life for normalizing the extraordinary. For this reason, even postmetaphysical thinking continues to coexist with religious practice – and not merely in the sense of the contemporaneity of the noncontemporaneous. This ongoing coexistence even throws light on a curious dependence of a philosophy that has fortified its contact with the extraordinary. Philosophy, even in its postmetaphysical from, will be able neither to replace nor to repress religion as long as religious language is the bearer of semantic content that is inspiring and even indispensable, for its content eludes (for the time being?) the explanatory force of philosophical language and continues to resist translation into reasoning discourses." Jürgen Habermas, *Postmetaphysical Thinking: Philosophical Essays* (Cambridge (Mass.): MIT Press, 1992) 51.

[23] As he explains, „[o]n the premises of postmetaphysical thought, philosophy cannot provide a substitute for the consolation whereby religion invests unavoidable suffering and unrecompensed injustice, the contingencies of need, loneliness, sickness, and death, with new significance and teaches us how to bear them." Jürgen Habermas, *Religion and Rationality: Essays on Reason, God, and Modernity* (Oxford: Polity Press 2002) 108

[24] *Ibid.*

This postmetaphysical therapeutic conception of religion gets developed further into a version of *public religion* when Habermas makes efforts regarding the political inclusion of religious opinions. This is the semantic context of religious traditions that is supposed to be canalised into the public political discourse.[25] Unlike Harrington who speaks of three stages of development,[26] I propose to distinguish at least *four* phases in Habermas's account of religion since the postsecular theory transforms the character of the postmetaphysical conception. Habermas evidently attributes a specific existential *truth-content* to the *potentialities of meaning* carried by the religious traditions, whose introduction into the political discourse renders it possible that these contents play a *moral* role in the life of the society and contribute at least to the motivational sources of democratic politics, thereby rendering postmetaphysical religion into a form of public religion. The basic condition of this political inclusion is the rational-secular translation of these meaning contents into a generally, that is rationally, available form.

4. Paradox of Secularism and Dialectics of Secularization: Threats of Idolatry in the Postsecular Context

The problem of the Habermasian demand regarding the rational-secular translation of the religious idioms could be the subject of an independent study. However, it is important to realize that, although Habermas speaks in terms of *epistemic challenge* here, it is evident that there is much more complex, paradigmatic dilemma behind the demand. I speak of the ultimate Habermasian claim

[25] „Unlike the ethical restraint that characterizes postmetaphysical thought – which eludes every generally biding concept of the good and exemplary life – holy writings and religious traditions articulate, subtly spell out, and hermeneutically keep alive over thousands of years intuitions about fall and redemption, about saving exit from life experienced as being without salvation. That is why something that has elsewhere been lost and that cannot be restored using the professional knowledge of experts alone remains intact in the life of religious communities, so long as they avoid dogmatism and the moral constraint of a prescribing conscience. By this something I mean sufficiently differentiated possibilities of expression and sensibilities for misspent life, for societal pathologies, for the failure of individual life plans and the deformation to be seen in distorted life contexts." Jürgen Habermas, „On the Relations Between the Secular Liberal State and Religion", in *Political Theologies: Public Religions in a Post-Secular World* (eds.: Lawrance E. Sullivan and Hent de Vries, New York: Fordham Universiyt Press, 2006) 251-260, 257.

[26] Austin Harrington: „Habermas and the 'Post-Secular Society'", in: *European Journal of Social Theory* 10/4 (2007) 543-560, 547. On the complexity of the Habermasian sources and aspects of the Habermasian discourse of concept of „religion" see Cf. Von Sebastian Maly: "Die Rolle de Religion in der postsäkularen Gessellschaft: Zur religionsphilosophie von Jürgen Habermas", in: *Theologie und Philosophie* 80 (2005) 546-565, 547. See also John Rundell's and Michael Hoelzl's papers in this volume.

for the preservation of the „dogmatic" core not merely of critical theory but the whole Enlightenment paradigm. This is vital for him to preserve the idea of autonomy and the accompanying vision of symmetrical relationship as the warranty for the integrity of the citizens of a democratic state. This element I interpret as a most problematic point in Habermas's theory of religion in general. This tension, however, proves to be even more challenging in the light of his postsecular shift and, in my interpretation, essentially contributes to an ambiguous point to which Pecora calls our attention, to a „lack of clarity about the precise meaning and function of the Western religion in his social philosophy."[27] One may wonder whether this ambiguity regarding the Habermasian program can be interpreted as a version of what the Indian social psychologist Ashis Nandy depicts as the *paradox of secularism.*[28] As stated by this thesis, secularism as an ideology can flourish only in a predominantly non-secular society, but once a society begins to get secularized and it is getting cleansed from religious ideas and perspectives of transcendence „people become anxiously aware of living in an increasingly desacralized world, and start searching for ideologies to give meaning to their life and to retain the illusion of being part of a traditional community."[29] Therefore, in Nandy's view this paradoxically combined movement of secularization and subsequent trends of „retraditionalization" – or, in certain cases, of ideologization[30] – constitute a complex cultural phenomenon that he determines as an essential factor in the sociocultural and political developments in the recent South Asian context.

My view is that Habermas' postsecular rediscovery of religion and his proposition for the dialectical reinvention of the socio-political role of religious stimuli can be interpreted considering the Nandian thesis. This paradox is to be connected to the Habermasian problem in that extent that the Habermasian inquiry seems to be oscillating among certain dilemmas derivable from the paradoxical conditions belonging to the secular agenda and its effect on the European context. On the one hand, he intends to set an inclusive framework regarding the *political* accommodation of the opinions of the religious citizens considering the principle of recognition. On the other hand, he hopes to draw on the potentialities of meaning as therapeutic reinvention of religious truth contents in a postmetaphysical milieu, and – as a postsecular development – he intends to render these „domesticated" contents accessible for the wider political community as possible sources of social solidarity. This latter process should be implemented among the framework of the dialectical conception of secularization.

The Nandian conception about the paradox of secularism can prove to be an apt interpretative tool to the Habermasian theory exactly in so far as Habermas

[27] Vincent P. Pecora, *Secularization and Cultural Criticism: Religion, Nation, & Modernity* (Chicago: The University of Chicago Press, 2006) 53.

[28] Ashis Nandy, *The Romance of the State and the Fate of Dissent in the Tropics* (New Delhi: Oxford University Press, 2003) 62.

[29] *Ibid.*

[30] *Ibid.*

tries to reinvent the religious sources of social solidarity as a reaction to the earlier mentioned crisis of the normative aspects of modern democratic culture and societal agenda. Nevertheless, as our foregoing investigation shows, Habermas' program remains equally influenced by an intensive worry about the possible threats implied by what we called ambiguous religion: threats stemming from the specific ways of the binding and normative functions of the sacred. It is by no means to say that these threats does not exist or should be underestimated. Even so, it seems to me that Habermas provides us with a narrow horizon in so far as the question of the religious options and strategies are concerned within such a postsecular context where the jeopardy resulting from ambiguous religion or the discrepancies of the sacred should be addressed too. My view is that these worries are shared by Levinas, hence the resonance between him and Habermas can be easily detected also in view of this specific question, but the solutions he proposes are very much different.

These concerns, as we have also pointed out, have essential implications regarding problems of idolatry and ideology. It is evident, at the same time, that in the eyes of Habermas a crucial element of these threats would be the reanimation of such models about interpersonal and societal relations that draw on the idea of heteronomy. These worries can be the source of his restatement of the dogmatic status of autonomy – a problem that, at the same time, is not easily integrated with a religious stance in general – and mark the limits of the Habermasian theory. However, as Maeve Cooke underlines, any sort of dogmatism „impedes learning experiences and blocks the creative rearticulation and reenactment" of the conceptual resources of critical theory. She admits that contemporary critical social theories „must acknowledge their commitment to the ideal of autonomy" but she argues that even this ideal may undergo modification in the course of the aforementioned process of rearticulation and reenactment.[31] However, it is a question whether the Habermasian dialectics of secularization would be able to accommodate such a rearticulation. At the same time, one may ask how far this rearticulation and reenactment can be generally brought about. It is, finally, also an important question whether the taken-for-granted secularist strategy – or even the postsecular introduction of a dialectics of secularization – should be accepted as the sole possible source of the criticism of the sacred and ambiguous religion. In what follows I will demonstrate that Levinas' desacralization and criticism of the sacred as idolatrous is a very important alternative for the Habermasian dialectical pattern. Levinas' criticism of the sacred, at the same time, implies the criticism of the Durkheimian framework itself, a paradigm whose applicability Habermas clearly admits and embraces as the basic theory in his discussion of the question of religion.

[31] Maeve Cooke, *Re-Presenting the Good Society* (Massachusetts-London: MIT Press, 2006) 208.

5. The Sacred as Idolatrous: Levinas on the Desacralization of the Sacred

Levinas's critique of the sacred expresses an obvious discontent with the late modern career – the terminological and hermeneutical triumph – of „the sacred", as well as with its consequences for the general religious discourse. This means that together with his Durkheimian sympathies Levinas is critical of certain trends in the heritage of the French sociology and science of religion.[32] This Leviansian criticism embodies not merely the disapproval for the theoretical discussion of religion but also articulates a conviction of directly religious and theological nature. This impression concerning the immediate religio-theological motives is strengthened by the fact that important elements of the Leviansian criticism of the sacred is developed in his Talmudic writings, and implemented together with politically relevant arguments.

In *Difficult Freedom* he straightforwardly declares that in late modernity „[t]he Sacred – together with the fear and trembling, as well as the ecstasy, aroused by its luminous presence – becomes the key word, if not the grand concept, of a whole religious renewal. What contemporary sociology discovered in the prelogical mentality of Australia and Africa assumes the status of a privileged religious experience. It is triumphantly set against the dry and mind-deadening moralism of the nineteenth century, that abomination of abominations."[33] Referring to a classic piece of religious studies and cultural anthropology written by Lévi-Strauss he asserts that „[m]odern atheism is not the negation of God, it is the absolute indifferentism of *Tristes Tropiques* [...] the most atheist book that has been written in our day, the most absolutely disorientated and disorientating book [which] threatens Judaism as much as does the Hegelian and sociological vision of history."[34]

Levinas declares that this phenomenon of the sacred and the human reaction it can engender are exactly what the Bible and the Talmud fight against as the very manifestations of *idolatry*. So, we can discover an interesting point of intersection between what, drawing on Adams, we detected as the Habermasian concern regarding the relatedness between the manifestation of the sacred and the threats of idolatry. At the same time, the Levinasian solution is radically different from the one proposed by Habermas. As we have seen, Habermas argues for a dialectical restatement (one may say, replication) of the secularizing tendencies as a safeguard against ambiguous religion and the „weight" of the sacred. Unlike the German thinker, Levinas gives a religio-theological answer to this challenge when he declares that „*saintliness* of God [...] stands in sharp contrast to the numinous meaning of this term, as it appears in the primitive religions

[32] Howard Caygill, *Levinas and the Political* (London-New York: Routledge, 2002) 10-11; 31-32.

[33] Emmanuel Levinas, *Difficult Freedom: Essays on Judaism* (Baltimore: The Johns Hopkins University Press, 1990) 101.

[34] *Ibid.*, 200-201.

wherein the moderns have often wished to see the source of all religion [and adds that] Judaism remains foreign to any offensive return of these forms of human elevation [and] denounces them as the essence of idolatry."[35] Similarly, in his *Desacralization and Disenchantment* he declares that Judaism has nothing to do with the Scared, on the contrary, the „sacred is the half light in which the sorcery which the Jewish tradition abhors flourishes."[36]

According to Levinas, the alternative for ambiguous religion is nor the formation of a therapeutically reformed version of religion, nor a dialectically restated version of secularization. For him it is *divine saintliness* – or perhaps we should term it as *holiness* – [37] that serves as the source and driving force of criticism of idolatry, and this critical power renders it possible to take up a very different sort of concept of religion. Not domestication of transcendence but the divulgement of its real meaning, not the therapeutically transformed way of religiosity but the radicalization of relation in the form of responsibility, not dialectics of secularization but *civilizing force called God*[38] – these are the Levinasian warranties against the threats of the idolatrous sacred. One even may wonder whether the last expression about the civilizing force of God can be interpreted as the Levinasian alternative for the generally embraced vision concerning the secular character of the so called civilizing process.

Declaring his indebtedness to Rosenzweig for inspiration of *Totality and Infinity*, Levinas points to a very important source of his model of Judaism – and, by the same token, of his conception about religion in a non-idolatrous or, to apply our categorization, non-ambiguous form. Hence, we can write about Levinas himself what he declares referring to his predecessor; namely, that he „reminds us of a notion of religion that is totally different from the one that secularism combats and is put forth, as though emerging in the economy of being, at the very level on which philosophical thought emerges."[39]

This demarcation made by Levinas is especially important for our present investigation because it provides an alternative form of thinking about those dilemmas that pertain to Habermas too. It is evident that his project concerning the regeneration of the contents of religious sources for moral and social discourse are accompanied by certain worries concerning ambiguous-idolatrous forms of religion and the devastating political consequences following from the attitudes attached to it. His demand regarding the dialectical repetition of secularization follows exactly from the fears generated by a notion of religion which secularism essentializes and combats – and, in fact, Habermas basically embraces.

[35] *Ibid.*, 14.

[36] Emmanuel Levinas, *Nine Talmudic Readings* (Bloomington: Indiana University Press, 1994 [1990]) 141.

[37] For the dilemmas regarding the English translation of the terms *le sacré* and *le saint* see Michael B. Smith, *Toward the Outside: Concepts and Themes in Emmanual Levinas* (Pittshburg (Pens.): Dunquesne University Press 2005) 249, Notes to Chapter 7, note 4.

[38] *Difficult Freedom*, 11.

[39] *Difficult Freedom*, 187.

The conviction concerning the rational translation of the religious meanings as the only safeguard against these perils of ambiguous religion can be interpreted as a *restatement* of the Enlightenment strategy for the normalization of these discrepancies.

However, in the light of the Levinasian conception we can find an alternative way by means of which to step outside the limits of the dichotomy belonging to the Enlightenment paradigm in general and Habermas' strategy in partiular. This alternative approach can be derived from the Levinasian criticism of the sacred as idolatrous and so it can be directly related to the Habermasian quandary.

6. „Beyond" the Violence of the Sacred

The most important element of this alternative path is that for Levinas revelation and Judaism are the antitheses of idolatry – and so, of ambiguous religion – and he explicitly declares that an essential alternative „that humanity has faced since Sinai [is] idolatry *or* religion."[40] Similarly, he asserts that the Torah is the „book of anti-idolatry, the absolute opposite of idolatry."[41] This declaration implies not merely that Levinas locates the root of non-idolatrous form of religion in Judaism, but – in consequence of this gesture – an important feature of his religious thought is revealed. Namely, that notwithstanding his universalistic orientation and the applicability of the *framework* set by Judaism for other forms of religious traditions or even for secular attitudes, the very *essence* and the (historical and theological) *manifestation* of this antithetic, non-ambiguous and non-idolatrous form of religion is attached to Judaism by Levinas.

In addition to the clarification of how monotheism can be related to the ambiguities of the sacred as a form of experience and as a conceptual instrument in treating questions concerning religion, Levinas explains that the phenomenality of the sacred expresses and animates an essential form of *violence*. It is worth noting that despite the differences this Levinasian thesis concerning the identity between violence and the sacred bear important resemblance with René Girard's theory, according to which „[v]iolence and the sacred are inseparable";[42] and which defines *mimetic desire*, the moment behind practices of sacral violence, as a quasi-Hobbesian principle.[43] A similar quasi-Hobbesian reading of the milieu of the sacred comes to the fore in Levinas when he defines the general human concern for salvation as a *mythic* gesture of the *biological* self. He asserts that while „Judaism [...] appeals to a humanity devoid of myths" the biological self „cannot dispense with mythology and

[40] Emmanuel Levinas, *In the Time of the Nations* (London: The Athlone Press, 1994) 58. Italics added.

[41] *Ibid.*

[42] René Girard, *Violence and the Sacred* (London: Continuum, 2005) 19.

[43] René Girard: *Je vois Satan tomber comme l'éclar* (Paris : Grasset, 1999) 25.

war."[44] What Levinas defines as mythical is in close relationship with the sacred in so far as both are attached to a violent immanentism, egology and communality. However, as John Llewelyn explains „[b]y war Levinas means a resistance and counter-resistance of energies, an allergy which is an opposition of powers analogous to the reciprocity of forces in the system of Newtonian mechanics."[45] The fear, trembling and ecstasy belonging to the halo of the sacred and fiercely criticized by Levinas as a mentality attached to the idolatrous form of religion and denounced as a primer category of sociology and science of religion evidently point to the political implications of this conceptual model. The sacred as a category for discussing religion and inter-human relationships gets under an uncompromising criticism in Levinas. According to him, this mythic-sacral form of religion – together with a complementary violent form of transcendence – is in a sharp contrast with the monotheistic principle from which a *real sense of transcendence* follows.[46] According to Levinas – and this is an evidently theological thesis – monotheism and its specific features imply the *desacralization of the sacred.*[47] Therefore, in place of the linguistification of the sacred and the dialectical secularization of the religious meanings Levinas proposes *monotheism* as the safeguard against the ambiguities of „the sacred" and the threats of idolatry. To clarify the relevance of these issues of the holy – and, consequently and complementarily that of the sacred and desacralization of the sacred – for Levinas it is enough to refer to his statement reported by Derrida; namely, that although he is mostly taken as a thinker interested in ethics, what really interested him was „in the end not ethics, not ethics alone, but the holy, the holiness of the holy."[48]

It is especially important for us that according to Levinas from the violent and alienating nature of the sacred an evident *socio-political ambiguity* results. As he declares „[v]iolence is a sovereignty, but also a solitude [and to] endure violence in enthusiasm and ecstasy and delirium is to be *possessed*"[49] and, we can add, this implies that from a form of social cohesion drawn from the trembling and alienating sacred nothing else can follow but the doubled version of unsocial sociability.[50] So, similarly to Habermas, Levinas finds that idolatry carries an essential and destructive *ambiguity* in so far as sociability and, we can add, democratic political cohesion is concerned. But Levinas argues that in contrast with idolatry and the elevating violence of the sacred, Judaism teaches that it is the *ethical relation* that appears as a *religious* relation,[51] and he proposes this

[44] *Difficult Freedom*, 48.

[45] John Llewelyn, *Appositions*, 7-8.

[46] Cf. *Difficult Freedom* 14-16.

[47] *Ibid.*, 18.

[48] Quoted in Michael B. Smith, *Towards the Outside*, 73.

[49] Ethics and Spirit, 9.

[50] One may wonder whether Schmitt's conception of the soverign has deep connections with this political version of "the sacred".

[51] *Difficult Freedom*, 16.

authentic religious attitude as way of quitting the jeopardy resulting from the influence of the sacred and ambiguous religion. In *Totality and Infinity* he asserts: „The ethical relation is defined, in contrast with every relation with the sacred, by excluding every signification it would take on *unbeknown* to him who maintains relation. [...] Everything that cannot be reduced to an interhuman relation represents not the superior form but the forever primitive form of religion."[52] The political relevance of monotheism is that, while the sacred offends human freedom in virtue of its trembling power,[53] due to the idea of a real transcendence and the „relation with Him Whom the soul cannot concern and without Whom the Soul cannot [...] hold itself together" human being *quits* the tremor of the sacred. In other words, real transcendence *liberates freedom*.[54] In consequence of this relation even my freedom shows itself as arbitrary[55] and learns that its real essence comprises in my *responsibility for the other*. While the immanence of mythology and the sacred belongs to ontology and materializes a specific form of *conatus* – together with the resulting *determinism* – the monotheistic principle and the accompanying idea of the real transcendence *liberates* the self for the responsibility for the other. Taken as a religious relation, responsibility is the exact opposite of the experience of the sacred and the resulting idolatry. In contrast with the *bad heteronomy* joined up with the ambiguous sacred it expresses a *good heteronomy* or, strictly speaking, the heteronomy, the anarchy of the Good.

Another important constituent arises in Levinas's assertion that „the relationship with the Divine crosses the relationship with men and coincides with social justice."[56] We can say that while the ethical orientation of Levinas's philosophy is located *outside the subject*,[57] the socio-political and religio-theological perspectives of this way of thought (together with the political theological implications) guide us entirely *outside the sacred*, that is, outside idolatry (as well as of „mythology", „war", and so on). As Regina Mara Schwartz puts it, according to Levinas „only when we have abandoned our idols can justice prevail."[58] In phenomenological terms, instead of the awe belonging to the phenomenality of the sacred the (non)phenomenality, that is the enigma, of the face of the other becomes the focus of thinking about the perspectives of sociability. So to speak: the *banality of Goodness* for Levinas resides in the marvellously banal fact of conversation that quits the order of violence.[59]

52 *Totality and Infinity: An essay on Extreiority* (Dordrecht: Kluwer 1979) 79.

53 R*Difficult Freedom*, 14.

54 *Ibid.*, 16.

55 *Ibid.*, 17.

56 *Ibid.*, 19.

57 Cf. Emmanuel Levinas: *In the Time of the Nations* (Standford: Standford University Press, 1993) and the essay bearing the same title in *ibid.*, 151-158.

58 Regina Mara Schwartz: *Sacramental Poetics at the Dawn of Secularism: When God Left the World* (Standford: Standford University Press, 2008) 27.

59 *Difficult Freedom*. 7

Viewed from the specific perspective of this paper – namely, the questions concerning „the sacred" and political idolatry – the differences between Habermas and Levinas turn out to be as relevant as the evident similarities. While in Habermas, as we have seen, a residuum of the sacred persist in the form of the linguistically approached consensus of autonomous and rational agents, Levinas's critique of the sacred disqualifies even this residual form of the sacred as the ultimate referent of political deliberation. He declares that „human autonomy rests on a supreme heteronomy and that the force [...] which institutes force, the civilizing force, is called God,"[60] and it implies that deliberation is preceded by the doubly enigmatic events of the *elective* moment of the face of the other and the *graced* element of justice.[61] Furthermore, this supreme heteronomy continuously calls into question every form of self-enclosed autonomy addressing it with a *paradox*.

At the same time, the deep-seated Levinasian criticism of „the sacred" as the proper religious, theological, social, or political principle opens a path towards *prophetic politics* – a politics which, in Bergo's terms, „gives a voice to the incomprehensible dimension of my relation to the other."[62] This is a *radically* democratic politics according to which neither democracy nor human rights can be divorced from their ethical and prophetic depths.[63] It is important to emphasize that in view of Levinas's criticism of the sacred and mythology even Habermas's therapeutically conceived political religion turns out to be a repetition of the ambiguous and violent religion of immanence and egology. We have seen that it was *consolation* that served as the key-element in postmetaphysical religion both in its private and public forms. In *Ethics and Infinity*, Levinas makes an important statement which we can interpret as the complement of his critique of the sacred and the biological striving for salvation. He asserts that „[p]rophecy and ethics in no way exclude the consolations of religion; but [...] only a humanity which can do without these consolations perhaps may be worthy of them."[64] Not therapy, but justice stemming from responsibility: this is a basic principle of a *religion for adults*[65] and the Levinasian postsecular politics. The ideal of this democracy resides in that universalism that intrinsically belongs to monotheism. But it is a universalism that cannot be divorced from the very event of the ethical: from the enigmatic surplus of meaning revealed by the face of the other, a surplus „that cannot be represented – cannot be

[60] *Ibid.*, 11.

[61] Cf. For justice and grace Bettina Bergo, *Levinas Between Ethics and Politcs: For the Beauty that Adors the Earth* (Dordrecht: Kluwer, 1999) 183.

[62] *Ibid.* 200.

[63] Emmanual Levinas, *Beyond the Verse: Talmudic Readings and Lectures* (London: The Athlone Press, 1994) xv. Cf. also Caygill, *Levinas and the Political*, 151.

[64] Emmanual Levinas, *Ethics and Infinity: Conversations with Philippe Nemo* (Pitthsburg: Duquesne University Press 1985) 117, modified translation from Hent de Vries *Minimal Theolgies*, 533.

[65] Cf. *Difficult Freedom*, 11-23.

presented – but that signifies in the imperative with authority or glory."[66] This universalism takes the form of a position which Levinas detects in Rosenzweig, but which without difficulty could be attributed also to him: „a universality of election, a *particularity existing for all*."[67]

7. Conclusions

In this paper I have tried to show how Habermasian and Levinasian thought can be seen in a resonating divergence if we try to unveil this specific relation in the light of their respective approaches to the problem of the sacred. As mentioned, this study can be understood as a preliminary step towards the analysis of their specific views on politics in general and the options of „postsecular" political strategies. Beyond doubt, a cardinal issue of such a study would be an analysis regarding the similarly resonating difference between their specific approaches to the question of justice, a question we only mentioned here. This study would reveal further nuances of the resonating divergence between these possible postsecular strategies too.

[66] Levinas: *Alterity and Transcendence* (London: The Athlone Press, 1999) 33.
[67] *Outside the Subject*, 61. italics added.

THE PERMANENCE OF THE ESCHATOLOGICAL: REFLECTIONS ON GIANNI VATTIMO'S HERMENEUTIC AGE

Matthias Riedl

Prefatory Remarks[1]

At some point in the early 1990s, Gianni Vattimo made his religious turn, initiating a series of prominent religious „conversions" or „outings" of contemporary thinkers, Terry Eagleton being only the most recent example.[2] Subsequently, Vattimo gained prominence in Europe and the United States as one of the foremost post-secular philosophers. Several volumes on religion, co-edited and co-authored with Jacques Derrida, Richard Rorty, and John D. Caputo contributed to his fame outside his Italian motherland.[3]

In the post-secular discourse of our days, Vattimo takes the opposite position to Jürgen Habermas. Both philosophers take recourse to the Christian religion, but for utterly different reasons. Habermas, departing from the German bioethics discourse,[4] acknowledges the role of the Churches as representatives of a life-preserving theological tradition. Moreover, in his eyes, the churches produce and provide meaning, normativity, and social solidarity as the vital resources, from which post-metaphysical constitutional democracies can draw.[5] Vattimo, on the other hand, departing from the anticlerical discourse of the Italian left, denounces the same tradition as evil and destructive for democracy.

[1] I would like to thank Irina Denischenko for corrections and constructive criticism.

[2] T. Eagleton, *Reason, Faith, and Revolution. Reflections on the God Debate* (New Haven 2009).

[3] *Religion. Cultural Memory in the Present* (ed. J. Derrida and G. Vattimo, Stanford 1998); R. Rorty and G. Vattimo, *The Future of Religion* (ed. S. Zabala, New York 2005); J.D. Caputo and G. Vattimo, *After the Death of God* (ed. J.W. Robbins, New York 2007).

[4] J. Habermas, *The Future of Human Nature* (Cambridge 2003) 29-41.

[5] J. Habermas, *Glauben und Wissen. Friedenspreis des Deutschen Buchhandels 2001* (Frankfurt am Main 2001) 20-25; J. Habermas and J. Ratzinger, *Dialektik der Säkularisierung. Über Vernunft und Religion* (6th ed., Freiburg 2006) 31-33; J. Habermas, *Zwischen Naturalismus und Religion. Philosophische Aufsätze* (Frankfurt am Main 2009) 106-118.

According to him, the official Catholic position in the bioethics debate is possible only through dogmatic insistence on metaphysics, while he identifies the essence of Christianity as the overcoming of metaphysics. Vattimo clearly relates his religious turn to the common post-secular experience:

> [...] it seems necessary to clarify from the outset that I have resolved to speak and write on faith and religion, because I take the subject matter to be more than a concern of my own renewed personal interest in this theme; the decisive factor is that I sense a renewed interest in religion in the cultural atmosphere around me.[6]

He went so far as to claim that his „itinerary toward the Christian faith" makes him „a statistical example, of which quite a few people who have had a training similar to mine also are part."[7]

It is not clearly identifiable at what point Gianni Vattimo's religious turn exactly happened; but at least since 1994 his philosophy can justifiably be characterized as a postmodern eschatology. At its basis is an insight which Vattimo, in his very personal book *Belief*, described as a religious experience. Experiencing the suffering, illness, and death of persons dear to him, and reflecting on René Girard's scapegoat theory, Vattimo gained the illuminatory insight that the overcoming of metaphysics in Nietzsche, Heidegger, and postmodern philosophy coincides with the message of the Christian gospel. This message is essentially the *kenosis* (Philippians 2:7), the self-divestment of God in the act of incarnation.[8] Moreover, postmodern thought is the true heir of the Jewish-Christian tradition:

> It is only as the heir of a Judeo-Christian tradition that conceives of the real in terms of creation and the history of salvation that postmodern thought has freed itself from the objectivistic metaphysics of scientism so that it can live up to its experience of cultural pluralism, namely of the historicity and contingency of existing.[9]

While Vattimo's thought remained relatively constant in the past fifteen years, the intellectual environment of European philosophy changed significantly. In the 1990s, it seemed as if Vattimo aimed to reconcile Christian eschatology and postmodern thought;[10] now, it seems as if he aims to save postmo-

[6] G. Vattimo, *Belief* (Cambridge 1999) 20.

[7] G. Vattimo, *After Christianity* (New York 2002) 2.

[8] The report of the experience is found in Vattimo, *Belief*, 36. The results are summarized as follows: „[...] the incarnation, that is, God's abasement to the level of humanity, what the New Testament calls God's kenosis, will be interpreted as the sign that the non-violent and non-absolute God of the post-metaphysical epoch has as its distinctive trait the very vocation for weakening of which Heideggerian philosophy speaks." *Ibid.*, 39.

[9] Vattimo, *After Christianity*, 7.

[10] For this earlier period see M. Riedl, „Säkularisierung als Heilsgeschehen: Gianni Vattimos postmoderne Eschatologie," in *Säkularisierung und Resakralisierung in westlichen Gesellschaften. Ideengeschichtliche Perspektiven* (ed. M. Hildebrandt et al., Wiesbaden 2001) 171-184.

dern thought for the post-secular age. The ambiguity of Vattimo's thought, which is more disguised in the earlier writings on religion than in the more recent ones, goes even further. Paradoxical as it may sound, Gianni Vattimo's postmodern eschatology aims to preserve, by means of radical hermeneutics and a very particular philosophy of history, what cannot be preserved by means of metaphysics: atheism. Under the post-metaphysical conditions neither the objective existence of God nor his objective non-existence can be claimed. Yet, what if God had really become man and died for us on the cross? Not to resurrect, to rule and to judge, but to be finally dead? The main thesis of this article is that Vattimo's postmodern eschatology celebrates God's death as a sacred global process, initiating the third age of hermeneutic liberty and aesthetic joy.

The following analysis of Gianni Vattimo's thought has a twofold goal. First, it aims to evaluate the philosophical consistency of Vattimo's thought, especially where he explicitly claims the heritage of ancient and medieval eschatology. Second, Vattimo's work serves as an example for what I call *the permanence of the eschatological.* My diagnosis runs counter to present-day mainstream social and historical research on religiosity which is determined by paradigms of change. For quite some time the secularization of society has been the primary paradigm of religious change; more recently it is re-sacralization or the resurgence of the religious. These perspectives certainly do have their own legitimacy. Yet, they fail to address a fact that is no less fascinating: the permanence of symbolic complexes over centuries and even millennia which, in their essence, remain untouched by processes of secularization and re-sacralization.

The analysis concentrates on Vattimo's 2002 book *After Christianity*, but refers to other works wherever necessary. *After Christianity* summarizes and clarifies the central arguments of Vattimo's earlier religious writings and may be considered as the standard work on postmodern eschatology.

THE POSTMODERN SITUATION

Philosophy in the postmodern situation must accept a twofold premise, says Vattimo. The objective structures by which metaphysics had described reality have ceased to be convincing. Theology can no longer refer to God as the highest principle of cosmic order; the metaphysical God is in fact dead, as Nietzsche claims.[11] Yet, proclaiming the death of God is not the same as declaring his non-existence. Declaratory atheism would be just another form of metaphysics, another claim about the objective structure of reality.[12] Vattimo therefore concludes:

[11] Vattimo, *After Christianity*, 3-4.

[12] „The end of metaphysics and the death of the moral God have liquidated the philosophical basis of atheism." *Ibid.*, 17.

> [...] since God can no longer be upheld as an ultimate foundation, as the absolute metaphysical structure of the real, it is possible, once again, to believe in God. True, it is not the God of metaphysics or of medieval scholasticism. But that is not the God of the Bible, of the Book that was dissolved and dismissed by modern rationalist and absolutist metaphysics.[13]

But who now is this non-metaphysical God of the Bible that is still trustworthy? The postmodern experience tells us about the pluralism of truths, about the contingency and historicity of our experience. Being can no longer be conceived of as mirroring the true structure of reality, as Heidegger, the prophet of the postmodern situation, had already acknowledged. Being is an event, as is already implied in the biblical account of the creation.[14]

Here and elsewhere Vattimo keeps silent about the most important implication of his argument: God as the creator is not thought separately from Being as creation; or, put differently, God creates himself and is, therefore, an event like all other Being. Only in this way can Vattimo subject him to the historicity of all Being and achieve congruity between the biblical account and Heideggerian *Seinsgeschichte.*[15] It is important to see that this underlying tacit pantheism is an essential prerequisite for Vattimo's theological hermeneutics. This is not to say that Vattimo is a pantheist in any naturalist manner; nonetheless it will become apparent that his hermeneutic eschatology implies the image of an immanent God. In a variation of Spinoza's formula: *Deus sive interpretatio.* For if God would transcend our interpretive efforts, if even the God who dies on the cross would be the hypostasis of a transcendent eternal God, he could not really die but would eternally remain in objective reality. Yet, the death of God is precisely what Vattimo's eschatology is about, not resurrection and eternal life as in traditional Christian eschatology. In order to fully understand what Vattimo means by the God of the Book, it is necessary to briefly look at his earlier works on hermeneutics.

HERMENEUTICS

In 1994, Vattimo gave a series of lectures, later published under the title *Beyond Interpretation.* The first lecture attempts a diagnosis of the contemporary intellectual situation and is entitled *The Nihilist Vocation of Hermeneutics.* Vattimo says that today hermeneutics is no longer necessarily accompanied by certain adjectives such as biblical, juridical, or literary. Already in Hans-Georg Gadamer it has become a general theory of interpretation which coincides with every possible human experience of the world.[16] There is no given experience

[13] *Ibid.*, 6.

[14] *Ibid.*, 6.

[15] *Ibid.*, 21.

[16] G. Vattimo, *Beyond Interpretation: The Meaning of Hermeneutics for Philosophy* (Stanford 1997) 4.

which is not an interpretive act.[17] Mass media and global communication, identified with Heidegger's *Ge-stell*, make us aware of the numerous narratives of the different cultures which are irreconcilable; they prove that there is no objective reality but only a multiplicity of regional realities.[18] However, according to Vattimo, the meaning of hermeneutics implies much more than Gadamer wanted to recognize. Hermeneutics properly understood is not only a theory of the historicity of horizons; it is itself a „radically historical truth."[19] In other words, after the metaphysical stadium of human history, we are entering the hermeneutic stadium.[20]

Vattimo himself describes the hermeneutic stadium as the fulfilment of the prophecies of Heidegger and Nietzsche.[21] On the one hand, it makes manifest the historicity of being, insofar as the history of modernity displays the weakening of Being. The fact that Heidegger, at least in the 1930s, prophesied the opposite, namely the adventure of Being, results, according to Vattimo, only from a wrong, rightwing interpretation of his own post-metaphysical revelations.[22] On the other hand, as already pointed out, the hermeneutic age fulfils Nietzsche's prophecy of the death of God, the protector and ontological guarantor of metaphysical propositions. In the process, the world and objective Being transmute into a fable and, consequently, demonstrate the interpretative character of the experience of truth. In other words, the history of Being brings about hermeneutics which is identical with the adventure of nihilism, that is, the dissolution of truth as objective evidence. The result of the weakening of Being is weak thought *(pensiero debole)*, as Gianni Vattimo, Aldo Rovatti, Umberto Eco, and others named their intellectual movement, opposing the strong thought *(pensiero forte)* of metaphysics.[23] The lecture ends with a modified version of Marx's eleventh

[17] *Ibid.*, 5.

[18] Vattimo, *After Christianity*, 15.

[19] Vattimo, *Beyond Interpretation*, 6.

[20] „[...] hermeneutics is not a philosophy but the enunciation of historical existence itself in the age of the end of metaphysics." *Ibid.*, 45.

[21] *Ibid.*, 6-7. „I argue [...] that the Nietzschean announcement of the death of God and the Heideggerian announcement (let me stress the character of *announcement*: neither a theory nor a thesis) of the end of metaphysics can provide the general framework for characterizing late-modern experience." Vattimo, *After Christianity*, 12; italics in the original.

[22] Vattimo, *Beyond Interpretation*, 13.

[23] The *pensiero debole* movement refers to Nietzsche, Heidegger, Gadamer, and other, predominantly German philosophers as prophetic precursors of their own post-modern revelations. "I saggi raccolti in questo volume, che difficilmente si potrebbero unificare sotto un'etichetta di scuola data la varia provenienza e i diversi orientamenti teoretici dei loro autori, hanno in commune l'idea che sia i discorsi italiani sulla crisi della ragione [...], sia molti versioni del post-strutturalismo francese [...], abbiano ancora nostalgia per la metafisica, e non portino davvero fino in fondo l'esperienza dell'oblio dell' essere, o della ‚morte di Dio', che soprattutto Heidegger e Nietzsche hanno annunciato alla nostra cultura.„ *Il pensiero debole* (ed. G. Vattimo and A. Rovatti, Milan 1988) 9.

thesis against Feuerbach. „[...] until now philosophers have seen fit to describe the world, now the moment has arrived to interpret it."[24]

The full meaning of Vattimo's hermeneutics discloses itself only in *After Christianity*. In most of Vattimo's earlier books on religion it has been intentionally concealed. Especially *Belief* is presented to the reader as the account of an aging philosopher who returns with some modifications to the faith of his youth. The opposite is true. Only one short passage in an essay published in the volume *Religion – Cultural Memory in the Present*, co-edited with Jacques Derrida, points to the core of Vattimo's thought:

> Beginning with St Augustine and his reflection on the Trinity, Christian theology is in its deepest foundations a hermeneutic theology: the interpretative structure, transmission, mediation and, perhaps, the fallenness do not concern only the enunciation, the communication of God with man; they characterize the intimate life of God itself, which therefore cannot be conceived in terms of an immutable metaphysical plenitude (in relation to which precisely, the revelation would merely be a 'subsequent' episode and an accident, a quoad nos).[25]

Vattimo objects to John Calvin's distinction between God's ineffable essence, his being *in se*, and God, as he reveals himself to us *(quoad nos)*.[26] As becomes more apparent in *After Christianity* and more recent writings, there is no God outside Scripture and exegetical tradition. We ourselves are the creatures of this tradition.[27] Our reception of revelation does not simply interpret the Gospel, but actually constitutes the Gospel.[28] The incarnation of Christ has not „actually" happened; it has reality only in its *Wirkungsgeschichte*, insofar as it is constitutive for our existence as an effect of tradition.[29] Only now it is apparent to what extent Vattimo's theological hermeneutics rests on a pantheist conception of the divine: the shifts and changes in our understanding of God are identical with the shifts and changes inside the divinity. God's inner life is hermeneutics. The relations of the divine persons to each other reflect our historically changing interpretation of the divinity. Nowhere but in our theological understanding do the Son and Spirit proceed from the Father. The development of our conception of God is therefore identical with the history of God:

[24] Vattimo, *Beyond Interpretation*, 14.

[25] Derrida and Vattimo, *Religion. Cultural Memory in the Present*, 88-89.

[26] For Calvin's terminology and its scholastic roots see P. Helm, *John Calvin's Ideas* (Oxford, 2005), 11-34.

[27] „[...] my dependence on God is my dependence only on the biblical tradition, on the fact that in the past they could not think without biblical conditions and meanings. So this is my creatural feeling." R. Rorty, G. Vattimo, and S. Zabala, „Dialogue: What is Religion's Future After Metaphysics?" in Rorty and Vattimo, *The Future of Religion*, 55-81: 77.

[28] Vattimo, *After Christianity*, 26-27.

[29] *Ibid* 112.

> [...] the God recovered in the postmetaphysical and postmodern epoch is the God of the Book. This is not only in the subjective sense of the genitive – meaning God as the author of the Biblical revelation – but also in the objective sense of the genitive: the God who is given to us in the Book and who does not 'exist' as an objective reality outside of salvation's announcement, is always handed over in historically changing forms offered, in the sacred Scriptures and in the living tradition of the Church, to the continuing reinterpretation of the community of the believers. [30]

This does not mean that before the hermeneutic age God had any objective reality. He always was nothing but interpretation. Yet only now, when the interpreters have come to acknowledge the Divine as human interpretation, have they become self-aware and therefore free. God has become man; the *kenosis* is complete. The ultimate consequence of Vattimo's hermeneutic pantheism, however, is that when we cease to believe in God's objective existence, he actually ceases to exist because he has no reality *in se*. This is what Nietzsche means when he says that the humans have murdered God. Vattimo does not deny the atheist implications of his hermeneutics: „So, when I say that 'thanks to God I am an atheist,' 'thanks to God' is very important, it means thanks to the history of the revelation, the salvation, the dissolution of Being that I'm an atheist and this history actually is my paradoxical foundation."[31]

The Process of Revelation

But how can Vattimo describe the death of God as a positive process of secularization and emancipation? How can he present the murder of God as the realization of the Christian essence, as, for instance, in the following quotation?

> [...] the [Nietzschean; M.R.] charge that the faithful have killed God has an even more radical and perhaps scandalous significance; secularization, the departure from the sacred characteristics of Western modernity, is an occurrence within the history of Western religiosity. It is not alien and hostile toward Western religiosity but rather characterizes it very deeply. If modern civilization secularizes itself, this is the positive mode in which it responds to the announcement of the religious tradition. My argument here is that the radical meaning of this occurrence is that the religious experience that has incorporated itself into Western culture – the land of the sunset, as Heidegger calls it, though we might call it the land of the sunset of the sacred – constitutes the long 'murder' of God, understood as a task that exemplifies the meaning of religion.[32]

[30] *Ibid* 8.
[31] Rorty, Vattimo, and Zabala, „Dialogue: What is Religion's Future After Metaphysics?," 63.
[32] Vattimo, *After Christianity*, 26.

At this point, Vattimo takes recourse to the Calabrian abbot Joachim of Fiore (ca. 1135–1202). Joachim occasionally comes up in several of Vattimo's writings,[33] but in *After Christianity* he devotes a whole chapter to him. For anyone familiar with the tradition of Italian anticlericalism, this move is hardly surprising. Joachim always served as the prophet of a future egalitarian church, from the Franciscan spirituals in the later Middle Ages up Ignazio Silone, the co-founder of the Italian Communist Party. Every literate Italian encounters his name frequently in the landmarks of national literature, from Dante to the self-proclaimed „people's poet" Dario Fo, the Italian Nobel laureate of 1997.[34]

As already pointed out, Vattimo's religious experience meant the sudden discovery that his ontology of the weakening of Being exactly coincides with the Christian revelation and that his post-modern philosophy is a transcription of the idea of the incarnation of God, the *kenosis*. In other words, even though he had considered himself an atheist, he had always preached the Gospel. With reference to the work of the French cultural anthropologist René Girard, he says that the sacred is intimately related to violence.[35] Vattimo discerns the remnants of archaic religion in metaphysics which violently insist on objective reality. The incarnation and crucifixion of Christ, however, may not be interpreted as the sacrifice of a human for the sake of mankind, as Catholic theology has it. The crucifixion rather has to be seen as the revelation of the connection between sacredness and violence with the aim of banning both from the sphere of human existence. In this way, Christ shows that there is a basic difference between religion and Christian faith.

This insight, however, could not prevail immediately after Christ's epiphany. Referring to Wilhelm Dilthey, Vattimo writes that a tendency toward subjec-

[33] Cf. Vattimo, *Beyond Interpretation*, 48-50; J.W. Jeffreys and G. Vattimo, „A Prayer for Silence. Dialogue with G. Vattimo," in Caputo and Vattimo, *After the Death of God*, 89-113: 100.

[34] For the Italian legacy of Joachim and a collection of references see M. Riedl, *Joachim of Fiore. Denker der vollendeten Menschheit* (Würzburg, 2004), 128-9.

[35] The central argument Vattimo refers to has been summarized by Girard as follows: „I think the most in fluential aspect of my work is to show that Judaism and Christianity exist in a continuity with archaic religions. […] In archaic society religion and culture are absolutely one, even when they don't seem to be. Religion, therefore, is a way that human beings learn, without realizing it, how to deal with violence in their midst. Here, sacrifice comes in as the killing of substitute victims. […] In a way, Christianity is the end of archaic religions because it reveals that the victim is innocent. When you understand Christianity correctly in its closeness and distance from archaic religion it is the same structure, the scapegoat phenomenon, that Jesus is victim of. Yet the text is intended to destroy your belief in scapegoat phenomenon instead of using it in order to have sacrifices. The relationship is very central and rational with all archaic religions in the past that may go back tens of thousands of years. This is very important. The religion of the Incarnation should be an anthropology as well as a theology. Incarnation means man and God together. Theology is pure God and is built on schemes that completely neglect what we call Incarnation in Christianity." www.firstthings.com/onthesquare/2008/11/an-interview-with-rene-girard, retrieved March 20, 2010.

tivity inheres in the Christian faith, as already apparent in the writings of the Church Father Augustine.[36] Yet, this tendency, which would inevitably lead toward the hermeneutic world-view, was suppressed by certain counter-processes. The Church was forced to take upon herself the burden of political responsibility after the ordering forces of the Roman Empire had declined. In this vein, the Church learned to appreciate the utility of metaphysics for guaranteeing an objective order of things. Only after the decline of metaphysics and the subsequent rise of hermeneutical philosophy could the full truth of the Christian gospel come forth and initiate the third age of the Holy Spirit, the age of free and non-dogmatic interpretation.

In this way, Vattimo establishes a link between Joachim's predictions and his own philosophy. Moreover, Joachim serves as a witness for the continuous hermeneutic undercurrent in Christian history, which has always contradicted the official dogma and which connects the epiphany of Christ with our own hermeneutic age:

> [...] alongside this dogmatic-disciplinarian view of the revelation [as held by the Catholic clergy; M.R.], which seems in the end to be discredited by its profound indebtedness to objectivistic metaphysics, the history of Christianity is traversed by another wholly different thread that one might well call Joachimist: for it was Joachim of Fiore who spoke of a third age in the histories of humanity and of salvation, namely, the reign of the spirit (following after that of the Father in the Old Testament, and that of the Son), in which the 'spiritual' sense of the scriptures is increasingly in evidence, with charity taking the place of discipline.[37]

The Eschaton

At this point one might wonder what concrete hopes Vattimo has for the hermeneutic age that was announced by Heidegger and now awaits its fulfilment. Once alienated from Catholicism because of his sexual orientation, Vattimo admits in *Belief*, that he hopes that these future social and ethical changes will also bring about the acceptance of his homosexuality. The precept of *caritas*, which, according to Joachim of Fiore, will govern the future Christian society, is not just the translation of the Greek *agape*, he says, but also of *eros*, in a very comprehensive sense.[38] In *After Christianity*, he pursues the issue further. The Church Fathers were not wrong when they established the connection between original sin and sexuality; since the same will to power over existence is at work in sexuality as in metaphysical questioning. The ultimate source of evil is the will of self-affirmation:

[36] Vattimo, „The age of Interpretation," in Rorty and Vattimo, *The Future of Religion*, 43-54: 46.

[37] Vattimo, *Beyond Interpretation*, 48-9.

[38] Vattimo, *Belief*, 72-74.

> […] the 'blessing' of sexuality in marriage, which grants that institution the same legitimacy as just war. It is a justice that can be called into question, that conceals violence – in the case of sex, the will of affirmation and the desire of fulfilling life – with the principle 'one must live on,' always invoked to justify the perpetration of the worst foul deeds.[39]

Consequently, truly Christian sexuality must be of the playful type, „the ludic, seductive, and aesthetic sexuality of Don Juan,"[40] exactly the opposite of what the Church commands. Even if it is not explicitly said, homosexuality appears as the even more perfect type, as it is completely free of reproductive interests.

This aesthetic sexuality, however, is only one element in the more general picture of an aesthetic eschaton. In the fullness of the hermeneutic age we will freely interpret all the meanings, we can freely choose from the tradition of our civilization. With the dissolution of objective realities God becomes an „ornament", as part of „salvation history insofar as it prepares for the transfer of reality on the plane of secondary qualities, of the spiritual, and of the ornamental; we might even add, the virtual."[41] It is preferable to render Vattimo's description of paradise in his own words, as they reveal the hedonism underlying the whole eschatological construct:

> Our civilization, which we have reached through mechanical and computer technology, political democracy, social pluralism, and the availability of goods necessary to ensure survival, offers us the chance to realize the kingdom of spirit, understood as lightening and poeticization of the real. […] Eternal life is nothing but the 'perfect' enjoyment of meanings and spiritual forms generated by the history of humanity, which now constitute the 'kingdom' of immortality. To draw closer to that life here and now would mean to realize the condition in which a more perfect aesthetic enjoyment of meaning can be increasingly given. The establishment of 'righteous' historical orders has only this aim.[42]

THE ANTICHRIST

Once the message of the Gospel and the content of salvation history have been identified as the overcoming of metaphysics, it is evident that all forces still insisting on objective reality are anti-Christian. Vattimo means the Catholic Church. Admittedly, the idea that the pope and his clergy are in truth the Antichrist is not a novelty. Already in the 14th-century controversy over Christ's poverty between Rome and the Franciscan Spirituals, the papal Antichrist

[39] Vattimo, *After Christianity*, 114.
[40] *Ibid.*
[41] *Ibid.*, 53.
[42] *Ibid.*, 54-55.

became a prominent mythical figure. Two centuries later, Martin Luther was to become the most prominent promoter of this idea.[43] The basic pattern remains unchanged: true Christianity, as lived in the Early Church, has been betrayed by the Catholic clergy. The Church, therefore, has become the greatest obstacle to the actualization of the Gospel.

Vattimo's original contribution is to integrate this narrative into his hermeneutic eschatology and into his reading of Heidegger. Heidegger (apparently quite unconsciously) moves into the role of the defender of authentic Christian experience against the objective claims of the Church. The whole concluding chapter of *After Christianity* is devoted to these synthesizing efforts:

> The Antichrist who continually tests the faithful and drives them to idolatrously indentify the Messiah with figures who falsify his meaning refers to representational, objectifying thought (which Heidegger later on calls metaphysical thought), which once it asserted itself in the Christian tradition, pushed into oblivion Christianity's authentic original context.[44]

From this perspective, Heidegger's thinking of historicity represents the early Christian experience of „authentic temporality,"[45] while the metaphysical theology is downright satanic.[46]

Critical Evaluation

Vattimo's philosophy stands and falls with its claim about the coincidence of post-metaphysical thought and the Christian Gospel. Otherwise, the huge construct of a hermeneutic eschatology, which he built up over two decades, would appear rather arbitrary. Therefore, it is essential that he rediscovers his own ideas in the thought of alleged dissidents within the Catholic tradition such as Joachim of Fiore.[47] Vattimo is, in many respects, right to refer to Joachim. The abbot does in fact present the Christian society of the third age as a community of love. Additionally, throughout his work he presents the growth of Christian

[43] B. McGinn, *Antichrist. Two Thousand Years of the Human Fascination with Evil* (New York, 1994), see especially 157-166 and 201-208.

[44] Vattimo, *After Christianity*, 133.

[45] *Ibid.*, 124-25.

[46] „Every attempt to read revelation as a teaching on the nature and attributes of God falls into the same [here the word „satanic" is left out in the English translation; M.R.] error of representational thought – the sin of objectifying metaphysics – against which we are called to recover the hearing of Being." *Ibid.*, 133.

[47] As I have shown elsewhere, Joachim did not consider himself a dissident but rather a Catholic reformer in the tradition of Pope Gregory VII. Riedl, *Joachim of Fiore*, 204.

knowledge as a growth of spiritual understanding *(intelligentia spiritualis)*, transcending all literal meaning of the Scripture.[48]

Is Vattimo therefore right when he describes the kernel of Joachim's teaching as „the idea that salvation takes place at a specific time – which is an intrinsically historical matter. And the idea that this history is still in progress, like the divine life that unfolds in the three persons of the Trinity?"[49] No, he is not. Joachim makes perfectly clear that the inner life of the Trinity, the *processiones*, in which the Father generates the Son, and the Father with the Son generate the Spirit, are eternal processes.[50] They have to be clearly distinguished from the *missiones*, the acts in which the divine persons are revealed to us which constitute the decisive events of salvation history (incarnation, dispensation of the Spirit).[51] In other words, the temporal reality of God's gradual self-revelation as *Deus quoad nos*, is absolutely distinguished from the transcendent reality of the coeternal an coequal persons as *Deus in se*. Thus, according to Vattimo's vague categories, Joachim's theology qualifies as „metaphysical", as it insists on the permanent objective reality of the divine. Consequently, there is no substantial ground for Vattimo's claim to the Joachimite legacy. There is generally *no* Christian tradition that would justify Vattimo's hermeneutic radicalism, which subjects the divine reality to human interpretation and ultimately identifies the two.

There are a number of other elements in Vattimo's philosophy that deserve critical evaluation. On the one hand, Vattimo insists on the pluralities of truth; on the other hand, he claims that only Christianity has the potential of a universal religion, as it is the only religion that can overcome its objectivism and embrace otherness. This results in invectives against „Jewish" philosophy – he thinks, for instance, about Emmanuel Levinas – that leaves God in a position of transcendence and otherness.[52] The same applies to Protestant theology. Another problematic consequence of Vattimo's thought is the canonization and religious veneration of Heidegger. Ultimately, the philosophy of Heidegger stands higher than the Bible, as it is the spiritual understanding of the letter of the Gospel. Consequently, any acceptable reading of the Bible in our days must be compatible with Heidegger's post-metaphysical revelations. Vattimo is no

[48] For a systematic account of Joachim's teachings: *Ibid.*, 253-308.

[49] Vattimo, *After Christianity*, 32.

[50] „Neque enim, quia Filium a Patre esse dicimus et a Patre et Filio Spiritum sanctum, idcirco aliquid prius posteriusve in Trinitate esse fatemur, sed confitemur totas tres personas coeternas sibi esse et coequales." Joachim of Fiore, *Psalterium Decem Chordarum* (ed. Venice, 1527), fol. 230vb.

[51] Riedl, *Joachim von Fiore*, 221-224.

[52] „There is a sort of predominance of Judaic religiosity in the return of religion into contemporary thought (let me make clear that this observation has no anti-semitic intention whatsoever). It is a fact that the total otherness of God with respect to the world appears to be affirmed at the expense of any recognition of novelty in the Christian event." Vattimo, *Belief*, 84; cf. Vattimo, *After Christianity*, 36-39.

less dogmatic than the Catholic Church, as any objective or metaphysical theology is declared an atavism and a violent onslaught on true Christendom. Lastly, Vattimo's picture of the Catholic theological tradition is a caricature, a generalization of certain Neo-Thomist trends prevalent after the First Vatican Council. Certainly, Thomas Aquinas did claim that the existence of God can be made evident by metaphysical proof; but even he denied that the essentials of Christian theology, such as the Trinity, would be accessible through metaphysical inquiry. Yet, when every objective claim is declared metaphysical, there is not much room for differentiations.

In the context of this volume, a juxtaposition of Vattimo and Habermas illustrates another, probably more important flaw in Vattimo's thought. Whatever one might think about Habermas's earlier work, his recent interrelated works on bioethics and religion are motivated by a genuine concern about the future of constitutional democracy, the most humane political order currently at our disposal. For instance, whether the biotechnological „instrumentalization of human nature changes the ethical self-understanding of the species in such a way that we may no longer see ourselves as ethically free and morally equal beings guided by norms and reasons."[53] Secondly, referring to the constitutional jurist Wolfgang Böckenförde, he asks whether secular democracy is dependent on normative resources it cannot provide on its own. Finally, he evaluates how secular democracy should react to (or make productive use of) the post-secular situation, that is, the obviously continuing existence of religion and religious communities.

Vattimo, on the other hand, quite cynically dismisses the bioethical problem because there is no objective violence in killing.[54] The only violence he can see in this regard originates from the Church that imposes its metaphysical argument on the believers, thereby influencing their political decisions. Secondly, the Böckenförde problem is nonexistent for him, because only democracy produces legitimate truths and, consequently, metaphysical truths must be banned for their undemocratic character.[55] Moreover, that democracy occurs in salvation history is a clear sign that profane and sacred history coincides.[56] So why should democracy be endangered? Finally, the conflict between secular institutions and

[53] Habermas, *The Future of Human Nature*, 40-41.

[54] „What about euthanasia? Once more, the reason the Church doesn't want to speak about this is because they believe there is an objective violence in killing. Yes, but what about God? If there is an objective violence to killing somebody, then it would follow that God is the biggest murderer of all. Violence, then, is the fact of no longer permitting the other to ask questions." Robbins and Vattimo, „A Prayer for Silence," 93-94.

[55] „The pluralistic world in which we live cannot be interpreted by an ideology that wants to unify it at all costs in the name of a sole truth [...]. This ideology would stumble against, among other things, any ideals of democracy. [...] the universal validity of an assertion can be construed by building consensus in dialogue, thought without claiming any right in the name of an absolute truth." Vattimo, *After Christianity*, 5; cf. Vattimo, „The Age of Interpretation," 50.

[56] *Ibid.*, 46.

religious communities will come to an end, once the believers hear Vattimo's message. They will learn that as true Christians they have to overcome dogma, authority, Church, truth, and God, in order to establish the future „religion of pure love".[57]

The problem here is not that Vattimo identifies *caritas* as the core of the Christian gospel, as the only limit of secularization and interpretation;[58] nor is it wrong that *caritas* needs to be defended against the institutional logic of the church(es). Similarly, his criticism of „metaphysical" dogmatic positions is overdrawn and imprecise but not always unfounded. The problem rather is that Vattimo fails to address the post-secular problem, namely that metaphysical questions and the theology of the transcendent God continue to attract a great number of people from within secular societies. The tension between the logic of secular democracies and experiences of transcendent truth cannot be solved by enforcing a pluralist creed supported by speculations on the course of salvation. The axiom that there is „no experience which is not an interpretative act", that our experiences can never transcend the historicity of our existence falsely claims self-evidence, precludes any authentic religiosity, and is no less intransigent than any other form of dogmatism.[59] Vattimo cannot avoid this conclusion by presenting his dogma as eschatological insight. It is true that an increasing confrontation with non-Western civilizational contexts may make us aware of the historicity of many or our positions and amplifies the need of hermeneutic skills. Yet in this respect Vattimo's mix of dogmatic hermeneuticism and eschatological fantasies devoid of empirical grounds is anything but helpful, as it replaces intellectual sincerity and political responsibility. These flaws cannot be counterbalanced by Vattimo's practical engagement in national and European politics, especially if this engagement is based on the same fantasies.[60]

[57] G. Vattimo, „Toward a Nonreligious Christianity," in Caputo and Vattimo, *After the Death of God*, 27-46: 44-45.

[58] Vattimo, *Belief*, 62-65.

[59] Accordingly, mystical experience is just as much qualified as antichristian as metaphysics. Vattimo, *After Christianity*, 135.

[60] In 2004 Vattimo, as a member of the European Parliament, answered to the questions of two journalists. When asked why he thought that Turkey as a non-Christian country should become a member of the European Union and why he spoke out against explicitly addressing the Christian legacy in the European Constitution, he answered: „Christianity is already incorporated in the principles, in the rights we will decide to include in the European Constitution. In this regard, the same applies to the occident and to Christianity: as long as it describes itself as 'Christian', as opposed to 'Buddhist' or 'Islamic', the occident still has an identity, which has not yet dissolved. The same goes for the Church. Therefore I say that the weak thought is the only philosophy which can save the Church. For either the church refrains from its dogmatic stubbornness, which has nothing in common with the proper message of the Gospel (the relation to God, *caritas*, fraternity) or it will perish. Christianity has a universal vocation and exactly therefore a vocation to dissolve itself in the sense of Joachim of Fiore. The same

Conclusion

The most striking phenomenon, illustrated in Vattimo's work, is the permanence of the eschatological. The basic symbolic forms of our civilization, such as eschatology, cosmology, and mysticism, seem to survive even the most decisive breaks and changes in intellectual history. Post-modernity has by no means left behind the grand narratives. There are a few moments in Vattimo's work where he quite lucidly reveals the true motive for his recourse to the eschatological tradition – that there is simply no other narrative at hand: „[...] we cannot even speak but from a Christian point of view. That is because we are fundamentally incapable of formulating ourselves, fundamentally incapable of articulating a discourse, except by accepting culturally conditioned premises."[61] One could therefore interpret Vattimo's hermeneutic eschatology as an attempt to make inevitability a virtue. Our categories are so strongly determined by the Christian tradition that we have to speak a Christian language even if we aim at the destruction and negation of the Christian God. In this respect, Vattimo, more than others, understands that secular eschatologies transport a Christian heritage. This, by the way, also applies to Habermas, whose deliberative theory of democracy entails the eschatological promise of a future cosmopolitan age.[62]

Ultimately, however, Vattimo fails to convince that the huge building of his hermeneutic eschatology has been constructed for reasons other than the voicing of his anti-clerical sentiments, preservation of an outmoded atheism, and support for the wishful thinking of a hedonist. In the end, of course, everything is interpretation. There is no reality *in se*, only *quoad nos*. When God speaks to us, we are actually speaking to ourselves in joyful and productive dialogues, unless we are interrupted by a fundamentalist who does not play by the rules. From there, however, we can build up any kind of *eschaton*, any „lightening of the real", and reconnect it to a vague tradition which, in its turn, is also subject to our interpretation.[63] One is reminded

goes for the occident. The occident must become the precursor of a larger unit, in which it dissolves, like the yeast in the sour dough, as the Gospel says." G. Vattimo, „Für eine multipolare Welt. Im Gespräch mit Martin Ross und Martin G. Weiß," in *Polylog* 12 (2004) 59-68; also available at http://them.polylog.org/5/dvg-de.htm; my translation.

61 Vattimo, „Toward a Nonreligious Christianity," 36; cf. Vattimo, „The Age of interpretation," 53-54.

62 See for instance the concluding lines of *Faktizität und Geltung*: „Der weltbürgerliche Zustand ist kein bloßes Phantom mehr, auch wenn wir noch weit von ihm entfernt sind. Staatsbürgerschaft und Weltbürgerschaft bilden ein Kontinuum, das sich immerhin schon in Umrissen abzeichnet." J. Habermas, *Faktizität und Geltung. Beiträge zur Diskurstheorie des Rechts und des demokratischen Rechtsstaats* (Frankfurt am Main, 1992) 660.

63 Vattimo, *After Christianity*, 51.

of the snobbish detachment from a problematic reality, as it is so nicely illustrated in the works of Oscar Wilde:

„*Jack*: Is that clever?

Algernon: It is perfectly phrased! And quite as true as any observation in civilised life should be."[64]

[64] O. Wilde, *Complete Works. Centenary Edition* (Glasgow, 1999), 371 (from the first act of *The Importance of Being Earnest*).

HABERMAS ON RELIGION: THE PROBLEM OF DISCURSIVE EXTRATERRITORIALITY

Nicholas Adams

There is no consensus as to whether Habermas has changed his mind about the role and significance of religious life in modernity. It has certainly become a more prominent theme in his writing since 2001.[1] Regardless of how this question of significant change is answered, I argue here that there are two continuing difficulties with Habermas' recent remarks on religion. These problems relate to the question: how can members of religious traditions genuinely argue in the public sphere, rather than merely rehearse their claims? I maintain that Habermas asks the right questions, but his answers stand in need of repair. I do not think his answers display logical fallacies or that he misrepresents the histories of religious traditions. Rather, I have argued in my *Habermas and Theology* that he needs to pay attention to the details of religious life all the way down: these details need to provide structures for addressing his questions, not merely provide 'contents' that can be 'rationally appropriated' by a general theory. It may be that in some respects Habermas has changed his views in ways that force a reconsideration of his relation to theology. I will try to show that the problems I identified in Habermas' earlier work persist, and even intensify, in *Between Naturalism and Religion* of 2005. I am not pursuing yet another critique of Habermas, as I did not in *Habermas and Theology*. Instead, I take seriously the specific repairs offered by Habermas, in response to real contemporary problems, and try to repair them in turn.

[1] Some of the most significant contributions since 2001 translated into English are 'Faith and Knowledge' in *The Future of Human Nature* (Cambridge: Polity, 2003), 101-115.; 'A Conversation about God and the World' in *Religion and Rationality* (Cambridge: Polity, 2002), 147-167.; 'Pre-political Foundations of the Democratic Constitutional State?' in *The Dialectics of Secularization* (San Franciso: Ignatius, 2006), 19-52.; all the essays in *Between Naturalism and Religion* (Cambridge: Polity, 2008). See also the important untranslated 'Replik auf Einwände, Reaktion auf Anregungen' in *Glabuen und Wissen: Ein Symposium mit Jürgen Habermas* (ed. R Langthaler and H Nagl-Docekal, Vienna: Oldenbourg, 2007), 366-414.

The two problems I wish to consider are (1) discursive extraterritoriality and (2) the notion of appropriating religious 'contents' or their 'semantic heritage'. I argue that Habermas' binary opposition between 'faith' and 'reason' has the effect (unintended by him) of conceding too much to the rhetoric of the religious right. I share Habermas' concerns about this rhetoric and wish to reinforce his arguments by querying the justification of some of their key assumptions about religious life in modernity.

Before doing so, however, there is a case where Habermas' recent work offers an evaluation of the place of religious traditions in modernity which is significantly different from the impression he gives in earlier work. This relates to my previous claim that Habermas describes religions as ancestors, in some way, of modern rational thought.[2] Habermas has recently explicitly suggested that it is a mistake to treat contemporary forms of religious life as if they are archaic remnants that persist into the present time:

> As long as secular citizens are convinced that religious traditions and religious communities are, as it were, archaic relics of premodern societies persisting into the present, they can understand freedom of religion only as the cultural equivalent of the convervation of species threatened with extension. Religion no longer has any intrinsic justification in their eyes.[3]

Habermas himself does by contrast wish to take religious contributions to contentious political issues seriously, and to participate in a cooperative search for truth. There is a sting however. He wishes

> to participate in a cooperative search for truth to determine whether they may contain elements that can be expressed in a secular language and be justified by rational arguments.[4]

The sting lies not in the requirement that claims must be justified by rational arguments: that should be a given. It is in the double problem of the notion of 'elements' and the implied reduction of the scope of 'rational' to common sense. Habermas problematically maintains that the ancient moral 'contents' of religious traditions are both (a) the origin of secular morality and (b) available in some way for rational appropriation:

> Religious traditions have a special power to articualte moral intuitions, especially with regard to vulnerable forms of communal life. In corresponding political debates, this potential makes religious speech into a serious vehicle for possible truth contents, which can then be translated from the vocabulary of a particular religious community into a generally accessible language.[5]

[2] Nicholas Adams *Habermas and Theology* (Cambridge: CUP, 2006) 66-91).

[3] 'Religion in the Public Sphere', 138. All references are to essays in the translated collection Jürgen Habermas *Between Naturalism and Religion* (tr. Ciaran Cronin, Cambridge: Polity, 2008).

[4] Ibid. 139.

[5] 'Religion in the Public Sphere', 131. See also 'The Boundary between Faith and Knowledge', 212.

I shall return to this. There is a further case where Habermas settles a matter that had been uncertain. I previously claimed that Habermas associates religious traditions with metaphysics, and wondered what qualities Habermas might attribute to postmetaphysical theology.[6] Recently, Habermas names Schleiermacher and Kierkegaard, and by extension Bultmann and Barth, as theologians working within a postmetaphysical frame.[7] Habermas identifies a long tradition of postmetaphysical theology. It remains the case, however, that there is no serious conversation between Habermas and important anti-liberal thinkers such as Stanley Hauerwas and John Milbank.

(1) Habermas insists upon the importance of maintaining a strong division between faith and reason, and faith and knowledge (space prevents considering the difference between them here). The purpose of this division is to aid in the clarification of which kinds of claim can be publicly debated, and which cannot. Such a division is a commonplace in German philosophy, extending back at least to Jacobi and Kant. Jacobi claims that reason leads to nihilism, and that the decision to base one's life on faith is a *salto mortale*. Kant claims his limits on pure reason made room for faith. Attempts to oppose this strict division go back just as far. Hamann claims that reason, like faith, is a matter of habitual use and that their authority derives from traditions of such use. Further back, in the thirteenth century, Aquinas and Scotus agree that what one can know of God from 'natural knowledge' (which has a family resemblance to late eighteenth century 'reason') is more limited than what one learns from 'supernatural knowledge', that is, from scripture interpreted in the church. The rules for debating 'natural knowledge' are different from the rules for debating 'supernatural knowledge'. In the first case, one draws on a wide range of arguments from ancient Greek, classical Roman and contemporary Islamic sources, and the rules for evaluating them are internal to those traditions themselves. In the second case, one draws on a more limited range of arguments from the Church fathers and their successors, and seeks to display the wisdom of scripture, the harmony of the tradition and one's considered obedience to them both. The rules for evaluating rival arguments depend on faithfulness to scripture and the church's traditions of its interpretation.

In both cases there are rules for handling disagreements, but the rules are different. In the context of Habermas' question about public argumentation, the key difference between the two cases, natural and supernatural knowledge, is the range of authorities admitted, and the scope of the readership to which one addresses oneself. Aquinas can address his interpretation of Aristotle's *Metaphysics*, and perhaps his arguments about divine simplicity, to a relatively broad readership, including contemporary Muslim scholars; he should address

[6] Adams *Habermas and Theology*, 195-6.

[7] 'The Boundary between Faith and Knowledge', 237.

[8] For an illuminating discussion of the issues at stake in Jacobi's contrast between immediacy and demonstration see Andrew Bowie *From Romanticisim to Critical Theory* (London: Routledge, 1997), 35-52.

his questions on the Trinity more narrowly, not merely to fellow Christians but fellow Christians in the Western tradition. The breadth of prospective readership is a 'more or less' matter, not a strict separation between whether one is considering matters of 'faith' *or* 'reason'. By the time of the eighteenth century, in Jacobi's hands, matters of faith are associated with immediacy – with what is already taken to be true. By contrast, matters of reason are associated with reflection and demonstration – with what one comes to accept.[8] For Hamann, against Jacobi and Kant, matters of faith and of reason are, alike, matters of language and tradition[9] One might say that they are as public as a language, although one should add that the existence of different traditions means there are different publics, and the range of authorities on which one draws will determine the scope of the readership that will find one's arguments persuasive.

We can notice some interesting features of Habermas' way of distinguishing between faith and reason in his more recent work. The following is exceptionally important:

> the conflict between one's own religious convictions and secularly justified policies or proposed laws can only arise because even the religious citizen is already supposed to have accepted the constitution of the secular state for good reasons. He no longer lives as a member of a religiously homogeneous population within a religiously legitimated state. Hence certainties of faith are interconnected with fallible convictions of a secular nature; they have long since lost their purported immunity to the impositions of modern reflexivity – in the manner of „unmoved" but not „unmovable movers". Religious certainties are in fact exposed to increasing reflective pressure in the differentiated architecture of modern societies. Religious rooted existential convictions, by dint of their if necessary rationally justified reference to the dogmatic authority of an inviolable core of infallible revealed truths, evade that kind of unreserved discursive examination to which other ethical orientations and worldviews, i.e. secular „conceptions of the good", are exposed.[10]

There are very serious historical questions to be asked of these contrasts. It is not clear where one would ever have found a 'religiously homogeneous population' unmarked by disputation and public argumentation. Every major theological text is best interpreted as an intervention in an ecology of public debates, and most were produced in situtations of disputatiousness. The production of 'religious certainties' is almost certainly a late modern phenomenon – more Jerry Falwell than Saint Francis.

Yet for Habermas the 'certainties of faith' are contrasted with 'fallible convictions of a secular nature'; an 'inviolable core of infallible revealed truths' is contrasted with the 'unreserved discursive examination' that secular conceptions of the good receive. Faith is thus accorded a state of 'discursive extraterritoriality':

[9] J. G. Hamann *Metacritique of the Purism of Reason* in Gwen Griffith Dickson *Johann Georg Hamann's Relational Metacriticism* (Berlin: De Gruyter, 1995), 520.

[10] 'Religion in the Publc Sphere', 129.

in other words, matters of faith are non-negotiable.[11] It is notable that the distinction is whether or not claims can be subjected to public argumentation, rather than being a question of the scope of the public to which one addresses oneself.

Habermas is caught up in Jacobi's contrast between the immediate and the demonstrable, but with a novel and unwelcome twist. Unlike Jacobi he does not explore the irreducible immediacy on which all demonstration rests. He performs a quite different manoeuvre, which is to drive a wedge between faith (immediacy) and reason (demonstration). For Jacobi there is no such wedge. This has four unfortunate effects. First, it makes it difficult to make sense of argumentation within a tradition, such as a church council. Are these not public in a sense? Second, it makes it difficult to make sense of argumentation between two traditions that share a significant belief, for example that there is one God. Is this not public in a sense? Third, there are probably no 'certainties of faith' or 'infallibly revealed truths' in any tradition that have not at some time provoked debate, and very few that do not continue to do so. When and how did they become 'discursively extraterritorial'? Fourth, it makes it easy for ideologues on the religious right to claim immunity from criticism when appealing to 'matters of faith'. How can they ever be wrong? Habermas' arguments have the unfortunate and unintended effect of shielding late modern purveyors of religious certainties, rather than forcing them (as he should) to confront the reality that all matters of faith are properly the domain of the contestable, and always have been. Theology is and has been the art of contestation.

Habermas might reply that there is no such thing as a 'limited public', and that arguments within religious traditions are thus not public in his sense. If so, this is the point at which severe criticism is called for. Surely public argumentation is a 'more or less', rather than a 'public' versus 'not public', matter. There are different publics, broader or narrower scopes of readership, and complex interrelations between them. Matters of faith should thus not be accorded 'discursive extraterritoriality', but should invite questions about who expects to persuade whom, of what, to what degree, in which contexts. Habermas himself suggests this way of thinking elsewhere, in discussing the difference between *Gültigkeit* and *Geltung*. It is unfortunate that when considering contributions by religious participants in public argumentation the idea of 'a generally accessible language', into which religious claims must be rendered, predominates rather than the more fruitful idea that 'the two-place relation of the validity [*Gültigkeit*] of propositions is extended [in reflexive communicative action] into the three-place relation of a validity [*Geltung*] that valid propositions have „for us"'.[12] These two words 'for us' have enormous significance for a sound understanding of the role of religious arguments in the public sphere. Claims have

[11] 'Religion in the Public Sphere' ,129-130., and also 143.

[12] Compare 'Religion in the Public Sphere', 120, 129, 131 and 'Communicative Action and the „Use of Reason"', 43.

validity for x. This is a powerful intellectual tool that renders unnecessary any attempt to decide whether claims 'have validity' or not. They may have validity 'for us' and not 'for you'. This seems to me to have some bearing on the question of what Habermas calls public discursive examination. Surely different communities will discursively examine claims, and their validity, differently.

This also permits a fruitful reconsideration of the idea of a 'generally accessible language'. One can readily see why Habermas might think this desirable. If one imagines a series of traditions, each with its peculiar customs and categories, attempting to propose, query and redeem validity claims it might seem there can be only chaos. The argument goes: surely a satisfactory form of argumentation requires the use of a uniform set of customs and categories, of rules and expectations? I would strongly argue that this is not so. Rather, a satisfactory form of argumentation requires each participant to learn the customs and categories of the others' forms of speech. Habermas is right to claim that translation is required, but it is not translation into a generally accessible language; it is translation between as many languages as are in play. If there are three traditions in conversation, there should be three sets of customs and categories in play, and a willingness on the part of participants in discussion to engage these.

Put differently, in order to address the important questions Habermas poses, one needs a well-ordered account of the relation between rationality and common sense. If the two are identical, as Habermas seems to imply, then a rational argument is one whose categories and logic are those of a common sense on which all are agreed. Similarly, one needs a well-ordered account of the relation between public discourse and common sense. Again, if the two are identical, then the only truly public argument is one whose categories and logic are those of common sense. It appears that for Habermas the identity of both pairs is affirmed. My own contrary view is derived from technical logical arguments advanced by the Jewish philosopher Peter Ochs.[13] Ochs' argument is simple in construction: an argument can quite properly be addressed to a collection of nested publics. His own arguments concern how to read the philosophy of C. S. Peirce.

> I present the hypotheses as a series of incremental interpretations and revisions of Peirce's pragmaticism, each increment of which should speak to an increasingly defined and narrow community of readers. In other words, the first interpretive move I make should be meaningful to a relatively broad collection of readers. ...The next move should be meaningful to only a subset of these, and so on.[14]

I propose that this can be generalised. It is not just that for each increment of an unfolding argument the scope of its readership can be progressively narrowed. It is that any increment, and indeed any argument, can be understood as

[13] Peter Ochs *Peirce, Pragmatism and the Logic of Scripture* (Cambridge: CUP, 1998). For commentary and explanation see Nicholas Adams 'Reparative Reasoning' in *Modern Theology* July 2008, 447-457.

[14] Ochs *Peirce*, 246.

addressing any particular reader directly, or somewhat tangentially, or rather indirectly, or even not at all. In terms that Habermas has himself enbraced, in his discussion of the relationship between *Gültigkeit* and *Geltung,* what is axiomatic for me might quite properly be taken as hypothetical for you. What Ochs shows clearly, but which is in doubt for Habermas, is that 'common sense' is itself a particular set of discursive rules which can be contrasted with other competing sets. Ochs himself goes further (as I would too) and indicates that claims that are vague when interpreted according to common sense rules can be rendered much more precise when interpreted by narrower more communally specific rules.[15] In other words, one can argue not just that an account of differentiated publics does better justice to the ways that specific claims are in fact variously interpreted, but that the meaning of a specific claim is likely to become much vaguer if it is presented and interpreted as a common sense utterance. It will thus not be a matter simply of 'translation into a generally accessible language' as Habermas thinks, but of increased vagueness which cannot be easily remedied.

It should be clear that what I mean here by 'common sense' is what Habermas calls 'generally accessible language', and not the assumptions about the world which we take for granted, and which scientific research interrupts and sometimes alters. Habermas calls both common sense.[16]

My argument admittedly generates its own problems, but I believe these are better problems to have. A few salient questions can be posed. When political leaders address their citizens, which customs and categories should their speech reflect? Which customs and categories should be reflected in legislation that applies to several traditions who together make up one state? Which customs and categories should be adopted in the education of young persons in institutions where many traditions are represented? When members of different traditions confront one another in court, which customs and categories should be reflected in the arguments and in the court's rulings? These are serious matters. I cannot solve such problems here: the problems vary from context to context, and different places have different histories that need to be investigated and understood. It seems to me that the requirement to generate a set of 'generally accessible' customs and categories is a false alternative to that patient historical, locally particular, interpretive work.

(2) Habermas suggests that philosophy should appropriate the 'possible truth contents' or 'semantic heritage' of religious traditions. With this suggestion, the 'contents' or 'heritage' of religious life appear to be separable from the religious traditions. This is a serious problem. In some of his work, Habermas makes it clear that he wishes to learn from religious traditions: their long histories of ritual, narrative, formation; above all the rich, meaningful lives that religious traditions make possible. This is evident in the first and last essays of the collection *The Future of Human Nature* of 2001. Habermas is equally attentive to

[15] Ochs *Peirce,* 316 ff.

[16] For the second meaning see Habermas 'Faith and Knowledge' 105ff.

the possibility that without the rich textures of living religious traditions, secular society itself might produce shallow attenuated institutions and would probably fail to produce of its own accord certain practices of care for the vulnerable and hope in the face of apparent disaster. In other parts of his work, including essays in *Between Naturalism and Religion*, Habermas seems to reproduce Kant's idea that religions have a 'core' or 'content' that is contained in a 'shell'.[17] This account stands in urgent need of repair.

The religious traditions of Judaism, Christianity and Islam (to name but three, but to encompass half the world's population) incorporate complex performances which include forms of discipline, repetition of certain habits (including prayer), modes of praise and lament, rhythms of work and rest, periodisations of the year with festivals, and so forth. To suggest that these complex performances have a 'content' that can be pried out of them, like shucking and consuming an oyster, suggests (surely unintentionally) a violent relation between philosopher and religious person. The ethnographer who describes a primitive rain dance in terms of the claims made about it by his informants ('we are trying to make it rain') or who tries to reduce it to his own claims ('they are trying to make it rain') fails from the start to notice the way in which language and ritual evoke a world in which rain may focus all sorts of concern, involve or exclude various participants, whose role in the community may be reflected or even determined by the part they play in the ritual, and so forth. It is a poor ethnographer who *already* knows what 'rain' signifies and tries to work out what claims about rain his informants might make. This is true *a fortiori* of practices of fasting, repetition of ancient prayers, burying the dead and so on. It is strange and slightly idiotic to try to get at the 'content' of a wedding or a baptism, especially when the central participants may themselves only discover what they were doing many years afterwards, if at all. Phrased even more critically, the distinction between 'shell' and 'content' is not native to the traditions themselves, but is imported from outside. From where? With what warrants is the distinction imported? Whose authority determines the way the distinction is made? Whose rules govern disagreements about what is shell and what is content? The list of questions can be extended indefinitely.

It is especially disappointing when this skewed perspective is reproduced and indeed amplified in the work of theologians. Something is badly wrong when the claim is made that 'propositional contents from religious life may crystallise within our discourses', without any reference to performance, or that 'the distinction between God and man' can be made without any reference to the notion of divine grace, or most bluntly: 'Philosophy is invited to listen to the propositional contents of religious traditions and to critically appropriate their semantic heritage.'[18] The impulse is understandable: there is a strong

[17] 'The Boundary between Faith and Knowledge', 213-4, 223.

[18] This particular example comes from the Christian Ethicist Stefan Heuser, but it is quite a widespread approach. See Stefan Heuser's review of my *Habermas and Theology* in *Political Theology* 9.4 (2008), 549. This particular example comes from the Christian Ethicist Stefan

liberal desire not only to be intelligible to a broad public, but to make a responsible and responsive contribution to that public's concerns. Yet Habermas himself is careful not to instrumentalise religious traditions so brutally: his interest is in how validity claims made within a tradition can be understood by those outside it, or how the density of religious practice enriches the lives of even resolutely secular members of society.[19]

Drawing attention to performance is not to deny, absurdly, that theology involves propositions, or to suggest, irresponsibly, that its propositions are of little importance. It is rather to insist that understanding those propositions means understanding the questions to which they are answers, and appreciating that those questions often arise because of uncertainties relating to the meanings of religious performance in the face of novelty or suffering.

Habermas asks the right questions, and articulates well-considered and important modes of repair in the face of urgent contemporary problems. His work is worth repairing in turn, for this reason. The best repairs are those that insist on closer attentiveness to the complexities of actual practice, and on more detailed historical investigations.

My two arguments can be brought together as a significant challenge to Habermas' recent work in relation to religious traditions. These are not merely a challenge to Habermas. To use Wittgenstein's terms, they challenge any impulse in philosophy that tries to distil the meaning of a proposition independently of the form of life, or more narrowly the language game, in which it arises. Religious claims are especially resistant to this distillation, not because they are a particular genus of claim but because they are often addressed quite precisely within and to a particular limited public. Others may listen in, especially when claims are made in public, but a proper engagement with those claims will entail learning the other's language and customs rather than attempting to reformulate the claims in ways that conform to the logic of common sense. To state the matter baldly, and simultaneously to address both questions – of 'discursive extraterritoriality' and of 'religious contents' – a flourishing sphere of public argumentation requires its participants to become ethnographers rather than theorists of communicative action.

Heuser, but it is quite a widespread approach. See Stefan Heuser's review of my *Habermas and Theology* in *Political Theology* 9.4 (2008), 549.

19 'Religion in the Public Sphere', 131.

WHAT IS RELIGION, AND WHAT IS RELIGION FOR? THOUGHTS IN LIGHT OF COMMUNICATIVE THEORY AND COMMUNICATIVE THEOLOGY

Edmund Arens

„In the beginning was the Word." (John 1, 1) That is not only the beginning of the Gospel of John. It is indeed a basic statement on communication, and it is a fundamental theological statement as well. There is no human existence without communication and action. Without communication, community is unthinkable. No society can survive or manage without communicative exchange, without discursive dispute and processes of understanding. Religion is also linked to communication in various respects. Religion and communication are profoundly connected with one another. It even can be claimed that religion *is* communication.[1]

Religion, I would like to affirm, is first and foremost not a „view of life," but rather a „way of life." In this respect, it is not primarily a world view, but fundamentally a performance or life practice. It is in this sense that the principle of the theological theory of action formulated by Helmut Peukert is to be taken: „Faith is itself a practice that, as a practice asserts God for others in communicative action and attempts to confirm this assertion in action."[2]

In the following, my approach to and conception of religion as communication and action are unfolded. This chapter takes five steps. The first sketches an understanding of religion as a practice coping with contingency and refers to positions that comprehend religion as essentially ritual practice. The second step briefly examines the relationship of religion and communicative action in conversation with Jürgen Habermas. The third section deals with the status of

[1] E. Arens, „Religion as Communication," in *Social Psychological Perspectives on Communication* (ed. D. Hook, B. Franks and M. Bauer, Houndsmill 2010). See also idem, *Gottesverständigung. Eine kommunikative Religionstheologie* (Freiburg 2007).

[2] H. Peukert, *Science, action and fundamental theology: Toward a theology of communicative action* (Cambridge 1984) 226. (German: idem, *Wissenschaftstheorie – Handlungstheorie – Fundamentale Theologie. Analysen zu Ansatz und Status theologischer Theoriebildung. Mit einem Vorwort zur Neuauflage und einem neuen Nachwort* (Frankfurt 2009) 331.

religion in post-secular society. In the fourth step, perspectives towards a communicative theological understanding of religion are addressed and significant forms of religious-communicative practice are developed. Finally, I conclude by pointing out some guidelines for communicative theology.

1. RELIGION AS PRACTICE COPING WITH CONTINGENCY OR RITUAL PRACTICE

In the modern age, the experience of the contingency of reality – including the contingency of one's own life – has become one of the basic problems of scientific theory and philosophical reflection. The German theologian Ernst Troeltsch already observed at the beginning of the 20th century that the problem of contingency contained all philosophical problems *in nuce* and simultaneously concerned religious questions.[3] The American philosopher Richard Rorty saw the problem of contingency as decisive for his position.[4] According to him, it is the experience that we are ourselves contingent, that we are what and how we are only by chance – be it through luck or unluck and from no rational ground and without general meaning or purpose. Everything that we know and have to accept is the „sheer contingency"[5] of existence.

For the German philosopher Hermann Lübbe the relevance, necessity, and future demand of religion are beyond doubt. In his well known work on *Religion after the Enlightenment,*[6] he pointedly maintains that in the process of modernization and secularization, religion does not just fundamentally fade and finally vanish, but merely changes its forms of cultural expression. Lübbe holds that religion, in the course of this process, basically rids itself of its political and social restrictions. By that it becomes able to adequately fulfil its genuine task. It is the task to cope with contingency. Lübbe describes this task as „practice coping with contingency." Colloquially, this would mean the practice of overcoming contingency. However, contingency in reality just cannot be overcome. He notes: „What shall then 'coping' mean? The answer is: Coping with contingency is accepting contingency."[7]

For Lübbe, religion deals with any contingency that bears on life's „indisposabilities." These indisposabilities are resistant to any enlightenment and emancipation. They are simply there, as we too are simply there. Lübbe emphasizes that it is nothing but sheer chance that we exist instead of not existing, that we are what we are and nothing else. This contingent fact does not in any way

[3] E. Troeltsch, „Contingency," in *Encyclopedia of Religion and Ethics*, Vol. IV (1911) 87-89, 89.

[4] Cf. R. Rorty, *Contingency, Irony, and Solidarity* (New York 1989).

[5] Ibid., 22.

[6] H. Lübbe, *Religion nach der Aufklärung* (Graz 1986); see also J. H. Franz, *Religion in der Moderne. Die Theorien von Jürgen Habermas und Hermann Lübbe* (Berlin 2009).

[7] Lübbe, ibid., 166.

allow to be transformed in any meaning of action. It must simply be taken as such and that means being accepted. According to him, this is precisely what takes place in the practice of religious life, which he conceives as intrinsically ritual. Rituals, he asserts, change nothing: They are there to confirm that which exists, to sanction and bless it. Lübbe refers to ritual ceremonies like the consecration of a new house, a new highway, or a new president. In such ritual-religious action, nothing is added to what the builder of the house or the highway have created: rather it is simply affirmed in the face of technical or institutional accomplishments that the event of the moment is nothing other than an island lapped by an ocean of contingencies and imponderabilities. According to Lübbe, the question does not concern whether such practice contains or refers to truth. He regards the question of truth as irrelevant in view of religion. What matters is whether religion really fulfils its function of coping with contingency through its acceptance of contingency.

On the one hand, Lübbe rightly calls religion a practice, a life practice, and he recognizes that it manifests itself above all in ritual. On the other hand, he strictly separates it from any moral, social, or political practice. He emphasizes that religion has nothing to do with action, but rather takes place in our head, in the spiritual acceptance of our sheer contingency. Contrary to Lübbe's own understanding, his conceptualization is obviously not simply analytic and certainly not value free. Rather, it affirms a bodiless, alienated „bourgeois religion"[8] separated from real life and action – neither putting it in question nor changing anything. Quite the reverse, it preserves, legitimates, and sanctions the given status quo. In this respect, the apparent affirmation of religion after the Enlightenment proves to be a distortion of at least Jewish and Christian, prophetic, biblical religion.

Religion is seen as ritual practice in Anglo-American social anthropology in particular. Of special interest are the works of Victor Turner, who studied the rites or rituals of passage and their characteristic features of what he calls the „ritual process."[9] From these rites of passage Turner determines three phases of ritual process, in which the religious dimensions and meanings of rituals simultaneously become evident.

The rituals of passage – which Turner studied with the Central African people of Ndembu – are, first, about one's removal of one from a given position in the group, community, or society; second, about a transitional phase in which the ritual subject no longer has the old, abandoned position, but does not yet have a new status; and, third, about the condition in which the passage is fulfilled, a new place or status reached, a new fixed position inside the group, community, or society is gained and occupied.

[8] Cf. J. B. Metz, *Jenseits bürgerlicher Religion* (Mainz 1980); idem., *Glaube in Geschichte und Gesellschaft. Studien zu einer praktischen Fundamentaltheologie* (Mainz 1977).

[9] V. Turner, *The ritual process: Structure and anti-structure*, (Chicago 1969); see also A. van Gennep, *Les rites de passages*, (Paris 1981); C. Bell, *Ritual Theory, Ritual Practice* (New York 1992); R. Rappaport, *Ritual and Religion in the Making of Humanity* (Cambridge 1999).

The middle or „margin" phase provides the key to understanding the ritual process, which Turner designates as „liminality." The characteristics of the „marginal condition" or „marginal person" are necessarily amorphous or undetermined. Marginal beings are „betwixt and between,"[10] they are neither here nor there; they are situated between socially fixed positions and are not integrated into the social structure. From this perspective they appear as outsiders, as frontier runners. In the condition of liminality, however, something fundamental happens for ritual subjects. They have the experience of an alternative form of human relations that is opposed to the social structure. Turner calls this „communitas." While the social structure represents a hierarchically arranged system of fixed positions, the *communitas* is an unstructured and relatively undifferentiated „communion of equal individuals who submit together to the general authority of the ritual elders."[11] In the ritual *communitas* there is no top and no bottom: In the intermediate stage of statuslessness, an egalitarian community is experienced and practiced. The „margin" condition of spontaneous, concrete *communitas* comes into opposition with the status system of the norm-regulated social structure.

Turner, indeed, discovers a religious, sacred quality in the margin phase. According to him, the religious quality of the marginal position in complex societies is conserved in religious performances and institutions. From his point of view, the quality of transitional religious life appears nowhere „more clearly marked and defined than in the monastic and mendicant states in the great world religions."[12] The monastic communities and orders would therefore be something like institutionalized liminality, or *communitas.* Turner is, in this context, expressly alluding to the rule of the order of the holy Benedict, and he treats Francis of Assisi's movement of voluntary poverty under the rubric of permanent liminality.

For theistic religions, worship obviously is a central ritual practice. The worship form of ritual action is often dealt with under the concept of the cult. The German philosopher Richard Schaeffler emphasizes three distinctive features of cultic action. The cult is first, according to him, the action of worship; second, ritual action; and third, religious celebration.[13] Viewed for a phenomenological point of view, the cult is a community action in which groups by means of external actions come into relation with supernatural powers. The cult is therefore an event of communication. It is, first, a community action of an action-community, whose members communicate with a supernatural power and

[10] V. Turner, „Betwixt and Between. The Liminal Period in Rites of Passage," in *The Forest of Symbols. Aspects of Ndembu Ritual* (Ithaca 1967) 93-111.

[11] Turner, *The ritual process,* 96.

[12] Ibid., 107.

[13] Cf. R. Schaeffler, „Der Kultus als Weltauslegung," in *Kult in der säkularisierten Welt* (B. Fischer et al., Regensburg 1974) 9-62; idem, „Kultisches Handeln. Die Frage nach Proben seiner Bewährung und nach Kriterien seiner Legitimation," in idem and P. Hünermann, *Ankunft Gottes und Handeln des Menschen* (Freiburg 1977) 9-50.

simultaneously interact with each other. This happens, as a rule, in the form of a regulated, ritualized action in which the areas of authority and roles of the participants are carefully distributed. Cultic community action is, secondly, spatially and temporary bound; it takes place in particular situations at fixed times in designated places. The cult, thirdly, makes use of definite media in which, among other things, language and music, gestures and gesticulations are in play and now and then join together in highly complex rituals and dramas. Fourthly, the objects of cultic action are supernatural powers, to whom or which worship or veneration are shown; they are communicated with, in the case of personally presented powers, through prayer and sacrifice. The goals of such cultic action are, fifthly, the magical influence and steering of material powers on the one hand, and on the other, personal communication with the deity. Face to face with the deity the cultic community experiences itself; it is thus constituted and articulated in worship, sacrifice, pleas, and gratitude.

Religious-ritual action creates, strengthens, and transforms community. However, it may not only establish *communitas*, but can also become neurotically compulsive in the Freudian sense; it can degenerate into magical effective-thinking and spiritless ritualism. The cult is thus constantly threatened with corruption and can degenerate into the demonstration of religious claims to power. To be sure, the question of power is deeply connected with ritual action.[14] Ritual action structured as or shaped by power brings about the critique of ritual. This critique contests either the very possibility and validity of cultic action in general, or it aims directly – like the prophetic critique of the cult – at „true worship," at the proper relation of cultic-ritual and ethical-communicative action.

2. Religion and Communicative Action

Jürgen Habermas, the outstanding contemporary representative of the Frankfurt School of Critical Theory, has developed a highly differentiated, comprehensive and furthermore globally discussed communicative theory of action.[15] The basic distinctions of the theory elaborated by Habermas contain

[14] Cf. Bell, *Ritual Theory*; D. J. Kertzer, *Ritual, Politics, and Power* (New Haven 1988); *Spektakel der Macht. Rituale im Alten Europa 800–1800* (ed. B. Stollberg-Rilinger, Darmstadt 2008).

[15] Cf. J. Habermas, *Theorie des kommunikativen Handelns.* 2 Bde. (Frankfurt 1981); idem, *Faktizität und Geltung. Beiträge zur Diskurstheorie des Rechts und des demokratischen Rechtsstaats* (Frankfurt 1992); idem, *Die Einbeziehung der Anderen. Studien zur politischen Theorie* (Frankfurt 1996); idem, *Wahrheit und Rechtfertigung* (Frankfurt 1999). Habermas's works have been taken up from a theological perspective in a growing number of publications. Cf. Peukert, *Wissenschaftstheorie;* E. Arens, *Christopraxis. Grundzüge theologischer Handlungstheorie* (Freiburg 1992); *Habermas und die Theologie. Beiträge zur theologischen Diskussion, Rezeption und Kritik der Theorie kommunikativen Handelns* (ed. idem, Düsseldorf ^{2}1989); *Kommunikatives Handeln*

essential elements for current social-, action-, and communications-theoretic theory-formation. Let me just mention some of those distinctions: first the opposition of agreement-oriented or communicative action and result-oriented or strategic action, then the difference between action and action-relieved discourse, further between real and ideal communication communities. Also important is Habermas's differentiation of validity claims of truth, truthfulness, and rightness; the analysis of the polarity of lifeworld and system, as well as communicative and instrumental rationality. The different elements of Habermas's theory can also be made religion-theoretically fruitful.

However, the Frankfurt philosopher has, for a long time, taken the view that religion and communication are incompatible.[16] In his main systematic work, *The Theory of Communicative Action*, he develops a sophisticated theory of society, action, communication, and rationality alongside a rudimentary theory of religion. His both religion-theoretical and religion-critical position at this stage contains the central thesis of the „linguistification of the sacred."[17] According to this thesis, the religious-metaphysical conceptions and worldviews become untenable in the process of social rationalization and the formation of modern structures of consciousness; they become, as he calls it, „obsolete." The stage of social evolution reached with modernity differentiates the once-combined dimensions of moral-practical rationality in religion into right and morals. In his view, the religious ethic of brotherliness cultivated especially in the Judeo-Christian tradition, entered into „a communicative ethic detached from its foundation in salvation religion."[18] Thereby religious ethic is both superseded and preserved in secular form.

According to Habermas, religious practice did not only have an ethical orientation, but a ritual shape as well. It became obsolete, when it passed its functions of social integration and expression, once fulfilled by ritual praxis, over to communicative action. The authority of the sacred was thereby progressively substituted by the authority of a justifiably held consensus. Consequently, communicative action is separated and released from sacredly protected normative contexts. The result of his understanding of the development of religion is that

und christlicher Glaube. Ein theologischer Diskurs mit Jürgen Habermas (ed. idem, Paderborn 1997); H. Düringer, *Universale Vernunft und partikularer Glaube. Eine theologische Auswertung des Werkes von Jürgen Habermas* (Leuven 1999); N. Adams, *Habermas and Theology* (Cambridge 2006); Moderne Religion? Theologische und religionsphilosophische Reaktionen auf Jürgen Habermas (ed. K. Wenzel and Thomas M. Schmidt, Freiburg 2009).

[16] Cf. E. Arens, „Kommunikative Rationalität und Religion," in idem, O. John and P. Rottländer, *Erinnerung, Befreiung, Solidarität. Benjamin, Marcuse, Habermas und die politische Theologie* (Düsseldorf 1991) 145-200; G. M. Simpson, *Critical Social Theory: Prophetic Reason, Civil Society, and Christian Imagination* (Minneapolis 2001).

[17] Cf. J. Habermas, *TheTheory of Communicative Action: Lifeworld and System.* Vol. II. (Boston 1989) 77-111.

[18] J. Habermas, *The Theory of Communicative Action: Reason and theRrationalization of Society.* Vol. I. (Boston 1984) 242.

religion belongs to a past stage of humanity, which has in the meantime been superseded by modernity. Religion thereby loses its cognitive, expressive, and moral-practical content; it resolves itself into a communicative ethic. Free and unrestricted communication thus takes the place of religion.

Habermas's view of religion has changed significantly in the last two decades. Already in his collected essays on postmetaphysical thinking, a notably clear change has come about in his interpretation. Although it speaks more of the necessary appropriation of religious thought, it nevertheless does so without maintaining their supersession and dissolution. As the Frankfurt philosopher points out, he does not believe that „we, as Europeans, can seriously understand concepts like morality and ethical life, persona and individuality, or freedom and emancipation, without appropriating the substance of the Judeo-Christian understanding of history in terms of salvation."[19] The rhetorical power of religious speech retains its privilege so long as there is found no more convincing expression for those experiences and innovations which it still preserves.

The change of Habermas's views became obvious in his famous Frankfurt Peace Prize speech on „Faith and Knowledge"[20] in October 2001. He, who still regards himself as „religiously unmusical," in his Frankfurt speech made it clear that religion hasn't gone. It still represents a relevant and highly ambiguous factor to be taken seriously in today's society. For him, the menacing dimension of religion had become conspicuous with the terror attacks of September 11, 2001, when the „tension between secular society and religion...exploded."[21] Nevertheless, in contrast to a fundamentalism that has become terroristic, there are also religious forms and religious communities that deserve the predicate of „reasonable." Habermas now acknowledges, not only that the egalitarian law based on reason has religious roots, but that the boundaries between secular and religious reasons is more fluid than he first envisaged. Thus, according to him, „the determining of these controversial boundaries should therefore be seen as a cooperative task which requires *both* sides to take on the perspective of the other one."[22]

Cooperation, to be sure, presupposes communication. Indeed, the great philosopher of communication reiterates that the resources of religion and its semantic potential have to be translated by philosophy. But even if he remains cautious in view of theology, he nevertheless accepts in the meantime that faith and knowledge, religion and reason, theology and philosophy are not simply antipodes of which one pole belongs to the future, while the other is now

[19] J. Habermas, *Postmetaphysical thinking* (Cambridge 1992) 15.

[20] J. Habermas, *Glauben und Wissen. Friedenspreis des Deutschen Buchhandels* (Frankfurt 2001); (English: J. Habermas, „Faith and Knowledge," in *The Frankfurt School on Religion: Key Writings by the Major Thinkers* (ed. E. Mendieta, Milton Park 2005) 327-337; see also *Glauben und Wissen. Ein Symposium mit Jürgen Habermas* (ed. R. Langthaler and H. Nagl-Docekal, Wien 2007).

[21] Habermas, *Faith* 327.

[22] Vattimo, *Beyond Interpretation*, 13.

disappearing into the Hades of history. Both are rather dependent on the reciprocal communication of each other as well as on the productive dispute with one another. In those disputes the issue is above all the basic questions of human life and survival. This once more became clear in the surprising debate between Habermas and former Cardinal Ratzinger about the „dialectics of secularization" which took place in Munich in January 2004.[23]

Religion is connected with and has to do with communication. Habermas puts it this way: „From the beginning, the voice of God calling into life communicates within a morally sensitive universe."[24] Even those who, like himself, do not believe in the theological premises of the concept of creation, can nevertheless understand its semantic potential and approve of its social consequences. The discourse between religious and secular forms of communication essentially concerns a socially pressing agreement about humane practice.

In the meanwhile, Habermas decisively opposes an „unfair exclusion of religions from the public sphere,"[25] and at the same time firmly insists that even the secular side has to „remain sensitive to the force of articulation inherent in religious language."[26] Inherent in religion is thus a communicative potential that is of undeniable importance, especially in the post-secular age of globalization and genetic technology, in which fundamentalist regression on the one side and scientific-technological transformation on the other pose serious challenges to society. Given the seemingly unbridgeable clash of social and cultural worlds that are in need to develop a common language, and given the polarized positions generated by the reproduction and possible bio-technological production of „human nature"[27], one begins to realize that religion is in no way merely a private matter. On the contrary, religion is part of the public sphere; it belongs into public discourse. Here it is able to demonstrate its argumentative power of persuasion and its performative power of change. Its potential and power consist not in coming to terms with past injustice and suffering, but rather in bringing to mind a „consciousness of that what is lacking"[28], in calling into question „immutables," for example, through the speech and acts of memory, forgiveness and the promise of salvation and reconciliation.

[23] Cf. J. Habermas and J. Ratzinger, *Dialektik der Säkularisierung. Über Vernunft und Religion* (Freiburg 2005); see also J. Habermas, *Between Naturalism and Religion* (Cambridge 2008).

[24] Habermas, *Faith* 336.

[25] Ibid., 332.

[26] Ibid.

[27] Cf. J. Habermas, *The Future of Human Nature* (Cambridge 2003).

[28] Cf. *Ein Bewußtsein von dem, was fehlt. Eine Diskussion mit Jürgen Habermas* (ed. M. Reder and J. Schmidt, Frankfurt 2008); Peukert, *Wissenschaftstheorie*; J. B. Metz, *Memoria passionis. Ein provozierendes Gedächtnis in pluralistischer Gesellschaft* (Freiburg 2006).

3. Religion in Post-secular Society

The controversial concept of „post-secular society" has been introduced in Habermas's Frankfurt Peace Prize speech.[29] By this concept he distances himself both from progressist-optimistic theories of secularization and their replacement model and from an expropriation model advocated leading to an „unsheltered modernity" lamented by conservative critics of modernity. According to Habermas, a society can be called post-secular if it „adapts to the fact that religious communities continue to exist in a context of ongoing secularization."[30] First of all, the concept acknowledges the social fact that neither religion vanished from modern society nor has it become strictly privatized and thus lost any public meaning. Secondly, a change of consciousness that is taking place in secularized societies is addressed. And thirdly, the concept marks a cognitive and normative challenge for the interrelation and interaction of the secular and the religious side.

Habermas discovers the fact of a worldwide return of religion. The „vitality of the religious" for him can be detected from the missionary vigour of the great world religions, where, to be sure, orthodox and conservative groups are gaining ground. He also mentions the political instrumentalization of religion which, in his view, leads to the unbinding of religious potentials of violence. The „post-secular" change of consciousness compasses three elements. On the one hand, there is a significant change of public mind achieved by the media presence of worldwide conflicts in which religious matters and activities are involved. On the other hand, religion regains relevance in the realm of national publics, in which religious communities intervene with their outspoken contributions. Finally, a post-secular consciousness is the result of the fact that more and more immigrants form countries with traditional cultures are present in modern immigration societies where dissonances between different religions go together with the challenge of a pluralism of forms of life.[31]

[29] Cf. Habermas, *Faith* 329ff; see the criticism by H. Joas, „Religion post-säkular? Zu einer Begriffsprägung von Jürgen Habermas," in idem, *Braucht der Mensch Religion?* (Freiburg 2004) 122-128; H.-J. Höhn, Postsäkular. Gesellschaft im Umbruch – Religion im Wandel (Paderborn 2007); S. Grotefeld, „Postsäkulare Gesellschaft und säkularer Staat. Über öffentliche Vernunft aus protestantischer Sicht," in *Religiöse Überzeugungen und öffentliche Vernunft* (ed. F.-J. Bormann and B. Irlenborn, Freiburg 2008) 281-303; E. Arens, „Was die moderne Gesellschaft von den Religionen erwartet. Der Ansatz von Jürgen Habermas," in *Orientierung und Innovation. Beiträge der Kirche für Staat und Gesellschaft* (ed. B. Nacke, Freiburg 2009) 149-165.

[30] Habermas, *Faith* 329.

[31] Cf. J. Habermas, „Die Dialektik der Säkularisierung," in *Blätter für deutsche und internationale Politik* 4/2008, 33-46. See also J. Casanova, „Are We Still Secular? Exploring the Post-Secular: Three Meanings of 'the Secular' and their possible transcendence," http://www.crs.uu.se/fledownload.php?id=275

In a post-secular society both secular and religious citizens face specific cognitive and normative challenges in view of their self-understanding and their interrelation with one another. In a post-secular society, believers, persons of a different faith and nonbelievers have to learn to get along with one another. Habermas, the thinker of communicative rationality, realizes that there is a necessity of cooperation between the secular and the religious side; the cooperative task, as mentioned already, „requires *both* sides to take on the perspective of the other one."[32] In the course of the modernization of public consciousness, both secular and religious mentalities become reflexive. Through this process for both sides the possibility emerges to see oneself and the other involved in a common and complementary process of learning in which both are enabled to take serious their contributions in the public sphere, and to do so inspite of their ongoing dissonances, differences and dissent.

3. Towards a Communicative Theology of Religion

The approach of Habermas's communicative theory of action provides not only a productive social- and action-theoretic apparatus. His reflections on the basic distinctions and intentions of communicative action are also significant from a religion-theoretic view. His considerations about religion are capable of being integrated into a communicative theology of religion.

In this respect, one should reject the confrontation of communicative reason and religion, which Habermas admittedly put forth several times before his Frankfurt Peace Prize speech. A contrasting of the two is from his own understanding of communicative rationality not tenable, because communicative reason cannot *eo ipso* exclude religion and distance itself from something which belongs to it. Within the bounds of a procedural communicative rationality alone can what religion has to bring to it be proved by participating in the procedure of argumentation and in conversation or discourse with those taking part. This could thus be found in a discourse with the members or representatives of various religions and mutually clarified in a cooperative search for truth. This cooperative search for truth now is agreed by Habermas when he calls for the establishment of an already fluid, disputed boundary between secular and religious reasons to be understood as a cooperative task, which has to be taken up by both sides.

Within a communicative approach, I suggest that the following claims can be made: Religion is itself a constitutive communicative practice, which is genuinely inter-subjective and agreement-oriented. Within a particular religion a variety of forms of communication take place, in the form of different speech acts enacted by its members. These speech acts go along with non-linguistic actions – e.g. gestures and other types of behaviour. All these performances or

[32] Habermas, *Faith* 332.

„doings" are embedded in a comprehensive life practice. Such life practice is carried out on the part of, as well as within a communication community. Religious communities of communication in these actions give expression to their obligations to and responsibility in view of a transcendent reality. And doing so, they create, maintain, question and change community.

If the agreement-orientation represents the distinctive feature of communicative action, then religious practice itself can be viewed as communicative – if and insofar as it is directed at a reality in which people do not deal with one another strategically, that means, do not functionalize, and misuse the other as an instrument for one's own purpose.[33] Genuine religious action is oriented at a reality, in which people mutually recognize, associate with, and experience each other in solidarity and in so doing act together. This community-related and agreement-oriented character of religion, indeed, implies a significant difference to magic. The decisive difference can be formulated in this manner: Whereas religion represents an inter-subjective, consensus-dependent, and agreement-oriented practice originating in and linked to communities, magic has a tendency towards strategic-instrumental dealings and rather „monological" (hier fehlt wohl ein Substantiv oder „dealings" gehört hierher verschoben) with the external, social, or rather inner „world."[34]

In communicative-religious action, semantic contents are always brought forth. Thus, religion must not be restricted to an inspiring and stimulating rhetorical power, as on several occasions Habermas proposed; but it is also semantic, that is, discloses and names a reality. This reality for human life and coexistence brings forth a crucial semantic dimension, namely the dimension of promise. It is the promise of a relieving and reconciling liberation from political, social, physical and psychic bondage and mortality's grip. In such religious speech and communal practices we find both a semantic and a performative-practical surplus. Of course, this surplus can be translated into philosophical speech, but cannot be transformed without residue. In communicative-religious speech and action, according to my understanding, there are different potentials involved: a *creative*, that is, a reality-disclosing potential; an *innovative*, namely a reality-transforming potential; and an *anamnestic* potential of memory and remembrance, which becomes aware of and tries to do justice to the reality of the victims of history. From the perspective of the religious communities, such innovative-anamnestic religious action can be understood as communicative faith practice.[35] Religion is performed in the

[33] Cf. E. Arens, „Quellen und Kräfte konsumtiver, kommunikativer und kritischer Religion," in *Bulletin ET (Special Issue: Consuming Religion in Europe? Christian Faith Challenged by Consumer Culture*, ed. L. Boeve) 17 (2006) 29-53; this Bulletin ET contains a critical conversation with: V. J. Miller, *Consuming Religion. Christian Faith and Practice in a Consumer Culture* (New York 2004) and a response by Miller: ibid. 164-178.

[34] This is important for example in order to understand Jesus's communicative practice of healing in the right way; cf. G. Theißen and A. Merz, *The Historical Jesus* (London 1998).

[35] Cf. Peukert, *Wissenschaftstheorie*; E. Arens (ed.), *Gottesrede – Glaubenspraxis. Grundzüge theologischer Handlungstheorie* (Darmstadt 1994); idem, *Gottesverständigung*.

communicative practice of people, who in their communicative, communal, and critical actions communicate either *with* or *about a* reality – in the theistic religions, with or about *a* reality called „God."

Within the monotheistic religions of Abrahamic origin, Judaism, Christianity and Islam, two basic forms of religious-communicative action are recognizable: the act of witnessing and of confessing. Witnessing points to the reality of God in a most personal way; the transcendent reality is made accessible via self-involving action of the witness. In his or her own action and by his or her own person the witness discloses and makes visible what is of utmost importance and relevance. The witness acts as a „human medium."[36] He or she gives testimony and communicates in order to convince others of this reality. Witnessing is either missionary, or diaconal, or prophetic, or pathic, that is, taking place in suffering. In the last case, *martyria* becomes martyrdom. I consider witnessing as agreement-oriented, that means: witnessing aims at convincing. This includes a decisive difference to confessing. Confessing does not aim at convincing; it, rather, publicly and obligingly gives expression to an already realized common conviction. Confessing involves achieving consensus, or rather, performing and thus communicating it: Confessing can only be done on the basis of an agreement, which manifests itself in the confessional text, for example the Jewish *Shema Israel*, the Muslim *Shahada* or the Christian Creed.[37] The consensus and commonality once professed is actualized in the acts of confessing or professing.

Besides these elementary actions of faith practice characteristic of monotheistic religions, namely that of witnessing and of confessing, various other forms of religious-communicative practice can be traced across a variety of religions. In the case of Abrahamic religions, those forms are interwoven with witnessing and confessing and therefore overlapping. Five religious speech-acts shall be dealt with: the practices of remembering, narrating, celebrating, proclaiming, and sharing.

Remembering is indispensable of human life and living together. Remembering is a fundamental individual and collective practice which links us to our personal and communal past. Our memory forms, contains and communicates answers to questions like who we are, where we come from, where we belong to, and what makes up our identity. As individuals, communities and societies are unable to exist without memory.[38] Religions also depend on traditions and practices of remembering. Religion indeed can be considered „as a chain of memory."[39] The cultural

[36] W. Faulstich, *Das Medium als Kult. Von den Anfängen bis zur Spätantike (8. Jahrhundert)* (Göttingen 1997).

[37] Cf. Rappaport, *Ritual*; E. Arens, *Bezeugen und Bekennen. Elementare Handlungen des Glaubens* (Düsseldorf 1989); idem, *Christopraxis*; J. Pelikan, *Credo. Historical and Theological Guide to Creeds and Confessions of Faith in the Christian Tradition* (New Haven 2003).

[38] Cf. P. Ricoeur, *Memory, History, Forgetting* (Chicago 2004).

[39] D. Hervieu-Léger, *Religion as a Chain of Memory* (New Brunswick 2000); see also *Erinnern. Erkundungen zu einer theologischen Basiskategorie* (ed. P. Petzel and N. Reck, Darmstadt 2003).

memory, in which the formative and normative events of the collective past which „must not be forgotten" are kept in mind, is enacted above all in festivities and ritual celebrations.[40] Religious remembrance includes the memory of the dead and it should comprise the memory of the victims and of their suffering. According to Critical Theory and Political Theology, it should not be restricted to the memory of one's own history but include the whole history of suffering. Remembrance thus becomes „memoria passionis" and it is enacted as „anamnestic solidarity."[41]

Religions tell stories. They do not only speak of God or of Gods, but also of the founders and paradigmatic figures of their religious traditions, whose actions they recount. The cosmic event „in the beginning", the creation of the world and of people, primeval times, the origin of death, as well as the beginnings of ones own tradition, are the subjects of religious narratives, from creation-myths and myths of primeval times to foundational stories.[42] Narrating plays an important role for the development and maintenance of both personal and social identity – and religious identity as well. In a way, we are what we have been told and what we tell our children, friends and fellow believers.[43]

Communicative-religious practice involves the narrating of stories of promise, liberation, exodus, faith and hope. Through these stories the semantic content of religion is communicated, preserved und passed on. Judaeo-Christian faith has a „narrative depth structure."[44] Narrating faith stories implies their interpretation and contextualization to the present situation of action. Indeed, narration makes an invitation to imagine the present situation in the light of the faith story and to act therein in a particular way. Telling God's story and faith stories is communicative-religious practice because religion lives, remains alive and is handed down in these stories; its contents and intentions are remembered and actualized by and in them.

Communicative-religious practice further comprises celebrating.[45] Service to God or worship in Christianity and other religions has the character of celebration. Liturgical celebration is a powerful expression of the participants' experiences of community, of their communal interconnectedness; it is an expression and

[40] Cf. J. Assmann, *Religion and Cultural Memory* (Stanford 2006); *Das Fest und das Heilige. Religiöse Kontrapunkte zur Alltagswelt* (ed. J. Assmann, Gütersloh 1991).

[41] Cf. Metz, *Memoria passionis*; Peukert, *Wissenschaftstheorie*. See also W. Benjamin, „Theses on the Philosophy of History," in *The Frankfurt School on Religion*, 265-273.

[42] Cf. the extensive work of M. Eliade, *A history of Religious Ideas*. 3 Vols (Chicago 1978-1985).

[43] Cf. P. Ricoeur, *Time and Narrative*. 3 Vols (Chicago 1984-1988); idem, *Oneself as Another* (Chicago 1992).

[44] Cf. Metz, *Glaube*, 18.

[45] Cf. *Celebration. Studies in Festivity and Ritual* (ed. V. Turner, Washington 1982); S. Garrigan *Beyond Ritual. Sacramental Theology after Habermas* (Aldershot 2004); E. Arens, „Liturgisches Handeln als performativer Vollzug und religiöse Praxis. Die Perspektive einer kommunikativen Religionstheologie," in *Liturgisches Handeln und soziale Praxis* (ed. J. Brademann and W. Freitag, Münster 2010).

practice of *communitas.* On the one hand, ritual-liturgical action often implies a manifestation and performance of hierarchical power relations; on the other hand, these relations are interrupted and transgressed. An imaginative participation and embedding into a greater or even unlimited community of memory and hope is experienced. Hence, an opening or widening of agency takes place. Liturgical celebration can be understood as „practice of hope". Celebrating is a decisive communicative-religious practice in which God's saving reality and surpassing action is actualized, narrated, lauded and performed.

A fourth form of communicative-religious practice is proclaiming. Thereby, religious content and meaning is communicated in order that it shall be shared. Proclaiming makes known the meaning of a religion and is in this respect informative. This happens of course in the sense of an engaged and evocative communication, which intends that the addressees make what is communicated their own. Proclaiming emphasizes impressing the prevailing religious message upon the addressees while taking into account the situation of its listeners. There is thus a missionary element within proclaiming. Proclaiming aims at persuading people into a religion or – in the case of those who already possess religious conviction – at reinforcing, defending, strengthening, or perfecting such conviction.

Besides the missionary aspect, another important moment of proclaiming is encountered in the Abrahamic religions. It led to their qualification as prophetic religions. In fact, prophetic proclaiming is an important element for Judaism, Christianity, and Islam. The prophet is first of all the one who proclaims God's word and will. Prophetic action is performed in speech acts, symbolic and subversive actions. The Biblical prophets first and foremost criticise their community „from within."[46] They raise critical objections against the prevailing political and religious powers in the name of God. They intervene in God's „lawsuits" with the world or with idols and take God's side. For the Biblical prophets God's side is the side of the powerless, the poor, and the victims. Prophetic practice uncovers and denounces political, social, economic, and religious injustice and oppression. Prophetic proclamation, at the same time, announces God's promise of a new, just, and benevolent order. Prophetic practice thus accompanies the „condemnation of sinful conditions" with the „heralding of a new world."[47] A fifth form of communicative-religious action is sharing. This is a general term for what in biblical Christian terminology is called diaconal action or *caritas.* Such practice of benevolence, compassion, pity, and solidarity is central for all religions; it belongs everywhere to the ethical, communicative core of religion. The practice of sharing creates, strengthens, and transforms community in particular ways. All religions have their ideas about how the goods of the earth – the material as the spiritual, the social as the communal goods –

[46] M. Walzer, *Interpretation and Social Criticism* (Cambridge 1990).

[47] J. Comblin, *Das Bild des Menschen* (Düsseldorf 1987) 37. See also G. Gutiérrez, *A Theology of Liberation* (Maryknoll 1988); *Prophetie in einer etablierten Kirche? Aktuelle Reflexionen über ein Prinzip kirchlicher Identität* (ed. R. Bucher and R. Krockauer, Münster 2004).

are to be shared. Sharing „is here not meant in the sense of occasional conduct, but rather as a definite form of living and dealing with each other. It is the expression of a deep-reaching consciousness of solidarity." It enables people to mutually engage in a liable, reliable and lasting life practice. „Sharing, thus understood, is the most radical form of communicative practice, in that those involved share with and participate in one another."[48]

4. Guidelines for a Communicative Theology

Communicative Christian theology, elaborated in conversation and discourse with existing conceptions of religion, ritual theory and Habermas's theory of communicative action, can be characterized by five marks:

First: Christian theology is both scholarly and public practice – the case is thus „doing theology". As scientific theology it takes place within the framework of the scientific community. It is bound to the principles and procedures of public scientific communication, and it aims at argumentative discourse and discursive agreement.[49]

Secondly: Christian theology is a communal practice which at the same time is done within an ecclesial framework.[50] Thus, theology serves the communication community called the church. It implies a critical analysis and reflection of communicative ecclesial faith practice. In doing so, it is oriented at inspiring and helping the church in her communication of the gospel and stimulates the Christian community to become even more communicative.

Thirdly: Christian theology is done within the horizon of the Judaeo-Christian tradition and in the context of other religions. In Catholic Fundamental Theology religion appears as an important and relevant subject.[51] Both, the history and presence of religion and religions form the background of biblical, systematic and practical theology. Theology is in need of conversation and dispute with other disciplines in general and with religious studies in particular. However, if theology no longer analyses and affirms the validity claims of truth, rightness and truthfulness implied in Christian faith, it does not achieve its purpose. Normative God-talk, consequently, turns into descriptive cultural studies.

Fourthly: Christian communicative theology tries to unfold, how communicative faith practice is done in a whole variety of forms and figures. It explains that faith practice takes place on a personal, a communal and a societal level; it

[48] N. Mette, „(Religions-)Pädagogisches Handeln," in *Gottesrede*, 164-184, 182.

[49] Cf. *Wieviel Theologie verträgt die Öffentlichkeit?* (ed. E. Arens and H. Hoping, Freiburg 2000).

[50] Cf. *Bindung an die Kirche oder Autonomie? Theologie im gesellschaftlichen Diskurs* (ed. A. Franz, Freiburg 1999); C. Sedmak, *Theologie in nachtheologischer Zeit* (Mainz 2003).

[51] Cf. D. Tracy, *Plurality and Ambiguity. Hermeneutics, Religion, Hope* (San Francisco 1987); J. Werbick, *Den Glauben verantworten. Eine Fundamentaltheologie* (Freiburg 2000); M. Knapp, *Die Vernunft des Glaubens. Einführung in die Fundamentaltheologie* (Freiburg 2009).

is done in different actions of faith. Theology seeks to elaborate that faith practice is directed at the reality of God. The communication of the reality of God pursues the goal that people will be persuaded of this creative, redemptive and liberating reality, and that the human, worldly, as well as cosmic reality will be transformed in the direction of this ultimate reality.

Fifthly: Christian Theology implies a communicative and critical theory of religion, which includes the analysis of strategic distortions and violent corruptions of religions and religious actions.[52] This means the uncovering of untruth, injustice and ideological veiling, the denunciation of power structures, the inclusion of the excluded, remembrance of the victims of history, society, and church. At the same time, Christian theology reflects on the communicative religious potentials, that is, those perspectives directed at justice, solidarity and sharing. These communicative potentials encompass the practical acknowledgement of others including other religions and the common search for truth and understanding.

[52] Cf. H. Peukert, „Kommunikatives Handeln, Systeme der Machtsteigerung und die unvollendeten Projekte Aufklärung und Theologie," in *Habermas und die Theologie*, 39-64; *The Frankfurt School on Religion*; R. J. Siebert, *Manifesto of the Critical Theory of Society and Religion*. 3 Vols (Leiden 2010).

TOWARDS A THICKER DESCRIPTION OF TRANSCENDENCE

Michael Hoelzl

Jürgen Habermas' Philosophy of religion

To what extent can we speak of a Habermasian philosophy of religion? If philosophy of religion is understood in a traditional sense of what in German academia is called *Religionsphilosophie*, then the answer will be a negative one. Despite some indications Habermas has not published a philosophy of religion which addresses phenomena like myth, ritual, the sacred or religious prohibitions so far. But, in a recent interview with Eduardo Mendieta the interviewer refers to a manuscript by Habermas called „The Sacred Roots of the Axial Age Traditions" that seems to be a proposal to fill that gap in Habermas' philosophy of religion. Habermas outlines the thesis of the manuscript, or to be precise „a chapter of work in progress", which is worth quoting at length:

> Religions do not survive without the cultic activities of a congregation. That is their 'unique distinguishing feature' [Alleinstellungsmerkmal]. In modernity, they are the only configuration of spirit [Gestalt des Geistes] that still has access to the world of experience of ritual in the strict sense. Philosophy can only recognize religion as a different and yet contemporary configuration of spirit if it takes this archaic element seriously, without devaluing it a fortiori. After all, ritual has been a source of societal solidarity for which the enlightened morality of equal respect for all does not provide a real, motivational equivalent—nor do Aristotelian virtue ethics and the ethics of the good. This of course in no way precludes the possibility that this source, protected in the meantime by religious communities, and often used toward politically questionable ends, will run dry one day.[1]

[1] J. Habermas, „A Postsecular World Society? On the Philosophical Significance of Postsecular Consciousness and the Multicultural World Society," 5. Available at: http://blogs.ssrc.org /tif/wp-content/uploads/2010/02/A-Postsecular-World-Society-TIF.pdf. [italics MH].

This quotation is revealing for at least three reasons. First, Philosophy is claimed to be coexisting with theology and philosophy has to accept the autonomy and independence of religion. Secondly, religions can only exist if they are centred on „the cultic activities of a congregation". To a certain extent Habermas, as will see in the next chapter, refers to rituals and cults once more in his work and therefore returns to his hypothesis of the transformation of the sacred into language.[2] It also shows his profound indebtedness to Emil Durkheim's definition and understanding of religion. According to Durkheim „[a] religion is a unified systems of beliefs and practices relative to sacred things, that is to say, things set apart and forbidden – beliefs and practices which unite into one single moral community called Church, all those who adhere to them. The second element which thus finds a place in our definition is no less essential than the first; for by showing that the idea of religion is inseparable from that of the Church, it makes it clear that religion should be an eminently collective thing."[3] For Durkheim a religion without a church or any form of institutionally organised community of believers is just magic. That of course is a controversial claim and it would be of interest whether Habermas is willing to follow Durkheim in this respect. In other words, the question is whether Habermas is willing to subscribe to such a strong collectivist understanding of religion, or whether his understaning of religion is informed by the hypothetical scenario of the one before God. Thirdly, Habermas still emphasises that there is no guarantee that religion will persist. Therefore it is not clear whether religious rituals as a 'source of societal solidarity' will 'run dry one day'.[4] The view of religion as a source of societal solidarity is once again very close to Durkheim's understanding of the social function of religion. Though the problematic question is whether with the end of religious rituals societal solidarity necessarily must also come to an end or whether society will find alternative mechanism to provide and produce solidarity. Furthermore, a constant problem with Habermas' understanding of religion or, as we will see later, theology is that he never qualifies or disqualifies certain religions with respect to their role they should play for society. Which concrete religion or religions and what kind of theology or theologies are acceptable and needed and which are not? And what are the normative criteria to make this distinction? These questions lead us to Habermas' conversation with theology. But beforehand some remarks on the shifts in Habermas' view on religion should be made.

[2] J. Habermas, *Theorie des Kommunikativen Handelns*, Vol 2 (Frankfurt: Suhrkamp, 1987 [4th ed] 118-119.

[3] É. Durkheim, *The Elementary Forms of the Religious Life* (New York: Collier Books, 1961) 62-3.

[4] For the problem this causes for the phenomenon of solidarity, or, in theological language 'the challenge of the sacrificial victim', see: M. Hoelzl, Recognising the Sacrificial Victim: The Problem of Solidarity for Critical Social Theory," *Journal for Cultural and Religious Theory*, vol. 6, no. 1 (2004) 45-64.

Philosophical Reservation

It is not true that Habermas begun to discuss religious phenomena and/or theology as late as 2001 when he delivered is widely respected speech *Glauben und Wissen*, causing great astonishment and consternation. This speech is now commonly referred to as the *Friedenspreis Rede*[5] and is considered by many as the religious turning point in Habermas' work. But in the second volume of his *Theory of Communicative Action*, published in 1981, we can already find a long treatise on the idea of the transformation and therefore liquidation of the sacred into language and communicative actions in particular. The ideas expressed in the *Friedenspreis Rede* are only an affirmation of the thesis of the transformation of the sacred into language on the one hand, and an adjustment of this thesis on the other. That is to say, that given his recent concern with religious and theological ideas, one has to bear in mind that he has repeatedly referred to them in his work for almost thirty years. Therefore it is quite misleading and a misappropriation of Habermas to talk about Habermas' 'new' interest in religion. Nevertheless, it is true, that since the publication of the *Theory of Communicative Action* in 1981, the conversation with theologians became more important in his thought and changes have been made to his earlier view expressed in the thesis of the transformation of the sacred into language. In this sense the *Friedenspreis Rede* marks a certain shift in his thinking about religion and theology.

But what does this shift entail? What does it actually mean? First, it is a very subtle shift and a very fine amendment of the thesis of the transformation of the sacred into language. Secondly, it is an ambivalent shift which is not easy to pinpoint.

The hypothesis, following Durkheim, Max Weber and also Rudolph Otto's concept of the holy, which is expressed in the second volume the *Theory of Communicative Action*, reads as follows:

> The disenchantment and disempowering of the sacred sphere will happen by a transformation into language [Versprachlichung] of the ritually secured normative common sense. This also means that the potential of rationality, of communicative action is set free. The aura of enchantment and fright caused by the sacred, the capturing power of the holy is transformed to the binding force of a validity clause that can be criticised and the holy is at the same time sublimated [sublimiert] and turned into an everyday experience [veralltäglicht].[6]

The key words used to describe the process of the transformation of the holy/sacred are sublimation and normalisation i.e. the turning of something extraordinary into an everyday experience. Sublimation (which literally means 'elevation') can either be understood in Freudian terms or in chemical terms. Given

[5] J. Habermas, *Glauben und Wissen.* Friedenspreis des deutschen Buchhandels 2001 (Frankfurt: Suhrkamp, 2001).

[6] J. Habermas, *Theorie des Kommunikativen Handelns*, Vol 2 (Frankfurt: Suhrkamp, 1987 [4th ed] 119. [All translation are mine except stated otherwise. MH]

Habermas' preference for the use of metaphors which are working on the basis of a borrowing from scientific *termini technici* I suggest that the latter is at stake here. Sublimation is called the process when a solid substance is transformed into gas phase without going through the stage of the liquid phase. In this context the sublimation of the holy by the potential of communicative rationality turns the solid, concrete, distinct and reified manifestations of the aura of the sacred into the sublime. Let me illustrate this by a chemical experiment.[7] If the chemical element iodine in its solid phase is heated on a Bunsen burner it will not become liquid but immediately evaporates and becomes a gas. In the reversed process (re-sublimation) the gas-like iodine becomes solid again immediately as it cools down (on a glass plate held over the heated iodine for example). Communicative rationality elevates religion, but at the same time normalises it. The ambivalence is, to use Habermas' metaphor that communicative rationality is at the same time heating and cooling religion, turning it into the sublime and normalising and therefore vulgarising it. In Habermas' words, the *tremendum* and *fascinosum* i.e. the qualities of the sacred are transformed to negotiable validity claims but with sublime qualities. By this process of transformation the holy loses its extraordinary, charismatic and untouchable nature of the sacred and therefore becomes a sublime everyday experience that is accessible. It is important to notice, that at this stage in Habermas' work the thesis of the transformation of the sacred is formulated as an assumption or prediction of the future of religion. Nevertheless, the ambivalence expressed in terms of normalisation and elevation remains and Habermas returns to it by introducing the idea of a 'transcendence from within' some years later.

[7] I follow here the example of Immanuel Kant who explains the purpose of the Critique of Pure Reason by referring to the chemical practices of reduction and oxidation: „Dieses Experiment der reinen Vernunft hat mit dem der Chemiker, welches sie mannigmal den Versuch der Reduktion, im Allgemeinen aber das synthetische Verfahren nennen sehr viel Ähnliches. Die Analysis des Metaphysikers schied die reine Erkenntnis a priori in zwei sehr ungleichartige Elemente, nämlich die Dinger der Erscheinungen, und dann der Dinge an sich selbst. Die Dialektik verbindet beide wiederum zur Einhelligikeit mit der notwendigen Vernunftidee des Unbedingten, und findet, daß diese Einhelligkeit niemals anders, als durch jene Unterscheidung herauskomme, welche also die wahre ist." I. Kant, *Kritik der Reinen Vernunft* (Stuttgart: Reclam, 1966) 31. It is beyond the scope of this essay to compare Habermas' indebtedness to Kant with regards to his understanding of 'reconstruction' and 'transcendence'. [„This experiment of pure reason has a great similarity to that ofthe chemists, which they term the experiment of reduction, or, more usually, the synthetic process. The analysis of the metaphysician separates pure cognition a priori into two heterogeneous elements, viz., the cognition of things as phenomena, and of things in themselves. Dialectic combines these again into harmony with the necessary rational idea of the unconditioned, and finds that this harmony never results except through the above distinction, which is, therefore, concluded to be just." Transl. by J. M. D. Meiklejohn].

See also J. Habermas, From Kant to Hegel and Back again – The Move Towards Detranscendentalization. In: *European Journal of Philosophy*. Jg. 7/2 (1999) 129-157.

In *Texte und Kontexte*, published 1991, Habermas responds for the first time to a group of theologians and sociologists of religion who have engaged with his work. In his respond he basically reiterates[8] his view which he has expressed in 1988 in his book *Nachmetaphysisches Denken*. The context of his statement is the question of the compatibility or incompatibility of a religious praxis with philosophical language in a post-metaphysical era. Once again the difference between extraordinary and everyday-life experiences is used to describe the difference between the sacred and the profane. But, this time it is philosophy that has lost its extraordinary status. Habermas says:

> After metaphysics philosophy has lost its extraordinary [außeralltäglichen] status. The explosive extraordinary experiences migrated to autonomous arts. Of course, even after this deflation the completely profaned everyday life is not immune to unexpected extraordinary events. From an outsider's perspective, religion, which has mostly lost it monopoly of providing the dominant worldview, is still inevitable for the handling of the extraordinary in everyday life. That's why even post-metaphysical thinking coexists with a religious praxis. [...] The continuing coexistence even sheds light on a strange dependence of a philosophy which has lost its connection to the extraordinary. As long as religious language presents inspiring and undeniable and necessary semantic contents, which cannot be translated into philosophical language (so far?) and which are still awaiting a translation in discourses based on reason, philosophy in its post-metaphysical shape can neither replace religion nor can it remove it.[9]

This passage summarises Habermas' 'translation thesis'. Contrary to the idea of a transformation of the sacred in to language or communicative actions, the translation thesis grants religious practice and religious language, which he does not seem to distinguish, an autonomous right of existence and even an undeniable value for post-metaphysical thinking. As long as post-metaphysical thinking cannot translate or does not provide the adequate conceptual tools for the expression of theological semantic insights, religion will prevail. It seems that it is no longer religion which needs to be transformed by communicative rationality and which needs to be sublimated. It is now post-metaphysical thinking that shows a deficit or is seen as being incapable of fulfilling the function of religion. But, and this 'but' cannot be stressed enough, it is left open whether philosophy might be able to translate the religious, enigmatic language into a universally understandable and rational discourse. That is exactly Habermas' philosophical reservation which he was never tired to point out. This is also evident from the passage taken from the interview with Mendieta at the beginning of

[8] J. Habermas, *Texte und Kontexte* (Frankfurt: Suhrkamp, 1991) 141-2. Another debate with theologians took place in 2005 in Vienna. The results are published in: R. Langthaler; H. Nagl-Docekal [ed], *Glauben und Wissen. Ein Symposium mit Jürgen Habermas* (Wien: Oldenburg, 2007).

[9] J. Habermas, *Nachmetaphysisches Denken* (Frankfurt: Suhrkamp, 1988) 60. [italics are mine MH]

this essay, when he acknowledges the undeniable value of religious practice i.e. the ritual's importance for providing the source of societal solidarity. And at the same time he insists that there is no guarantee that this might not change one day.

At this point we can summarise three essential aspects of Habermas' 'philosophy of religion'. First, he has never withdrawn from his reservations regarding the future of religion and the everlasting importance of religious language and practice in times of post-metaphysical thinking. Secondly, the shift in Habermas' understanding of the significance of religion can be seen in his change from his earlier *theory of transformation* to the more cautious *theory of translation.* Transformation is a process which is driven by rationality and is not unlike Weber's understanding of the course of secularisation, whereas translation means a process of the 'relocation' of a semantic content i.e. to move from one language to another. According to the latter, religion is granted a right of coexistence and is admitted to have a positive function, not just in terms of providing the source of solidarity for society, but also in terms of offering a supplement for an impoverished postmetaphysical philosophy which has not yet managed to invent a language for the extraordinary i.e. the sacred. That is exactly what Habermas, following the current debate about the revision of secularisation theory[10], calls the *post-secular condition.* Furthermore, as it is with all translations, the target language and the language of the original exist in their own right and it is commonly accepted that whenever a text is translated from one language into another there will always be something which has not been translated, is untranslatable and therefore remains inaccessible to the one who is not bilingual. On the other hand, translations can also provide an added on value, because certain semantic contents seem to work better in the targeted language than in the original.[11] Exactly this last point i.e. that what will always remain untranslatable is referred to in Habermas' *Friedenspreis Rede.*

In this speech, given in the light of the events of 9/11 in 2001 Habermas talks about the „ever glowing kernel of the problem of theodicy"[12] with reference to the famous exchange of letters between Horkheimer and Benjamin in 1937[13] where the problem of final justice is raised, the *telos* of history and whether

[10] See the excellent overview article b: J. Sweeney 'Revising Secularisation Theory' in *The New Visibility of Religion. Studies in Religion and Cultural Hermeneutics* (London: Continuum, 2008)

[11] This raises the question of the epistemological *meta-phorical* use of language or 'creative mistakes'. See: P. Ricœur, *Die lebendige Metapher* (München: Wilhelm Fink, 1991); P. Ricœur, *From Text to Action. Essays in Hermeneutics, II* (Evanston: Northwestern University Press, 1991).

[12] J. Habermas, *Glauben und Wissen. Friedenspreis des deutschen Buchhandels 2001* (Frankfurt: Suhrkamp, 2001) 21.

[13] Helmut Peukert has pointed out, that Habermas cannot account for evil in the past with reference to this exchange of letters. Consequently he suggests being in 'anamnetic solidarity' with the victims. H. Peukert, *Wissenschaftstheorie – Handlungstheorie – Fundamentale Theologie. Analysen zum Ansatz und Status theologischer Theorienbildung* (Frankfurt: Suhrkamp, 1988 [2nd ed]). Habermas accepted this criticism and this is reflected in the *Friedenspreis Rede.*

justice can be comprehended without the notion of God.[14] The insistence on the ever remaining theological problem of theodicy suggests that there will always be theology. But, as mentioned before, that would suggest that Habermas has changed his mind and gave up his reservations. I do not think this a correct interpretation because as we have seen in the interview with Mendieta, Habermas repeats his reservation with regards to religion. Before we are going to discuss Habermas' 'thin description of transcendence' and contrast it with a possible 'thick description of transcendence', I will briefly answer the question we have raised above: What kind of religion and theology has Habermas got in mind?

CRITICAL THEOLOGY

What kind of theology now is the one that is the most preferred by Habermas, let alone Helmut Peukert's attempt to lay the foundations of practical theology on the basis of a theory of communicative action enriched by the concept of 'anamnetic solidarity'?[15] The answer I suggest is best given by listening to the end of the interview that Mandieta has conducted with Habermas.

> ED:[16] *„There are, as you expressed it, two forms of political theology: one that is anti-Enlightenment and an-other pro-Enlightenment. Could I say, then, that Metz's version of political theology embodies the kind of postmetaphysical religious enlightenment that you advocate in your own political philosophy? Is Metz your ideal religious postsecular dialogue partner?"*
>
> JH: „That is to express it in a catchy phrase, but it is not entirely mistaken. Metz's great merit is to have thematized the temporal sensitivity of postmetaphysical thinking without any contextualist blackouts, in such a way that the theme can serve as a bridge to contemporary theology. In part by way of Metz's influence, a younger generation of theologians emerged in Germany. This generation no longer shares the view that was expressed by the Pope in his Regensburg speech. The members of this generation start theologically, as it were, after Kant's critique of reason, so they do not lament nominalism as the gateway to modernity's history of decay. Rather, they also recognize in postmetaphysical directions of thought the learning processes from which these directions emerged."[17]

In fact Habermas and Johann-Baptist Metz are friends and their projects share the same political goal ie. to promote and support liberal democracy and its

[14] J. Habermas, *Texte und Kontexte* (Frankfurt: Suhrkamp, 1991) 110-26.

[15] H. Peukert, *Wissenschaftstheorie – Handlungstheorie – Fundamentale Theologie. Analysen zum Ansatz und Status theologischer Theorienbildung* (Frankfurt: Suhrkamp, 1988 [2nd ed]).

[16] ED stands for Eduardo Mendieta and JH for Jürgen Habermas [MH].

[17] J. Habermas, „A Postsecular World Society? On the Philosophical Significance of Postsecular Consciousness and the Multicultural World Society," 14. Available at: http://blogs.ssrc.org/tif/wp-content/uploads/2010/02/A-Postsecular-World-Society-TIF.pdf

implied set of values according to which there is still some room for theology and religion.[18] The absolute loyalty to democratic forms of government is crucial for Metz's 'New Political Theology' because he definitively seeks to distance himself from Carl Schmitt's understanding of Political Theology and does want to be confused with the latter.

Habermas idea of theology is that of a 'critical theology'. What does he mean by critical theology? In a discussion with Helmut Peukert, David Tracy, Charles Davis, Francis Schüssler-Fiorenza and Fred Dallmayr, he outlines this concept:

> With a non-*dogmatic understanding of transcendence und belief* this engagement takes seriously innerwordly aims and human rights and it connects itself in polyphonic arena to other forces which push forward radical democratisation. Against the background of a praxis which nobody will not respect we encounter a critical theology, which interprets the self-understanding of such praxis in way that our best moral intuitions are expressed; *without cutting the bonds with secular languages and cultures.*[19]

At a first glance critical theology seems to repeat Kant's project of a religion within the limits of pure reason i.e. the attempt to reduce the belief in God to a non-dogmatic, universally acceptable notion of transcendence. The novelty though is the democratic set of values and of a specific morality that is advocated. We have already mentioned that Habermas' genuine interest in religion and religious rites in particular is to provide the sources of societal solidarity. From the quotation above it is evident that critical theology should additionally provide the linguistic tools that enable us to express our noblest moral intuitions. These moral intuitions must be democratic, according to Habermas and also Metz. To a certain extent Habermas' proposal of a critical theology seem to be a third way between Tocqueville's concept of 'republican religion' and Rousseau's civil religion.[20] Two quotations should illustrate this suggested family resemblance. In Tocqueville's Democracy in America he states: „Religion in America takes no direct part in the government of society, but it must be regarded as the first of their political institutions; for it does not impart a taste for freedom, it facilitates the use of it."[21] And Rousseau in the famous concluding chapter of his *Social Contract* written almost eighty years earlier outlines what a civil religion should be like: „The dogmas of civil religion ought to be few, simple, and exactly worded, without explanation or commentary. The existence

[18] For a detailed discussion of Metz's New Political Theology see the contributions of Peter Losonczi in *From Political Theory to Political Theology*, P. Losonczi and A. Singh [eds.] (London: Continuum, 2010) as well as in the forthcoming volume, *The Future of Political Theology*, P. Losonczi, M. Luoma-aho, A. Singh [eds.] (London, Ashgate).

[19] J. Habermas, *Texte und Kontexte* (Frankfurt: Suhrkamp, 1991) 130. [italics are mine MH]

[20] See: M. Hoelzl, G. Ward [ed], *Religion and Political Thought* (London: Continuum, 2006) 123-36; 149-60.

[21] A. Tocqueville, in: M. Hoelzl, G. Ward [ed], *Religion and Political Thought* (London: Continuum, 2006) 156.

of a mighty, intelligent and beneficent divinity, possessed of foresight and providence, the life to come, the happiness of the just, the punishment of the wicked, the sanctity of the social contract and the laws: these are its positive dogmas. Its negative dogmas I confine to one, intolerance, which is part of the cults we have rejected."[22]

Habermas, like Tocqueville and Rousseau does not distinguish between religion and theology. If it is correct, that his concept of critical theology stands in the tradition of civil and republican religion, then this theology is reduced dogmatically to the lowest common denominator in order to avoid dogmatic zeal, social fragmentation and marginalisation. But, that would also mean that critical theology must be no direct political force. It must not be political as such it rather supports democratic politics. Two further observations can be made here about Habermas' concept of critical theology. First, critical theology is of Judaeo-Christian origin. In *Religion and Rationality* he admits this Judaeo-Christian legacy: „[u]niversalistic egalitarianism, from which sprang the ideals of freedom and a collective life in solidarity, the autonomous conduct of life and emancipation, the individual morality of conscience, human rights and democracy, is the direct legacy of the Judaic ethic of justice and the Christian ethic of love".[23] Secondly, it is an offspring of the Enlightenment and the Enlightenment's death blow to metaphysical thinking. The latter poses a problem. How should we understand transcendence without metaphysics i.e. in postmetaphysical thinking? We will discuss Habermas' answer to the problem in the next chapter. At this point I want to draw attention to another connotation of *critical* theology. What does critique mean in this context?

Eduardo Mendieta has published an anthology on religion and the Frankfurt School which illuminates the meaning of 'critique' at stake.[24] The list of contributors reads like a family tree of critical theology: Ernst Bloch, Erich Fromm, Leo Löwenthal, Herbert Marcuse, Theodor W. Adorno, Max Horkheimer, Walter Benjamin, Johann Baptist Metz, Jürgen Habermas, Helmut Peukert and Edmund Arens. Nevertheless, it is evident from this genealogy that critical theology should be understood as 'critical theory' and not as 'traditional theory' in the sense of Max Horkheimer.[25]

[22] J.-J. Rousseau, in: M. Hoelzl, G. Ward [ed], *Religion and Political Thought* (London: Continuum, 2006) 135.

[23] J. Habermas, E. Mendieta [ed], *Religion and Rationality. Essays on Reason, God, and Modernity* (Cambridge: MIT Press, 2002) 149.

[24] E. Mendieta, *The Frankfurt School on Religion. Key Writings by the Major Thinkers* (New York: Routledge, 2004).

[25] M. Horkheimer, „Traditionelle und Kritische Theorie" in: *Zeitschrift für Sozialforschung*, Jg. VI/2. 245-292.

THIN AND THICK DESCRIPTION OF TRANSCENDENCE

God is not merely a regulative idea as Kant proposes, nor can God be reduced to the concept of transcendence. By borrowing from Clifford Geertz the distinction between thin and thick description of cultures, I suggest to call Habermas' idea of a 'transcendence from within' a thin description opposed to a thick description. The difference between a thin and thick description becomes apparent if we look at Geertz's definition of religion and his methodological approach to religion. For Geertz religion is „(1) a system of symbols which acts to (2) establish powerful, pervasive and long lasting moods and motivations in men by (3) formulating conceptions of general order of existence and (4) clothing these conceptions with such an aura of faculty that (5) the moods and motivations seem uniquely realistic."[26] And subsequently: „The anthropological study of religion is therefore a two stage operation: first, an analysis of the system of meanings embodied in symbols which make up the religion proper, and, second, the relating of these systems to socio-structural and psychological processes."[27]

Compared to Durkheim's definition of religion which Habermas, as I have suggested, seems to have adopted, the emphasis in Geertz is on the symbolic whereas in Durkheim and Habermas the collective or community aspect is highlighted. Furthermore, from an anthropological perspective the functions of religion are not evaluated morally. Ideally anthropologists attempt to describe religions and their social functions without normative prejudices. As we have seen with Habermas' proposal of a critical theology there is a clear option for democracy and its implied set of values. Clearly, Habermas is not an anthropologist. But, as it is indicated in the conversation about his latest manuscript or book project his interest turned (again) to rituals, myths etc. For the moment we can only refer to his already published concept of a transcendence from within which we can call a thin description since it does not take into account any symbolic systems that are essential to religious phenomena and their theological interpretation.

According to Habermas, it is impossible to return to metaphysical thinking, therefore to assume a transcendence from outside is also impossible. There are no good reasons for the assumption that there is a transcendence from outside, completely separated from this world that is relevant for the immanent. But, Habermas does not conceive post-metaphysical thinking absolutely incompatible to transcendence; at least a different kind of transcendence. He states:

> On the premises of postmetaphysical thought, philosophy cannot provide a substitute for the consolation whereby religion invests unavoidable suffering and unrecompensed injustice, the contingencies of need, loneliness, sickness, and death, with new significance and

[26] C. Geertz, 'Religion as Cultural System', in: Religion and Ideology [R. Bocock, K. Thompson eds.} (Manchester: Manchester University Press, 1985) 67.

[27] C. Geertz, The Interpretation of Cultures (London: Fontana Press, 1993) 125.

> teaches us to bear them. But even today philosophy can explicate the moral point of view from which we can judge something impartially as just or unjust; to this extent, communicative reason is by no means equally indifferent to morality and immorality. However, it is altogether a different matter to provide a motivating response to the question of why we should follow our moral insights or why we should be moral at all. In this respect, it may perhaps be said that to seek to salvage an unconditional meaning without God is a futile undertaking, for it belongs to the peculiar dignity of philosophy to maintain adamantly that no validity claim can have cognitive import unless it is vindicated before the tribunal of justificatory discourse.[28]

There is nothing to gain from a speculation about the motivation for Habermas' ambition to retain the notion of transcendence despite the post-metaphysical condition we are supposed to live in. It could be argued that he does not want to see a biological materialism to triumph, as he criticises it in his *Friedenspreis Rede,*[29] or that he follows the late Horkheimer and his return to 'theology', or even, as it has been suggested, that he simply returns to religion just because of his old age.[30]

The notion 'transcendence from' might raise eyebrows among philosophers and theologians alike. For philosophers transcendence by definition is a contradiction to immanence and for Christian theologians they are somehow reminded of incarnation. Habermas develops the notion of transcendence from within in conversation theologians and he even uses the word logos to explain its nature. Possible theological irritations stem from the fact that, according Habermas, unlike the doctrine of incarnation, transcendence from within is not an act of *kenosis*, it is an effect that is produced by the people themselves. In this sense transcendence from within causes a double metaphorical effect i.e. it causes a semantic impertinence for both, theologians as well as philosophers.

Transcendence from within is similar to a regulative idea, because

> we orient ourselves to validity claims that we can raise only as a matter of fact in the context of our language, of our form of life, whereas the redeemability implicitly co-posited points beyond the provinciality of the given historical context. Whoever employs a language with a view to reaching understanding lays himself open to a transcendence from within.[31]

And „with every successful act of communication, they must orient themselves towards transcending validity-claims."[32] We are „exposed to the movement of a transcendence from within, which is unavailable for us in the same sense

[28] J. Habermas, E. Mendieta [ed], *Religion and Rationality. Essays on Reason, God, and Modernity* (Cambridge: MIT Press, 2002) 108.

[29] J. Habermas, *Glauben und Wissen. Friedenspreis des deutschen Buchhandels 2001* (Frankfurt: Suhrkamp, 2001) 31.

[30] E. Arens, „'Ich bin alt aber nicht fromm geworden'. Habermas und seine neuen Verehrer", in: *Herder Korrespondenz* 63 (2/2009) 79-83.

[31] J. Habermas, E. Mendieta [ed], *Religion and Rationality,* 108.

[32] J. Habermas, E. Mendieta [ed], *Religion and Rationality,* 123.

like the fact that the factuality of the spoken word does not make us masters over the structure of language (or over the Logos)".[33]

Communicative actions and the communicative rationality it releases create a transcendence from within that literally transcends the horizon of the participants in communicative actions. In communicative actions we orientate ourselves towards validity claims and we must assume a moment of transcendence because the redeemability of them transcends our provincial situation. We are not only exposed to this transcendence from within, we are, if we want to say it hyperbolically with Levinas, hostages of the transcendence from within.

One should not forget that Habermas' concept of communicative action is a philosophical reconstruction of an ideal speech situation and its conditions. In his theory he does not intend to analyse a concrete and real act of communication. This is why I suggest calling the concept of transcendence from within a thin description of transcendence. It is an abstraction from its concrete situation and its purpose is to clarify the conditions of the possibility[34] of communicative actions.

What then could be a thick description of transcendence? First of all, those authors who have recently attempted to give thick descriptions of transcendence which is not just restricted to religion or theology, question the assumption of post-metaphysical thinking as the nonnegotiable paradigm.[35] Is it really anachronistic to think in metaphysical categories if they still have explanatory power and if they are still in use? Moreover, Habermas' idea of a critical theology refers only to Catholic theologians like Metz, Arens, Peukert etc. It is still questionable how Catholic theology which is rooted in a sacramental worldview is possible without metaphysics. The second element of a thick description of transcendence is to take into account the symbolic structure of its expression. Contrary to a Habermasian reconstruction of the conditions of the possibility of communicative actions the analysis of the symbolic structure is always an act of interpretation rather than philosophical reconstruction.[36] Therefore, it operates with a different concept of rationality. This type of rationality I would like to call narrative rationality because it is related to the third crucial element of thick descriptions of transcendence i.e. narratives. All religions are expressed in narratives and Habermas has rightly pointed out, their semantic potential cannot (yet) be fully translated into philosophical language.

[33] J. Habermas, *Texte und Kontexte* (Frankfurt: Suhrkamp, 1991) 142.

[34] See also J. Habermas, *Kommunikatives Handeln und detranszendalisierte Vernunft* (Stuttgart: Reclam, 2001).

[35] A good example of a collection of such attempts is: R. Schwartz [ed], *Transcendence. Philosophy, Literature, and Theology Approach the Beyond* (New York: Routledge, 2004).

[36] I follow here Ernst Cassirer's philosophy of symbolic forms and his definition of man as '*animal symbolicum*'. According to Cassirer: „A genuine human symbol is characterized not by its uniformity but by its versatility. It is not rigid or inflexible but mobile." E. Cassirer, *An Essay on Man* (New Haven: Yale University Press, 1944) 36. The mobile nature of a human symbol, once more, underlines the importance of the interpretive nature of a thick description of transcendence.

Let me illustrate the difference of a thin and thick description by an example. Since all theology is about love, we might ask what love is. One possibility is to follow Hegel and to conceive love as the process of simultaneous and mutual recognition of each other and at the same time the recognition of this reciprocal act of recognition. This would be a thin description of love. A thick description could start with Shakespeare's *Romeo and Juliet.* It would begin with a narrative and the analysis of its different interpretations throughout history and across all genres of arts and literature.[37] It would be impossible to present a definitive and accurate interpretation of it as it is impossible to just a give a definite and contingent list of adjectives to answer why a person loves another person.

My aim in this essay is not to provide yet another critique of Habermas' enterprise and to complement and improve it by confronting it with something he never intended to do. I rather tried to show the development of Habermas' understanding of religion and theology and to suggest that a movement can be seen; irrespective whether Habermas will follow this movement from thin descriptions of transcendence to thick descriptions of it.

If we understand secularisation as the process of reducing the thick descriptions of transcendence to its thin descriptions, then post-secularity is the name of the reversed process. This does not simply mean a return and going back to pre-secular thinking. It also does not mean that secularisation was just a mistake which needs to be corrected. Nor does it mean that a model of cooperation, coexistence or a dialogue between philosophy and theology, between secular and religious praxis is adequate to solve the tensions between them.[38] The movement towards a thicker description of transcendence intends not to nullify thin descriptions of transcendence, it rather sublates them in a Hegelian sense and provides an attempt to facilitate the beginning of a new narrative of an old story.

[37] A fascinating attempt to discuss 'Religion before and after secularism' by referring to Shakespeare's *Romeo and Juliet* has been undertaken by Graham Ward: G. Ward, *True Religion* (Oxford: Blackwell, 2003) 5-34. The author concludes: „My claim here is that the role religion plays in postmodernity is the final working out and that we already beginning to enter another radical transformation of the understanding of what religion means. [...] As we have seen with Luhrmann, the end does not signal the falling into disuse or the oblivion of the religious. Rather, it signals exactly the opposite: the extension and hype of the religious as the ultimate vision of the excessive and the transgressive." 34.

[38] A dialogical model of co-operation between philosophy and theology has been also recently suggested by Alasdair MacIntyre: „Because what is required of us is dialogue and debate, both within the tradition and between the protagonists of the tradition and those with whom we are in philosophical disagreement, what we are committed to is a large cooperative venture." A. MacIntyre, *God, Philosophy, Universities: A Selective History of the Catholic Philosophical* Tradition (London: Continuum, 2009) 179. The author obviously follows John Paul II's conviction expressed in the opening sentence of the encyclical *Fides et Ratio* according to which: „Faith and reason are like two wings on which the human spirit rises to the contemplation of truth; and God has placed in the human heart a desire to know the truth – in a word, to know himself – so that, by knowing and loving God, men and women may also come to the fullness of truth about themselves."

HUMAN DIGNITY AND GENETICS IN A POSTSECULAR AGE: HABERMAS' IDEAS CONCERNING PRE-IMPLANTATION GENETIC DIAGNOSIS AND ENHANCEMENT IN THE CONTEXT OF THEOLOGICAL TRADITION HERMENEUTIC AGE

Gábor Viktor Orosz

This essay deals with a particular aspect of *The Future of Human Nature* published by Jürgen Habermas, first in 2000 and 2001 in German, the English translation being available since 2003. This book, revealing his opposition to the human determination of human nature, is complex and conservative. The book discusses many issues of contemporary relevance from pre-implantation diagnosis to sex selection, stem cell research, and human dignity.

Habermas's principal focus in this text is on the moral and political significance of prenatal genetic engineering or enhancement, which, he argues, could damage the affected person's autonomy. The intention of Habermas's book can easily be understood having as a background the German history, to quote Johannes Rau's words: „The experience that we had with National Socialism, in particular with research and science in the Third Reich, must play an important role for ethical judgment – and not only among us [Germans]."[1] On the contrary, Bernard G. Prusak, at the beginning of his article about Habermas's Bioethics suggested: „Germans have much to learn from liberal-minded Anglo-American bioethical discourse, rather than Anglo-Americans and others much to learn from Germany's history."[2] For Habermas, the understanding of the bioethical questions can only be found by reading them in the light of the German historical experience of the Second World War and taking into account the German philosophical tradition. The book under discussion

[1] J. Rau, Berliner Rede. Wird alles Gut? Für einen Fortschritt nach menschlichem Mass http://www.bundespraesident.de/Anlage6193/Die_Rede_im_PDF-Format.pdf

[2] B. G. Prusak, "Rethinking "Liberal Eugenics". Reflections and Qestions on Habermas on Bioethics", Hasting Center Report, 6 (2005) 31-32.

makes an attempt to expose the difficulties and the advantages that spring from the „dual nature" (German and Anglo-American) of the bioethical controversies.

The path that I have chosen in this study is new in several ways. First, my concept on Habermans's bioethics is based on his ideas of solidarity. Second, I argue that Christian theological tradition is able to make compromises on questions such as human genetic engineering and enhancement, even if it uses a strong definition for Human dignity. Before we discuss Habermas's concept on human dignity, pre-implantation diagnosis and enhancement, first we will focus on Habermas's ideas concerning solidarity, which might be a relevant basis for our essay.

SOLIDARITY: TRANSLATIONS OF THE SPIRITUAL INTO THE SECULAR?

Over the past decade, a new term has entered our vocabulary, that of the 'post-secular age.'[3] The changing role of religion in a pluralistic public sphere was discussed by Jürgen Habermas and Josef Ratzinger (Pope Benedict XVI) on January 19, 2004 at the Bavarian Catholic Academy in Munich, and both of them agreed that we have entered in a postsecular age.[4] At that time, Habermas formulated that religion is an indispensable source of *social solidarity*. This includes an increasing skepticism towards the absolutist claims of science, meaning: there is a great need for the translation of spiritual insights into secular language, first of all in the concept of Human dignity. Habermas offers examples of the translation of the spiritual into the secular.

The most *common reference* is to the familiar Christian notion of man created in the image of God translated in the secular sphere into the notion of *inalienable human dignity* that serves as the moral basis of many modern defenses of human rights. With this instance of a translation that still salvages the substance of the original term, he provides a pragmatic test to assess the degree of success in executing such translations: „this goes beyond the borders of one particular religious fellowship and makes the substance of biblical concepts accessible to a deliberating public that also includes those who have other faiths and those who have none."[5] This sentence is obviously based not only on biblical tradition, but also on Kant's understanding of dignity. Dignity to Kant was something beyond valuation and without equal.[6] Man should be an end unto himself, never the means to an end. This constitutes the dignity of man, his inner value. Without any

[3] J. Bowman, „Extending Habermas and Ratzinger's Dialectics Of Secularization: Eastern Discursive Influences On Faith And Reason In A Postsecular Age" In *Forum Philosophicum* 14 (2009) 39-55.

[4] J. Habermas and J. Ratzinger, *The Dialectics of Secularization*, (San Francisco: Shambala, 2005)

[5] Ibid., 46.

[6] M. Honeckre, Dignity in Law And Morality. In K. Bayertz (Ed.), *Sanctity of Life And Human Dignity.* (Dordrecht: Kluwer, 1996) 261.

doubt, thus dignity becomes synonymous with autonomy. One can say that in terms of dignity, the biblical view of man as an image of God, as well as Kant's understanding of autonomy and the longing for dignified humane existence come together. This is a reasonable argument for using human dignity as a common reference, but it is also true that on the basis of its origin, no Christian or other group can claim a monopoly on the interpretation of the term of human dignity.[7] In this context, Martin Honecker argues that individually dignity of man is inviolable[8]. For instance, there is the guarantee of personal freedom, the ban on discrimination, protection of life and equality. From this point of view, we can consider that the positive guarantee of dignity requires a corresponding order. Back to Habermas:

> An unambiguous definition of the moral status – be it in terms of Christian metaphysics or of naturalism – is possible only in facts, which a pluralistic society is well advised to leave to controversy are submitted to a description impregnated by one worldview or another. Nobody doubts the intrinsic value of human life before birth – whether one calls it „sacred" or refuses to sanctify something that is an end in itself. But neither the objectivating language of empiricism nor the language of religion can express the normative substance of the protection to which pre-personal human life is entitled in a way that is rationally acceptable to all citizens.[9]

In this way goes Habermas's next example, which has been brought about by the onset of new genetic technologies. He argues that in a secular public most non-believers would seem to be compelled by moral reasons to reject the idea of 'man playing God' via new genetic technologies, for instance, as found in the secular law of the German constitution and Article 3 of the EU Fundamental Charter of Rights through their respective bans on human cloning and the non-instrumentalization of the person.[10] From these citations and as I have argued above, a certain and short conclusion can be drawn: human dignity allows for a certain amount of leeway both in terms of realizing human dignity and in terms of specifying individual human rights. But first of all: human dignity as a common reference point sets limit to arbitrary behavior with each other.

In the arena of the postsecular, the distinction between secular and religious is complicated, not only concerning human dignity. As we have seen, one of the difficulties is that religiously embedded arguments are often advanced as if they were secular – claimed H. Tristram Engelhard, Jr. in his book *Bioethics and Secular Humanism: The Search for a Common Morality.*[11] Engelhard mentioned for example the Roman Catholic tradition, which ranging from issues of social

[7] See detailed M. Honeckre, *Dignity in Law And Morality*, 262.

[8] Ibid., 262.

[9] J. Habermas, *The Future of Human Nature* (Cambridge: Polity Press 2003) 32.

[10] Ibid., 21-23.

[11] H. T. Engelhard, Jr. : *Bioethics and Secular Humanism: The Search for a Common Morality* (London: SCM Press, 1991) 102-103.

justice to euthanasia and suicide, is justified in terms of natural law. This means that this theological tradition has been regarded as based on reason, and not on faith. The same can be said about many secular philosophers and ethicists. Engelhard asks the question: is there a philosophically justifiable foundation for bioethics that can be shared by all people?[12] The problem is how to choose the correct moral sense. In a postsecular age in terms of Habermas we live together with the post-modern skepticism regarding the weakness of humanism and human rationalism. But on the other hand, it means that there is a *transitus* between religiously justified morality and secular morality. That transitus by Habermas is the *complementary learning process*, which can be based on human dignity. The Latin word „compleo" means to fulfill something, to fill up, making it whole. In this sense the complementary learning process conducts to whole-making the solidarity.

We can consider that the implicit content of the complementary learning process is the traditional pairing of nature and grace, reason and revelation, autonomous humanity and the enduringly personal image of God.[13] The biblical teaching of *imago Dei* is the first and most important indication of human nature. It means that the dignity, value, and sanctity of human life is essentially inherent in the relationship to God. In his dialogue with Ratzinger, Habermas argues:

> The balance achieved in the modern period between the three great media of social integration is now at risk, because the markets and the power of the bureaucracy are expelling social solidarity (that is, a coordination of action based on values, norms, and a vocabulary intended to promote mutual understanding) from more and more spheres of life. Thus it is in the interest of the constitutional state to deal carefully with all the cultural sources that nourish its citizens' consciousness of norms and their solidarity. This awareness, which has become conservative, is reflected in the phrase: 'post secular society'.[14]

Habermas also finds that these fellowships carry a current of reflexivity whereby both believing and non-believing citizens undergo a *complementary learning process* in taking up a performative *attitude with respect to one another's reasons as offered* concerning *controversial public issues.*[15] It is needed because throughout modern times, new technological developments (first of all biotechnology) have created new regulatory, ethical and sociological needs and that means „moralizing human nature" in terms of a dubious sanctification.[16]

[12] Ibid., 103.

[13] J. R. Nelson, *On the New Frontiers of Genetics and Religion* (Grand Rapids: Eerdmans, 1994) 107-109.

[14] J. Habermas and J. Ratzinger, *The Dialectics of Secularization,* 45-46.

[15] See J. Bowman, *Extending Habermas and Ratzinger's Dialectics Of Secularization* , 5.

[16] J. Habermas, *The Future of Human Nature,* 24-25.

Human Dignity as a Regulative Principle

As we mentioned above, the image of God translated in the secular sphere into the notion of *inalienable human dignity* serves as the moral basis of many modern defenses of human rights. There is the relevance of the principle of human dignity in the context of genetic engineering regarding the discernment of the ethical and legal aspects of the principle and keeping a close watch on the possibilities and difficulties of its application. The principle of human dignity is the basis of the protection of human life but it would be a mistake to reduce it only to this role. Nevertheless, as a regulative principle it is the fundament of the objective basic rights, however it is not the type of principle from which the solution of conflict situations could be derived directly, but it is able to boost solidarity.

In addition to these, we can say that in the era of the genetic revolution the notion of human dignity *seems to be foreign* in a twofold way. On one hand, it is foreign because when we speak about „genetic revolution" we refer to the extension of knowledge in the sphere of biology and the natural sciences to such a degree that it is comparable to the breakthroughs in the field of space research or to the spreading of computers. In the ethical context of the new spheres of knowledge and their application, the exact role and function of the principle of human dignity is controversial. Recurrently, it appears as a „rhetoric weapon" far from the actual problem solving or it is simply regarded as an empty phrase. On the other hand, we speak about an alien dignity when we look for an answer to human value and determination in Christian theology. This dignity is alien since it is not present as something „written into" the human being, does not depend on the characteristics of the human being, but the creator and redeemer God bestows it on him / her – whom God made just slightly smaller than Godself.

Human dignity: a „Strong" Concept from German Theological Tradition

To see a detailed landscape of using human dignity in Christian tradition we will discuss Helmuth Thielicke's[17] protestant point of view of the mid-twenties to illustrate what dignity as alien dignity means. Because the dignity is alien, for

17 Helmut Thielicke is one of the most outstanding theologians of the German Lutheran Church. He was dismissed by the Nazi regime from his post of Professor of Theology at Heidelberg in 1940. After the war he served as professor and Rector at the University of Tubingen until 1954, when he accepted the post of Rector at the University of Hamburg, the first Protestant theologian to hold this position. He died in 1986.

some ethicists[18] it falls under the pre-ethical, pre-juridical category and it can serve as a common moral basis.

We take the „model of Thielicke", a paradigm that makes possible the reduction of the theological interpretation of the principle of human dignity. On the other hand, Thielicke's interpretation of the principle of human dignity reflects the theological paradigm that re-interprets the principle of human dignity on the basis of the two world wars in the theological and social context of its own age and culture. The dignity of human beings – in accordance with the traditions of the reformers – is an *alien dignity* (dignitas aliena). On the basis of Thielicke's paradigm the following statements are obviously right. The twofold nature of man[19], a being „en sarki" (in body) but not „kata sarka" (according to the body), represents a *source of tension* but at the same time a *willingness to make compromise*, as well, in relation to every technical novelty that is directed towards human beings. At the same time, in relation to the conceived human life it presents itself in a particular way in the field of genetics. In this tension, the principle of human dignity protects the human being as a *iustitia passiva* determined by the relation to God. The dignity and value of the human being cannot be relativized by bodily and genetic characteristics *(Eigenschaften)* since they rest on „those that are beyond" *(Aussenschaft)*[20] of the human being. The dynamism involved in the personal existence of the human being arises from this „beyondness": he/she is not a person by him/herself, but always becomes one through the relation with God. This vertical determination manifests itself in the relations with the horizontal spheres of life. The acknowledgement of personal existence becomes concrete in the inter-subjective relation with the other human being and in the social dimension of the human being.

It can be accountable for the fact that the *willingness to make compromise* should be met with Habermas's ideas about *complementary learning process* on the part *of Christians.*

For instance, in many church declarations dealing with the relation between alien dignity and modern bioethics, it is precisely the willingness to compromise presented in the paradigm of Thielicke that is left out of examination most of the time. To quote a non-Germanic, adequate example for this approach, here is an excerpt from a Statement from the Evangelical Lutheran Church in America:

[18] D. Ritschl, "Ethical Maxims from Theological Concepts of Human Dignity?" In D. Kretzmer – E. Klein (Ed.): *The Concept of Human Dignity in Human Rights Discourse* (Hague: Brill, 2002) 92.

[19] H. Thielicke, *Theologische Ethik. Bd. I. Dogmatische, philosophische und kontroverstheologische Grundlegung*, (Tübingen: J.C.B. Mohr, 1951) 9.

[20] H. Thielicke, *Mensch sein – Mensch werden* (München, 1976), 102. *Being Human – Becoming Human: An Essay in Christian Anthropology* Translated by Geoffrey W. Bromiley (Garden City: Doubleday, 1984).

[21] Draft Social Statement on Genetics. For Study and Response Prior to October 15, 2010. ELCA Task Force on Genetics Church in Society Evangelical Lutheran Church in America, March 2010., 25.

> Respect is a directive grounded in the dignity and integrity of created life. For Lutheran Christians, this respect follows from God's creative activity and God's regard for all life as precious, from the amoeba to the person. Human beings cannot love as God does, but the minimal response to other members of the community of life is to recognize their givenness and integrity. The claim to integrity is reinforced as creatures across the multitude of forms exhibit both purposiveness and interdependence. The community is sustained by individual activity and mutual interdependence as they function together within a complex whole. Respect constitutes a moral baseline to restrain all relationships, decisions and actions. The placement of the directive to respect before the directive to promote indicates that we must give priority first to claims of givenness and dignity in the community of life.[21]

To put it in a nutshell: isn't the complementary learning process a dialogue concerning human dignity, which is integrated in many different cultural and historical traditions? Likewise, can we say that God, or the religious conviction, is not a borderline in such a discussion, but a constitutive part of this dialog in a postsecular age? I think, yes.

PRE-IMPLANTATION GENETIC DIAGNOSIS AS A BACK DOOR TO ENHANCEMENT

Habermas points out that the „pre-implantation genetic diagnosis is hard put to it to strictly keep to the line separating the selection of undesirable hereditary factors from the optimization of desirable ones."[22] Optimization in this context is an intervention which has impact on human functioning, an enhancement is clearly anything that makes a change for the better. On this point Habermas makes it clear:

> If there is more than one potentially 'spare multicellular organism' to be chosen among, the decision implied is no longer a binary of yes or no. The conceptual distinction between the prevention of the birth a severely afflicted child and the optimization of the genetic makeup, that is, a eugenic choice, has become blurred.[23]

If we look back at the original goal of the pre-implantation genetic diagnosis (PGD), one fact will be clear: it is a reproductive technique that was developed for couples facing the risk of having a child with significant genetic variation known to be associated with genetic disease[24]. This technique involves the use of IVF to create embryos that are then selected based on their genotype or

[22] J. Habermas, *The Future of Human Nature*, 24.

[23] Ibid.

[24] Handyside and his colleagues reported the first confirmed human pregnancies following this technique in 1990. Handyside, A.H., Kontogianni, E.H., Hardy, K., et al., „Pregnancies from biopsied human preimplantation embryos sexed by Y-specific DNA amplification". *Nature* 344 (1990) 768–770.

karyotype and transferred into the uterus with the aim of establishing a pregnancy with a fetus free of the genetic condition for which it was at risk.[25] In other words: *PGD was used by couples at risk of having a child with severely debilitating early-onset conditions* such as cystic fibrosis, spinal muscular atrophy and Tay Sachs disease. The range of indications for its use has since broadened and as Habermas argues, it would set us a downward path, toward liberal eugenics. It seems to be the backdoor to human enhancement.

The term „eugenics" literally means „good genes" and can simply indicate the study of hereditary improvement by genetic control. However, it usually refers to any intentional strategy to direct the course of the human species through encouraging the transmission of „desired" traits while discouraging the „undesired" ones. In this sense Habermas starts by being almost right about „the procedures of pre-implantation genetic diagnosis and research on human embryonic stem cells demand the adoption of attitudes which, in their effect, tend to promote the transition from a negative to a positive eugenics,"[26] and that is, from practices concerned with preventing the transmission of severely disabling conditions to practices aimed at optimizing a child's genetic makeup.[27] This is a reasonable argument, human embryonic stem cell research and PGD „would clear the path to a liberal eugenics," which would be distinguished from an old, authoritarian eugenics by a great measure of state neutrality, with parents enjoying a free hand in „the choice of the goals of gene-modifying interventions to the individual preferences of market participants."[28]

John Harris in his book *Enhancing Evolution. The Ethical Case for Making Best People* deals with Habermas's ideas concerning the critique of human enhancement and wrote:

> Parents cannot evade or avoid responsibility for how their children will turn out, at least insofar as they have the power to leave things as they are or make them different. The power to make things different means that parents have a choice to do or forebear with highly probable but different consequences attending either future possibility following their decision. They have to do their best. What they should not do is their worst for their kids, and leaving their kids with a handicap of unknown and highly speculative advantage but known disadvantage would be, to put it mildly, problematic in almost anyone's philosophy.[29]

However, the parental choice can easily drive a new relation of dependence between parents and children. This might be the case, because the parents,

[25] B. M. Knoppers, S. Bordet, R. M. Isasi, „Preimplantation genetic diagnosis: an overview of socio-ethical and legal considerations". *Annual Review of Genomics and Human Genetics* 7 (2006) 201–221.

[26] J. Habermas, *The Future of Human Nature*, 96.

[27] See B. G. Prusak, *Rethinking Liberal Eugenics*, 31.

[28] J. Habermas, *The Future of Human Nature*, 19.

[29] J. Harris, *Enhancing Evolution. The Ethical Case for Making Best People* (Princeton: Princeton University Press, 2007) 142.

through their idea of a healthy child and technological realization of it, will directly be responsible for the genetic constitution of their offspring. Although parents are responsible for their children in several other ways (environment, education), the problem is if one puts the emphasis solely on the genetic characteristic, it might lead to total misunderstanding of genetic determinism.

In the followings, we take up Bernhard G. Brushak's observations for a while and examine how Nicholas Agar – because Habermas often relies on Agar arguments – relates to the limits of permissible genetic intervention. Brushak shows that Habermas thinks that Agar does not pursue his analysis far enough.[30] After rejecting the relevance of the two conventional distinctions in shaping people, Agar argues that „[t]he liberal juxtaposition of eugenics with education suggests a more suitable guide to the improving efforts of prospective parents."[31] The idea is: „In allocating educational resources to an individual we do not limit ourselves to the avoidance of disease, [but] rather we are concerned with the person's well-being, welfare or quality of life. So it should be with the goods of genetic engineering."[32] In this case, the genetic code of a human being is modified, at the very beginning of a human life, to produce the desired composition of genetic predispositions. The genetic engineering would be applied at the very beginning of a new human life. Therefore I think that this case is different in a significant way. On this point Habermas proposes that the manipulation of the makeup of the human genome might change our ethical self-understanding:

> The conditions, that is, of nature-like growth which alone allow us to conceive of ourselves as the authors of our own lives and as equal members of moral community. Knowledge of one's own genome being programmed might prove to be disruptive, I suspect, for assumption that we exist as a body or, so to speak, 'are' our body, and thus may give rise to a novel, curiously asymmetrical type of relationship between persons.[33]

Habermas's argument is that the contingency of our genetic makeup – the fact that there is a rooted categorical distinction between the subjective and objective, the grown and the made[34] – might well be necessary for a person to be capable of regarding himself as equal member of the moral community, as an autonomous being, who is more than his body. As we have seen, genetic engineering is concerned with future people under problematic identity and autonomy. Moreover, as Habermas has noted, there are also backward-looking cases such as affirmative action or compensation and apology for past crimes which raise the problem of autonomy. The question of autonomy concerning genetic engineering in our context is more, as Brushak argues: „They [parents] will

[30] B. G. Prusak, *Rethinking Liberal Eugenics*, 34.

[31] Ibid.

[32] N. Agar, *Liberal Eugenics in Bioethics. An Anthology* ed. H. Khuse, P. Singer (Oxford: OUP, 1999) 174.

[33] J. Habermas, *The Future of Human Nature*, 42.

[34] Ibid., 71.

have gotten their expectations for her not only 'into her head,' so to speak, but through her genes into her very body, to the very tips of her fingers."[35]

According to Habermas: „Irrespective of how far genetic programming could actually go in fixing properties, dispositions, and skills and in determining the behavior of the future person, *post-factum* knowledge of the circumstances may intervene in the self-relation of the person, the relation to her bodily or mental existence. The change would take place in the mind."[36]

On this point we turn back to Habermas's ideas of solidarity. Because it shows the difficulty in discussing solidarity, since it is qualitatively different and a more encompassing notion than enhancement, PGD as a type of deliberate quality control brings in a new aspect. Quoting Habermas: „the instrumentalization of conditionally created human life according to the preferences and value orientations of third parties."[37] In other words, selection is guided by the prospective parents. If genetic engineering enabled us to replace chance (grown) with choice (made), the „gifted character of human powers and achievements would recede, and with it, perhaps, our capacity to see ourselves as sharing a common fate."[38] So the explosion of responsibility for our own fate, and that of our children, may diminish our sense of solidarity with those less fortunate than ourselves[39] and the routinely practiced genetic enhancement „would make it harder to foster the moral sentiments that social solidarity requires."[40]

From a theological point of view, we can see the case of genetic enhancement in the analogy to creator and co-creator.[41] The above-mentioned social solidarity might be attempted by Paul Nelson's mentioned cartoon.[42] The cartoonist has altered Michelangelo's famous Creation of Adam on the ceiling of the Vatican's Sistine Chapel to show the extended fingers of God and Adam meeting on a DNA molecule. Even though he is the creature of God, Adam is also a co-creator with God. This idea of co-creator is not new. There are numerous ways to illustrate human creativity, but none drives more enthusiasm for the notion of co-creatorship than the methodical manipulation of genes. In short, we can observe the role of humanity in two ways. The first one sees humanity in the role of a steward, the second one in the role of a co-creator. But is there really a contrast? In both cases there is the responsibility before God, which in Judeo-Christian context means respect and solidarity for each other. If the man uses his ability to manipulate his own genetic makeup to enhance his offspring,

[35] B. G. Prusak, *Rethinking Liberal Eugenics*, 35.

[36] J. Habermas, *The Future of Human Nature*, 53.

[37] Ibid., 30.

[38] M. J. Sandel, *The Case Against Perfection. Ethics in the Age of Genetic Engineering.* (Cambridge: CUP, 2007) 92.

[39] Ibid., 87-89.

[40] Ibid., 91.

[41] Ph. Hefner, *The Human Factor. Evolution, Culture, and Religion,* (Minneapolis: Augsburg Fortress, 1993) 32.

[42] J. R. Nelson, *On the New Frontiers of genetics and Religion*, 110-111.

then, at the same time his responsibility will be bigger and much more complicated in the future. More responsibility requires more moral sense. For example, this is the case in the statement of the United Church of Canada: „We are called to be co-creators with God, working for wholeness in our communities and each person."[43] What we have discussed above has appeared recently in the ELCA Draft Study on Genetics:

> It also must be noted that this God-given calling does not mean that every possible enhancement or innovation should be pursued. Promotion must not violate the baseline established by respect, and this church does not support striving after some imagined perfection or idealized state of human life. Further, such efforts must be evaluated by the concern for justice before being pursued. Qualified by these concerns, the ELCA encourages the use of human imagination and innovation through genetic knowledge and its application to heal afflictions, relieve human suffering and improve the human situation. It supports efforts to promote general well-being and creative means to restore the environment. It supports investment in such goals.[44]

This citation shows that harm outside of family context is also possible because choosing an idealized state of human life must necessarily imply a preference for the specific characteristic. To prefer something plays a major role in rational choice theory when the implicit value structure of individual is determined from his explicit preferences.[45] As we have seen, the roll of human dignity might be to make a matrix for the exchange of different preferences and so promote a social discourse.

HUMAN DIGNITY AND SOLIDARITY

The critical idea of human dignity in public discussion highlights that all stakeholders should have the opportunity to make their concerns part of the agenda, and even to make the very rules of the debate a topic in itself. Such a discussion will encourage people to think about which arguments might be valid to everyone and not only from the point of view of a particular interest. Human dignity can be used to distinguish claims based on narrow self-interests from those conducive to the general public interests. So we can consider that in case of genetic enhancement the use of human dignity might be a *regulative principle.*

43 "A brief to the Royal Commission on new reproductive Technologies on behalf of The Division of Mission in canada of the United Church of Canada" approved by the Executive of the Division of Mission (January 17, 1991) 14

44 Draft Social Statement on Genetics. For Study and Response Prior to October 15, 2010. ELCA Task Force on Genetics Church in Society Evangelical Lutheran Church in America March 2010. 28.

45 S. Hølm, "Ethical Issues in Pre-implantation Diagnosis", In John Harris – Soren Hølmes (Ed.), *The Future of Human Reproduction* (Oxford: OUP, 2000) 187.

I think Habermas's theory about complementary *learning process* and solidarity has two strong messages or interpretations for the Christian theology and churches (in general to the people with religious worldview).

The first one is that it can be established that the relation of the principle of human dignity and the doctrine of justification[46] makes possible the realization of taking responsibility through compromises: *the alien dignity of the human being is the regulative principle of the willingness to make compromise.* The principle of human dignity of the human being becomes realized in the context of social coexistence, in the horizontal relation where the „verticality" (relation to God, religiosity) of the human being presents itself as hope: life and its dignity entrusted to the human being within the limits of birth and death are in the hands of God. The efforts made to solve the problems in a responsible way – especially in the era of the genetic revolution – reflect that the Christian person was created in the Image of God.

The second one, from the part of the churches it is necessary to ponder and guide morally the potentials involved in the new procedures, as well as to articulate and expound its particular aspects, since with the introduction of IVF a completely new situation has been generated in the field of human reproduction. The possibilities of application of this new situation grow wider with the augmentation of knowledge in the field of genetics and a retrocession *status quo ante* cannot be expected.

In conclusion, I would like to make a general remark. In my paper I have discussed the interpretation of human dignity reflecting Habermas's concept of solidarity and human enhancement and offered some opinions concerning the relationship between the willingness to make compromise and the complementary learning process. Thereby, I avoided the term „sanctity of life" because I have difficulties in using „sanctity of life". The word „sacred" means „belonging to God" and this is a statement of faith, of one's creed. The obvious goal of bioethics is an ethical consensus about life and not a religious interpretation of life. For this reason, the common and open terms as human dignity, solidarity etc. are more adequate for the religious and non-religious thinker. As a final remark I can only say that the solidarity I mentioned will be realized when men and women start to consciously reflect on the contingency of their fate.

[46] The interpretation of human dignity through the *doctrine of justification* (following from its forensic character) opens a critical and constructive perspective for the formulation of theological opinion, since the questions of the clinical application of human genetics raise questions to a „legal unity".

Schnittpunkte – Intersections

hrsg. von Dr. Jutta Hausmann, Dr. Tamás Lichtmann, Dr. Péter Losonczi (Goldziher Institut Budapest)

Péter Losonczi; Géza Xeravits

Reflecting Diversity

Historical and Thematical Perspectives in the Jewish and Christian Tradition

The term "interreligiosity" is a characteristic invention of the postmodern discourse of religious studies. But the feature it denotes-the mutual connections between religions, whereby they can share new view-points and paradigms-is not modern at all. One can say that religiosity and interreligiosity are correlative conceptions: when speaking of religion as a social entity, one is immediately and everywhere confronted by interreligious aspects. The present volume contains various essays exploring such interreligious aspects found within the history and traditions of Judaism and Christianity.

Bd. 1, 2007, 240 S., 24,90 €, br., ISBN 978-3-8258-0508-1

LIT Verlag Berlin – Münster – Wien – Zürich – London

Auslieferung Deutschland / Österreich / Schweiz: siehe Impressumsseite